Dr. Richter's
CommonSensediet

A complete guide to the fruits
and vegetables that help you
Get Fit *and Feel Great!*

©2005 Try-Foods International, Inc.
All rights reserved. No part of this book
may be reproduced or transmitted in
any form or by any means, electronic or
mechanical, including photocopying,
recording, or by any information storage
and retrieval system, without permission
in writing from the publisher.

The nutritional values supplied are
approximations and have been provided
because of consumer interest. Try-Foods
International, Inc. can make no warranty of
their accuracy. In an instance when a
nutrition fact was not available it is noted as
n/a. Recipe ingredients listed as optional have
not been computed into the nutritional
analysis.

The contents herein are no substitute for your
physician's advice and/or prescription. Nor, is
produce a cure or treatment for any ailment,
disease, or chronic disorder.

Try-Foods International, Inc.
207 Semoran Commerce Place
Apopka, Florida 32703 USA
Printed in the United States of America
To reorder, call 1-800-421-8871

D0564872

The U.S. Department of Agriculture's Dietary Guidelines for Americans tells us, "Eating fewer calories while increasing physical activity are the keys to controlling body weight." I couldn't have said it better myself. *It's just common sense.*

Fad diets come and go. Nutrition experts and physicians today believe the healthy way to control weight includes increasing consumption of low-calorie fruits and vegetables. Balanced with low-fat dairy products, lean meat and seafood, and whole grains, a new way of eating emerges. To modify your diet, take advantage of the menu plans, healthy recipes, and complete A to Z produce guide in the following pages. While shopping for and serving wholesome food for your family can be a challenge, I offer a no-fail supermarket strategy: Simply start in the produce department and focus on your store's fresh food perimeter. At home, look to this book for answers on preparing delicious and healthy meals. My program includes a 28-day diet program to help you get started, recipes designed for the busy cook, information on nearly 300 fresh produce items, and more.

But a healthy lifestyle is not just about food. It is a balance between being active and eating smart to support your activities. So, my commonsense plan also includes a target of 30 minutes of exercise daily. To help you reach this goal, the following pages include ideas to get you moving and keep you motivated.

The commonsense message: produce is the backbone of healthy eating and exercise is the foundation of sustained weight loss and good health.

To your great health,

Henry J. Richter, MD, FACEP

C O N T E N T S

Dr. Richter's
CommonSensediet

the
power of produce

A body of scientific research provides compelling evidence that a diet high in vegetables and fruit may reduce the risk of many chronic diseases as well as some forms of cancer—a long-term health benefit. Eating lots of fruit and vegetables also boosts the immune system, which means you're likely to stay healthier and have fewer colds and minor infections—an everyday health benefit.

Real food trumps supplements

Fresh fruit and vegetables contain a complex mix of nutrients and micronutrients, some known and others not yet identified, that help fight disease. You'd probably need a supplement the size of a golf ball to capture all the benefits. Scientists believe the phytochemicals, vitamins, minerals, and fiber in fruit and vegetables work synergistically to promote health and reduce disease. That's why experts recommend nutrients come primarily from foods, with an emphasis on fruit and vegetables—from five to thirteen servings a day.

Fiber

Fresh produce provides fiber, a substance that cannot be absorbed by the body, and has no calories, yet offers many health benefits. Soluble fiber can reduce blood cholesterol levels and help stabilize blood sugar. Vegetable and fruit sources include apples, dried beans, beets, carrots, cranberries, red currants, gooseberries, grapefruit, Concord grapes, oats, oranges, peaches, pears, and prunes. Insoluble fiber absorbs a lot of water and "bulks up," a characteristic that can help when you're trying to lose weight because you feel full faster without eating as much. It may also improve digestion, and help prevent some types of gastrointestinal disease. Good sources include fruit and vegetables with the skin on, whole grains, and peanuts.

Phytochemicals

Vegetables and fruit are not only rich in essential vitamins and minerals and fiber; they're also rich in compounds called phytochemicals that provide benefits beyond basic nutrition. Phytochemicals are found only in plants. Many phytochemicals are pigments that give plants their color. They act as antioxidants—substances that protect the body from free radicals (by-products of everyday metabolism) and toxic substances that damage cells and cause disease.

Glossary

Here's a guide to some of the beneficial compounds and produce families garnering lots of interest in the scientific community and popular press.

ALLIUM VEGETABLES: A class of vegetables in the onion family that contain organosulfer compounds thought to protect against cancer and reduce the risk of heart disease. **Sources: chives, leeks, garlic, onions, shallots**

ANTHOCYANIDINS: Antioxidants linked to improved blood vessel health in animals and humans. **Sources: blue/purple and red fruit and vegetables, such as berries, plums, red onions, and red potatoes**

BETA-CAROTENE: An antioxidant and precursor to vitamin A, a nutrient important for vision, immune function, and skin and bone health. **Sources: yellow/orange and dark green leafy vegetables**

CAROTENOIDS: Fat-soluble phytochemicals with a vitamin A-like structure and strong antioxidant and other potentially protective properties. Beta-carotene is one of the better known. **Sources: many fruit and vegetables, especially yellow/orange and dark green leafy produce, such as pumpkin, sweet potatoes, carrots, kale, and spinach**

CRUCIFEROUS VEGETABLES: A class of vegetables in the cabbage family with anticancer properties. **Sources: vegetables such as broccoli, Brussels sprouts, cabbage, kale, and cauliflower**

ELLAGIC ACID: a type of phytochemical called a polyphenol. It acts as an antioxidant and may reduce the risk of certain types of cancer. **Sources: berries**

LUTEIN: A carotenoid that concentrates in the macula of the eye. Lutein in foods may prevent age-related eye disease and may also reduce the risk of heart disease and protect against certain cancers. **Sources: green leafy vegetables such as collard greens, spinach, and kale**

LYCOPENE: A carotenoid that's a potent antioxidant and may help prevent heart disease and reduce the risk for many cancers, especially prostate cancer. **Sources: red fruit and vegetables such as tomatoes and cooked tomato products, watermelon, and red peppers**

PROANTHOCYANIDINS: A phytochemical that may reduce the risk of cardiovascular disease and cancer. Some proanthocyanidins may protect against urinary tract infections. **Sources: many berries, grapes, cranberries**

QUERCETIN: A flavonoid (a subclass of phytochemicals) that may reduce the risk for asthma, lung cancer, and fatal heart disease. **Sources: onions, apples, broccoli, cranberries, grapes**

RESVERATROL: A polyphenol that may help lower the risk of heart disease, cancer, lung disease, and asthma. **Sources: grapes**

ZEAXANTHIN: A carotenoid with antioxidant power that is deposited in the eye's macular region. Zeaxanthin may help prevent age-related eye disease and certain cancers. **Sources: green leafy vegetables and yellow/orange fruit and vegetables such as spinach, kale, collard greens, corn, tangerines, and nectarines**

Source: www.5aday.org

the diet

Dr. Richter's CommonSense Diet program is an easy-to-stick-to plan that incorporates the latest research on healthy eating and the U.S. Department of Agriculture's guidelines with some good old-fashioned common sense. It's a program designed with you in mind — a person who loves good food, who wants to be fit and healthy, but who needs a program that's easy because you have a busy life to live.

Our program includes everything you need to know about healthy eating to lose weight. You'll find a 28-day diet plan complete with recipes, a journal to track your progress, produce descriptions and preparation tips, commonsense suggestions for incorporating exercise into your life, and more! In short, Dr. Richter's CommonSense Diet has everything you need to start living a healthy lifestyle today!

Dr. Richter's
CommonSensediet

eating out

Just because you're trying to lose weight doesn't mean you can't enjoy a meal in a restaurant. Here are a few tips for staying on the program when eating out:

- Have the restaurant fax you a menu or log on to their Web site ahead of time. Preselect a healthy meal before you arrive so you won't be tempted to stray from your diet.

- Watch out for these dangerous-to-your-diet words: au gratin, scalloped, hollandaise, parmigiana, fried, flash-fried, pan-fried, scampi, Bolognese, butter sauce, wine sauce, rich, creamy, or buttery.

- Ask the server to remove the bread basket after you've taken one slice. Or, request no bread be served.

- Make choices—do you want a glass of wine or a small dessert?

- Salad bars can be great places to fill up on low-calorie, nutrient-dense vegetables. But don't turn veggies into high-fat treats by piling on fatty salad dressing, cheese, bacon, eggs, and luncheon meat. Avoid prepared salads that already have the dressing added.

- Ask for salad dressings, croutons, and sauces on the side so you can control how much you eat.

- Many restaurant portions are too large for dieters. Ask the server to bring a to-go box along with your entrée. Put half of the entrée in the container before you start eating.

- Order a salad as a starter, then an appetizer or side as an entrée.

- Ask the cook to grill or cook your meal without added butter or oil.

- Resign from the clean plate club. Stop eating when you're satisfied. Just because you paid for it doesn't mean you have to eat it all. Take it home for later, or leave it on the plate.

rely on skillpower, not willpower

Dr. Richter's CommonSense Diet contains a 28-day plan to start you on the road to your best weight and a healthy lifestyle. After the 28 days, you may repeat the weekly menus or use what you've learned to create your own healthy eating plan. Here are a few guidelines to give you the skills to ensure success.

FOLLOW THE PLAN
Each week's menus are nutritionally balanced and low in calories and fat while providing enough food to fuel your body and give you a feeling of fullness. Don't skip or add meals or snacks.

HYDRATE
Drink at least eight 8-ounce glasses of water each day. Unsweetened tea or decaffeinated coffee can account for two of those servings.

PICK PRODUCE
Fresh produce is delicious and low in calories and fat. The high fiber content of most fresh produce will leave you full and satisfied. When designing your own meals, make fresh produce one-half to three-fourths of what fills your plate.

EAT BREAKFAST
Numerous studies show that breakfast eaters are more likely to lose and maintain weight loss. Eating breakfast revs up your metabolism and helps keep you from overeating later in the day.

SEASON SMART
Look to low-sodium, high-flavor seasonings such as herbs and spices, vinegar, flavored vinegars, and lemon juice instead of salt. Limit salt to no more than one teaspoon per day—less if you have high blood pressure.

COOK HEALTHY
Grill, broil, microwave, steam, boil, or stir-fry with unsaturated oils instead of deep-fat frying. Use a nonstick skillet to reduce the need for oil.

CONSIDER A MULTIVITAMIN
It's a good idea to take a multivitamin supplement when on a low-calorie diet to ensure meeting the required daily amounts (or daily value or RDA) for all nutrients.

EXERCISE
Exercise is critical for losing weight and staying healthy. To lose weight, more is better. Check with your healthcare provider before starting an exercise program. If she or he agrees, aim for at least 30 minutes most days.

top diet 10 do's

Being fit and feeling great is not about deprivation. It's about creating healthy habits and living a healthy lifestyle. Use these simple strategies to help you stick to the program and successfully achieve your weight loss goals.

1. **Make a commitment.** Declare to yourself, "I'm going to live a healthier lifestyle."

2. **Separate food from mood.** Are you really hungry, or are you just bored, stressed, lonely, tired, angry, or even happy? If you aren't truly hungry, find constructive nonfood ways to manage your moods, such as exercising, reading, journaling, watching a movie, or calling a friend.

3. **Spring clean the cupboards.** Clear all temptations out of your kitchen cabinets. Discard high-sugar and high-sodium packaged snacks. If it's not there, you won't eat it.

4. **Pay attention to portions.** Learn to recognize standard serving sizes so you won't overindulge.

5. **Focus on fresh.** Fresh produce is high in fiber, low in calories, and nutrient dense. If you must substitute canned vegetables or fruit, check the labels and avoid any with additional sugar and sodium.

6. **Budget wisely.** Think of calories as dollars. Spend them where you'll get the most bang for the caloric buck. For example, if you're going to splurge on a chocolate bar, select the best. Or, eat a treat you truly enjoy and add in extra exercise to burn off the calories. Keep in mind, you may have to exercise an hour or more to burn off a 300-calorie treat.

7. **Plan ahead.** Plan for parties and other special occasions. Eat some fruit or vegetables beforehand so you won't be overly hungry when you arrive. Don't deprive yourself; just plan ahead, eat smart, and get a little extra exercise before or after.

8. **Strategize.** Develop strategies for resisting late-night snacks. Try flossing and brushing your teeth right after dinner. Or, sip lemon water through a straw.

9. **Get back on track.** Remember that if your eating plan is interrupted, it doesn't mean your whole day or week is shot. Just get right back on the program, at the very next snack or meal.

10. **Chart your progress.** See the journal on pages 18 to 21.

size wise

As portion sizes have grown in American kitchens and restaurants, so have American waistlines. Don't let portion distortion sabotage your diet. Here's what an accurate serving size looks like:

- ½ cup = one serving of fruit, vegetables, pasta, or rice
- 2 to 3 ounces = one serving of cooked meat, poultry, or fish
- 1 cup = one serving of milk or salad greens

Note that a serving of pasta, for example, is only a half cup. That means the giant plate of pasta served in many restaurants could equal as much as five or six servings. Measure portions when you can. When you can't measure, estimate. Here's how:

- 3 ounces of cooked meat, poultry, or fish = a deck of cards
- 3 ounces of cooked fish = a checkbook
- 1 cup of milk, yogurt, or fresh salad greens = a baseball
- ½ cup of fruit, vegetables, pasta, or rice = a small fist
- 1 ounce of cheese or 1 tablespoon salad dressing or peanut butter = a woman's thumb
- 1 teaspoon butter or oil = the size of a woman's thumb tip (from the first joint)

Day 1

BREAKFAST

1 cup crispy wheat cereal squares or other unsweetened whole grain cereal with **1 cup calcium-fortified skim milk**

1 cup sliced fresh strawberries

LUNCH

Pita salad sandwich

Fill ½ of a whole wheat pita with ½ cup baby spinach leaves tossed with 1 tablespoon fat-free Italian dressing, cucumber slices, tomato slices, and 1½ ounces thinly sliced reduced-fat, reduced-sodium Swiss cheese.

1 medium apple

SNACK

⅓ cup mixed unsalted nuts

1 cup green tea

DINNER

Honey mustard salmon (about 3 ounces cooked) Combine 1 teaspoon lemon juice and 2 teaspoons honey mustard and brush on salmon before broiling or grilling.

½ cup cooked quick-cooking brown rice

¾ cup steamed sugar snap peas tossed with **1 teaspoon light butter** and a sprinkle of fresh or dried basil

SNACK

1 prepackaged single serving fat-free vanilla pudding

1 small banana

CALORIES: 1343

SATURATED FAT: 8%

SODIUM: 1255MG

DIETARY FIBER: 25G

CALCIUM: 1187MG

Day 2

BREAKFAST

Fluffy scrambled eggs

Beat 1 egg and 1 egg white with 2 teaspoons water. Cook in a small nonstick skillet with 2 teaspoons light butter.

½ cantaloupe or **Crenshaw melon**

1 slice whole wheat toast with **2 teaspoons no-sugar-added fruit spread**

1 cup orange juice

LUNCH

Fresh "antipasti"

Arrange 4 whole wheat crackers, 1 ounce thinly sliced reduced-calorie, reduced-sodium Swiss cheese, 2 celery stalks cut into sticks, 8 baby carrots, and 2 tablespoons fat-free ranch dressing for vegetable dipping sauce.

1½ cups fresh blueberries

DINNER

Italian chicken

Brush 4-ounce chicken breast with 1 tablespoon fat-free Italian dressing before broiling or grilling. (Cook extra chicken for day 3 lunch.)

Spinach-apple salad

Arrange ½ cup apple slices, 2 tablespoons raisins, and 2 teaspoons chopped unsalted peanuts over 1½ cups baby spinach leaves. Drizzle with 1 tablespoon fat-free raspberry vinaigrette.

Sesame broccoli

Steam 1 cup broccoli until crisp-tender. Heat 1 teaspoon sesame oil in a medium nonstick skillet. Add broccoli and sauté until tender. Sprinkle with ⅛ teaspoon sesame seeds.

SNACK

1 cup calcium-fortified skim milk

1 piece whole wheat bread spread with **1 tablespoon reduced-fat peanut butter**

CALORIES: 1349

SATURATED FAT: 8%

SODIUM: 2094MG

DIETARY FIBER: 25G

CALCIUM: 1014MG

Day 3

BREAKFAST

1 cup toasted oat O-shaped cereal with **1 cup calcium-fortified skim milk**

½ banana

LUNCH

Honey mustard chicken sandwich

Spread 1 tablespoon honey mustard on cut sides of a medium (about 3 ounces) whole wheat bun. Place lettuce, tomato, and onion on bottom bun half. Top with 3 ounces cooked chicken (leftover from day 2 dinner), warm or chilled, and remaining bun half.

Four-fruit salad

Combine ¼ cup each sliced strawberries, grapes, diced mango, and blueberries.

DINNER

Veggie Black Bean Soup (See recipe on page 100. Save leftovers for day 6 lunch.)

Tomato and cheese toast

Arrange 1 ounce reduced-calorie Cheddar cheese over ½ of whole wheat bun. Top with tomato and broil until cheese melts.

Ranch and greens salad

Toss 1 cup salad greens with ¼ cup sliced celery, 2 tablespoons grated carrot, ¼ cup sliced sweet red pepper, and 1 tablespoon fat-free ranch dressing.

SNACK

2 cups air-popped or **97% fat-free microwave popcorn**

¾ cup low-sodium vegetable juice

CALORIES: 1214

SATURATED FAT: 5%

SODIUM: 2462MG

DIETARY FIBER: 32G

CALCIUM: 1177MG

Day 4

BREAKFAST

Honey oatmeal

Cook ½ cup quick-cooking oats with 1 cup calcium-fortified skim milk. Stir in 1 teaspoon honey.

½ cup calcium-fortified skim milk

½ pink grapefruit or **Ugli® fruit**

LUNCH

Mixed greens and bean salad

Toss together 1½ cup salad greens, ½ cup grape tomatoes, ⅓ cup rinsed, canned garbanzo beans, ¼ cup grated carrot, and 1 tablespoon fat-free Italian dressing.

4 whole wheat crackers, or a whole wheat roll, or ½ of a whole wheat pita cut into wedges

DINNER

Cumin-Spiced Sirloin with Tomatillo Salsa (See recipe on page 100. Save leftovers for day 5 lunch.)

Balsamic grilled veggies

Brush ½ each small zucchini, yellow squash, and sweet red pepper with 2 teaspoons olive oil. Grill until tender. (Cook extra veggies for day 7 lunch.) Flavor with a splash of balsamic vinegar, if desired.

½ cup cooked couscous

SNACK

Fruit and yogurt parfait

Combine ½ cup sliced strawberries, ½ cup cubed mango, and 1 tablespoon of honey. Layer fruit mixture in a parfait glass with ½ cup nonfat vanilla yogurt.

CALORIES: 1334

SATURATED FAT: 5%

SODIUM: 854MG

DIETARY FIBER: 26G

CALCIUM: 1574MG

Day 5

BREAKFAST
Strawberry-banana smoothie

Combine ½ cup strawberries, ½ cup sliced banana, ½ cup nonfat vanilla yogurt, and 2 tablespoons orange juice in blender. Process until smooth.

1 slice whole wheat toast with **1 teaspoon light butter**

LUNCH
Steak and salsa wrap

Arrange 1½ ounces Cumin-Spiced Sirloin and 2 tablespoons Tomatillo Salsa (leftover from day 4 dinner), ¼ cup shredded romaine lettuce, and 1 tablespoon fat-free sour cream on a whole wheat tortilla and fold in sides.

1 medium orange

DINNER
Shrimp marinara over linguine

Heat ¾ cup low-sodium pasta sauce or marinara sauce until hot. Stir in 4 ounces peeled, cooked shrimp. (Call ahead and ask your grocer to peel and steam the shrimp for you or use frozen cooked shrimp to keep preparation time to a minimum, if desired.) Serve over 1¼ cups cooked linguine; sprinkle with 1 tablespoon grated Parmesan cheese.

Italian tossed salad

Toss together 1 cup salad greens, ½ cup grape tomatoes, ½ cup sliced cucumber, ¼ cup rinsed, canned artichoke hearts, and 1 tablespoon fat-free Italian dressing.

SNACK
¾ cup toasted oat O-shaped cereal with **¾ cup calcium-fortified skim milk**

CALORIES: 1348
SATURATED FAT: 5%
SODIUM: 1517MG
DIETARY FIBER: 26G
CALCIUM: 1042MG

Day 6

BREAKFAST
½ cup 1% fat cottage cheese
1 slice whole wheat toast with **1 teaspoon light butter**
1 medium peach
¾ cup low-sodium vegetable juice

LUNCH
1 cup Veggie Black Bean Soup (leftover from day 3 dinner)
4 whole wheat crackers
½ cup each broccoli florets and **sweet red pepper strips** with **2 tablespoons Ranch dressing**

DINNER
Orange-curry pork tenderloin

Rub ¾ pound pork tenderloin with 1 teaspoon curry powder, ½ teaspoon ground coriander, and ¼ teaspoon garlic powder before baking. While pork is baking, brush with 1 tablespoon orange juice. (Reserve 3 ounces of orange-curry pork tenderloin for day 7 dinner.)

Brown sugar and butter sweet potato

Bake 1 small sweet potato. Dress with 1 teaspoon each light butter and brown sugar.

1 cup steamed green beans drizzled with **1 teaspoon olive oil** and sprinkled with **fresh or dried basil**

SNACK
1 cup calcium-fortified chocolate soy milk
1 banana or **¼ cantaloupe**

CALORIES: 1360
SATURATED FAT: 9%
SODIUM: 2537MG
DIETARY FIBER: 30G
CALCIUM: 1057MG

Day 7

BREAKFAST
1 Raisin Bran Muffin
(See recipe on page 100.)
1 cup calcium-fortified skim milk
1 apple

LUNCH
Grilled vegetable pita pizza

Spread ⅓ cup low-sodium pasta sauce or marinara sauce over one 6½-inch whole wheat pita. Arrange ½ cup coarsely chopped, grilled vegetables (leftover from day 4 dinner), ¼ cup rinsed, canned artichoke hearts, and 3 tablespoons feta cheese over pasta sauce. Bake until thoroughly heated.

1 cup grapes

SNACK
Crunchy snack mix

Combine 2 tablespoons each unsalted mixed nuts and raisins with ¼ cup crispy wheat cereal squares or other whole grain cereal.

DINNER
Pork Fried Rice
(See recipe on page 100.)
Stir-fried bok choy

Stir-fry 1 cup bok choy in 1 teaspoon sesame oil in a nonstick skillet until wilted.

SNACK
½ cup 1% fat cottage cheese
½ cup blueberries

CALORIES: 1357
SATURATED FAT: 6%
SODIUM: 2341MG
DIETARY FIBER: 25G
CALCIUM: 1118MG

adding flavor without adding fat

Kicking up the flavor in a dish doesn't have to mean loading it with fat; there are plenty of ways to add pizzazz to your food without adding inches to your waistline. Cut down on oil by making your own salad dressing and going heavier on the vinegar and lemon juice, or by sautéing veggies in reduced-fat broth or juice. Try substituting fat-free yogurt or cottage cheese for the mayonnaise or sour cream in your favorite recipe. Above all, make herbs your new best friend—experiment with exotic combinations in casseroles, curries, and soups, and coat uncooked meats with a dry rub rather than dousing in rich sauces or oily marinades.

diet plan Week 2

Day 1

BREAKFAST

1 container low-fat vanilla yogurt

1 cup fresh raspberries

1 hard-cooked egg

¾ cup orange juice

LUNCH

Turkey-avocado roll-up

Spread 1 tablespoon fat-free cream cheese on a whole wheat tortilla. Layer with 2 ounces thinly sliced smoked turkey, ¼ cup alfalfa sprouts, and 4 slices avocado (about ¼ avocado). Roll up.

1 medium apple

DINNER

Pan-seared chicken with braised mushrooms

Flatten 4 ounces chicken breast and sprinkle with salt and pepper. Brown chicken in a nonstick skillet with 2 teaspoons olive oil. Remove chicken from skillet. Add 2 tablespoons reduced-sodium chicken broth and ¾ cup mushrooms to skillet; cook until mushrooms are tender. Sprinkle with fresh or dried thyme, if desired. Spoon mushrooms over chicken.

Roasted asparagus

Toss 6 asparagus spears with 1 teaspoon olive oil. Broil until tender. (Broil extra spears for day 3 lunch.)

Cranberry couscous

Stir 1 tablespoon dried cranberries into ½ cup cooked couscous.

SNACK

1 cup calcium-fortified skim milk

1 small banana

1 tablespoon reduced-fat peanut butter

CALORIES: 1348

SATURATED FAT: 5%

SODIUM: 1495MG

DIETARY FIBER: 25G

CALCIUM: 1079MG

Day 2

BREAKFAST

1 cup toasted oat O-shaped cereal

1 cup calcium-fortified skim milk

1 tangelo or orange

LUNCH

Toasted pita wedges and vegetables with hummus

Cut 1 whole wheat pita into 8 wedges. Coat wedges with olive oil flavored cooking spray and bake until crisp. Serve pita wedges, 4 baby carrots, 4 cucumber slices, and 3 radishes with ⅓ cup store-bought hummus.

1 cup cherries or seedless grapes

DINNER

Grilled lemon pepper tuna

Brush 4 ounces tuna with 1½ teaspoons olive oil and sprinkle with salt-free lemon pepper seasoning before grilling. (Grill extra tuna for day 3 lunch.)

Steamed artichoke with tarragon aioli

Combine 3 tablespoons fat-free mayonnaise with 1 teaspoon lemon juice, ½ teaspoon Dijon mustard, and ⅛ teaspoon dried tarragon. Serve as a dipping sauce with steamed artichoke.

½ cup cooked barley or quick-cooking brown rice

SNACK

1 Raisin Bran Muffin (leftover from week one)

½ cup calcium-fortified skim milk

CALORIES: 1342

SATURATED FAT: 4%

SODIUM: 1858MG

DIETARY FIBER: 33G

CALCIUM: 1198MG

Day 3

BREAKFAST

½ whole wheat bagel spread with 1 tablespoon fat-free cream cheese and 1 tablespoon no-sugar-added fruit spread

¾ cup calcium-fortified skim milk

1 medium pear

LUNCH

Tuna niçoise salad

Thinly slice 2 ounces grilled tuna (leftover from day 2 dinner), and 2 small boiled new potatoes. Arrange tuna, potato, 6 roasted asparagus spears (leftover from day 1 dinner), 2 tablespoons sliced red onion, and 2 tablespoons sliced red bell pepper over 1½ cups salad greens. Drizzle with 2 tablespoons fat-free raspberry vinaigrette.

½ cup raspberries

DINNER

Vegetable Bean Tostadas (See recipe on page 102.)

¼ honeydew melon drizzled with lime juice

SNACK

⅔ cup calcium-fortified chocolate soy milk

¼ cup unsalted almonds

CALORIES: 1355

SATURATED FAT: 4%

SODIUM: 1458MG

DIETARY FIBER: 38G

CALCIUM: 1040MG

Day 4

BREAKFAST

Honey oatmeal

Cook ½ cup quick-cooking oats with 1 cup calcium-fortified skim milk. Stir in 1 teaspoon honey.

½ cup blueberries

LUNCH

Roast beef and mozzarella sandwich

Assemble sandwich using 1 tablespoon each fat-free mayonnaise and Dijon mustard, 2 ounces low-salt thinly sliced roast beef, 1 ounce thinly sliced part-skim mozzarella cheese, lettuce, tomato, and 2 slices whole wheat bread.

1 cup cherries

DINNER

Eggplant Ratatouille (See recipe on page 104.)

½ cup cooked polenta

Tossed salad

Toss 1 cup salad greens, ¼ sweet red bell pepper cut into strips, ¼ cup coarsely chopped cucumber, and 3 halved yellow teardrop tomatoes or cherry tomatoes with 1 tablespoon fat-free balsamic vinaigrette.

SNACK

Cranberry spritzer

Combine ¾ cup cranberry-apple drink with ¼ cup seltzer water. Squeeze in a wedge of lime.

Crunchy snack mix

Combine ¼ cup crispy wheat cereal squares, 2 tablespoons dried cranberries, and 1 tablespoon unsalted peanuts.

CALORIES: 1264

SATURATED FAT: 6%

SODIUM: 2232MG

DIETARY FIBER: 30G

CALCIUM: 1202MG

Day 5

BREAKFAST

Breakfast burrito
Scramble 1 egg and 1 egg white in a small nonstick skillet coated with vegetable cooking spray. Arrange egg down center of a whole wheat tortilla. Top with 2 tablespoons shredded reduced-fat Monterey Jack cheese and 1 tablespoon salsa. Sprinkle with chopped fresh cilantro, if desired. Fold up edges.

1 tangelo or orange

LUNCH

Bagel with peanut butter
Spread half of a whole wheat bagel with 1½ tablespoons reduced-fat peanut butter.

1 cup calcium-fortified skim milk
¼ honeydew

DINNER

Indonesian Chicken and Vegetable Kabobs
(See recipe on page 102.)

Seasoned kale
Steam 2 cups kale or spinach until wilted. Toss with 1 teaspoon light butter and a dash of malt vinegar.

½ cup cooked quick-cooking brown rice

SNACK

Lemon-berry smoothie
Combine ⅔ cup raspberries, ½ cup low-fat lemon yogurt, and 2 tablespoons orange juice in a blender and process until smooth.

CALORIES: 1363
SATURATED FAT: 6%
SODIUM: 1952MG
DIETARY FIBER: 25G
CALCIUM: 102MG

Day 6

BREAKFAST

1 cup bran flakes cereal
1 cup calcium-fortified milk
1 small banana

LUNCH

Fruit and cheese plate
Arrange ½ cup 1% cottage cheese, 1½ ounces reduced-fat Cheddar cheese, ½ cup grapes, 1 peeled and sliced kiwi, and 1 sliced carambola (star fruit) on a plate.

6 Melba toast rounds or whole wheat crackers

DINNER

Filet mignon with shallot-cherry sauce
Sprinkle 4-ounce filet with ⅛ teaspoon salt and ⅛ teaspoon pepper. Heat a small skillet over high heat until hot. Add steak and cook 2 to 3 minutes per side or until desired degree of doneness. Remove steak from pan. Reduce heat to medium-high. Add 1 teaspoon olive oil. Add 1 tablespoon diced shallots and ⅛ teaspoon minced garlic; cook until tender. Stir in 2 tablespoons water, 2 tablespoons cherry juice, and ¼ teaspoon beef bouillon granules. Cook until mixture reduces slightly. Serve over beef.

Citrus carrots
Steam ½ cup sliced carrots and toss with 1 teaspoon light butter, 1 teaspoon orange juice, and a dusting of grated fresh orange rind.

Rosemary roasted new potatoes
Cut 3 small new potatoes (4 ounces) in half. Place on a baking sheet. Coat with olive oil-flavored cooking spray. Sprinkle with ½ teaspoon dried rosemary, ⅛ teaspoon garlic salt, and a dash of pepper. Bake at 425°F until tender.

SNACK

¾ cup low-sodium vegetable juice cocktail
¼ cup unsalted almonds

CALORIES: 1337
SATURATED FAT: 8%
SODIUM: 1960MG
DIETARY FIBER: 25G
CALCIUM: 1112MG

Day 7

BREAKFAST

Honey oatmeal
Cook ½ cup quick-cooking oats with 1 cup calcium-fortified skim milk. Stir in 1 teaspoon honey.

1 small banana

LUNCH

Cheesy Artichoke Pasta Salad
(See recipe on page 104.)

1 medium apple

DINNER

Greek-style tilapia
Combine 2 teaspoons orange juice, 1 teaspoon lemon juice, 2 teaspoons olive oil, ½ teaspoon dried oregano, ⅛ teaspoon salt, and a dash of pepper. Drizzle over one 5-ounce tilapia fillet before baking.

Tomato and feta bulgur
Stir 2 tablespoons chopped tomato, 1 tablespoon crumbled feta, 1 tablespoon fat-free balsamic vinaigrette, 1 teaspoon lemon juice, and 2 teaspoons fresh parsley or mint into ½ cup cooked bulgur.

Minted peas
Stir 1 teaspoon light butter and 1 teaspoon chopped fresh mint into ½ cup cooked peas.

SNACK

Fresh pear with vanilla-almond dip
Stir ⅛ teaspoon almond extract and a dash of nutmeg into ¼ cup low-fat vanilla yogurt. Serve with a sliced pear.

CALORIES: 1366
SATURATED FAT: 7%
SODIUM: 1723MG
DIETARY FIBER: 30G
CALCIUM: 1013MG

---

choosing a cereal can be a challenge

Even healthy looking cereals can be deceiving. Avoid refined cereals and pick one made with whole grains instead, which may help fight heart disease, diabetes, and certain types of cancer. You'll get all three parts of the grain, including the fiber-rich bran and the nutrient-packed germ. A bonus—since fiber takes a while to digest, you'll feel full longer. Look for vitamin- and mineral-fortified products, and scrutinize the ingredients. Anything with partially hydrogenated oil contains cholesterol-raising trans fats, while sugar can lurk in the guise of "corn syrup," "maltose," or "dextrin." Most important, experiment until you find a cereal you really like—no matter how healthy it is, it'll stay in the box if you don't enjoy eating it.

diet plan Week ❸

Day 1

BREAKFAST

Whole grain waffles with sweetened strawberries

Coat 1 cup sliced strawberries with 2 teaspoons honey. Toast two frozen whole grain waffles. Top toasted waffles with strawberry mixture.

³/₄ cup calcium-fortified skim milk

LUNCH

Bacon, lettuce, and tomato sandwich

Combine 2 tablespoons fat-free mayonnaise and 2 teaspoons grated Asiago or Parmesan cheese. Spread evenly on 2 slices toasted whole wheat bread. Arrange 4 tomato slices, 3 pieces cooked turkey bacon, and a lettuce leaf over mayonnaise mixture on one slice of bread. Top with remaining bread slice, mayonnaise side down.

2 plums

DINNER

Sage pork chops with caramelized onions

Rub ¹/₈ teaspoon ground sage and ¹/₈ teaspoon pepper over one 4-ounce boneless center loin pork chop. Cook in a nonstick skillet coated with vegetable cooking spray until done. Remove from skillet. Add 1 teaspoon olive oil and ¹/₃ cup vertically sliced onion. Sauté until tender. Sprinkle with 1 teaspoon balsamic vinegar and ¹/₂ teaspoon sugar. Cook until golden. Add water if needed to keep onions from sticking. Stir in ¹/₂ teaspoon fresh thyme. Serve onions over pork.

Baked acorn squash with maple and cinnamon

Bake or microwave half of an acorn squash until tender. Brush with 1 teaspoon maple syrup and sprinkle with cinnamon.

Spinach-apple salad

Arrange 3 apple slices, 2 tablespoons sliced celery, and 1 tablespoon chopped pecans over 1¹/₄ cups baby spinach leaves. Drizzle with 1 tablespoon fat-free balsamic vinaigrette.

SNACK

Figs with ricotta

Stir 1 teaspoon honey into ¹/₄ cup part-skim ricotta cheese. (For a smooth cheese mixture combine mixture in a blender.) Serve with 2 halved figs.

CALORIES: 1371

SATURATED FAT: 8%

SODIUM: 2095MG

DIETARY FIBER: 25G

CALCIUM: 1092MG

Day 2

BREAKFAST

1 cup crispy wheat cereal squares or other unsweetened whole grain cereal with **1 cup calcium-fortified skim milk**

2 apricots

LUNCH

Greek salad

Toss together 2 cups romaine lettuce, ¹/₃ cup chopped green pepper, 4 red onion rings, 3 tablespoons feta cheese, 2 tablespoons sliced black olives, and 1 sliced plum tomato. Combine 1¹/₂ tablespoons lemon juice, 2 teaspoons olive oil, ¹/₈ teaspoon crushed garlic, and a pinch each of sugar, salt, and pepper. Drizzle over salad.

1 pear

1 whole wheat roll

DINNER

Mushroom-Beef Burgers (See recipe on page 106. Reserve leftover for day 4 lunch.)

Sweet potato wedges

Cut a small sweet potato into wedges. Arrange on a baking sheet. Coat with olive oil-flavored cooking spray. Sprinkle with ¹/₈ teaspoon salt and a dash of ground red pepper. Bake at 450°F until tender, turning occasionally.

¹/₂ cup canned, drained three bean salad

SNACK

1 snack-size container fat-free vanilla pudding

1 peach

CALORIES: 1230

SATURATED FAT: 6%

SODIUM: 2445MG

DIETARY FIBER: 28G

CALCIUM: 1057MG

Day 3

BREAKFAST

1 cup toasted oat O-shaped cereal

1 cup calcium-fortified skim milk

¹/₂ cup blueberries

LUNCH

Papaya Seafood Salad (See recipe on page 106.)

6 whole wheat crackers

SNACK

2 clementines

1 small handful of unsalted pistachios or mixed nuts (about 3 tablespoons)

DINNER

Chutney chicken

Combine 1 tablespoon mango chutney, 1 teaspoon rice vinegar or white vinegar, and ¹/₂ teaspoon coarse-grained mustard. Brush on 4 ounces chicken breast before baking.

Lemon-buttered broccoli

Steam 1 cup broccoli. Toss with 1 teaspoon light butter and 1 teaspoon lemon juice.

Quinoa with dates

Stir 1 tablespoon chopped dates and ¹/₈ teaspoon orange rind (optional) into ¹/₂ cup cooked quinoa or cooked quick-cooking brown rice.

SNACK

Honeyed banana frosty

Freeze 1 small sliced banana and ¹/₃ cup calcium-fortified skim milk. Combine frozen banana and milk in a blender with ¹/₄ cup low-fat vanilla yogurt and 2 teaspoons honey. Process until blended.

CALORIES: 1313

SATURATED FAT: 4%

SODIUM: 1020MG

DIETARY FIBER: 27G

CALCIUM: 1157MG

Day 4

BREAKFAST

Breakfast parfait

Coat ²/₃ cup strawberries with 1 tablespoon honey. Layer strawberries in a parfait glass with ¹/₂ cup low-fat vanilla or fruit-flavored yogurt. Top with ¹/₄ cup low-fat granola cereal and 2 teaspoons toasted slivered almonds.

LUNCH

Mushroom-Beef Burger (leftover from day 2 dinner)

Raw vegetables with blue cheese dip

Serve ¹/₂ cup broccoflower florets, ¹/₂ cup sweet red pepper strips and 4 baby carrots with 2 tablespoons fat-free blue cheese dressing.

1 medium apple

DINNER

Honey-Ginger Tofu and Veggie Stir-Fry (See recipe on page 106.)

¹/₂ cup cooked quick-cooking brown rice

2 clementines or 1 orange

SNACK

1 cup calcium-fortified skim milk

1 cup strawberries

CALORIES: 1339

SATURATED FAT: 4%

SODIUM: 1465MG

DIETARY FIBER: 30G

CALCIUM: 1221MG

Day 5

BREAKFAST
Peaches and "cream" waffles

Coat 1 sliced peach with 2 teaspoons honey. Toast two frozen whole grain waffles, and top with ¼ cup part-skim ricotta cheese and peach mixture.

1 cup calcium-fortified skim milk

LUNCH
1 cup prepared canned reduced-sodium tomato soup

Open-faced cucumber sandwich

Combine 1 tablespoon fat-free cream cheese with 1 teaspoon chopped fresh or ¼ teaspoon dried dill weed. Spread over ½ toasted whole wheat English muffin. Arrange 4 cucumber slices over cheese mixture. Garnish with fresh dill, if desired.

1 medium apple

DINNER
Lemon-caper swordfish

Grill 4 ounces swordfish. While fish is grilling, melt 2 teaspoons light butter; stir in 1 teaspoon lemon juice and ½ teaspoon small capers. Spoon sauce mixture over grilled fish.

Braised fennel and leeks

Combine 1 cup reduced-sodium chicken broth in a small skillet. Bring liquid to a simmer. Add half a trimmed fennel bulb and half a cleaned leek, and simmer until fennel and leek are tender. (For a flavor boost, add a couple peppercorns, 1 sprig of fresh thyme, and 1 clove garlic to simmering liquid; strain before serving.) Remove vegetables from liquid. Bring liquid to a boil, and boil until mixture reduces to ¼ cup. Stir in 1 teaspoon light butter.

Papaya and raspberries with lime

Arrange 1 cup papaya slices and ¼ cup raspberries on a plate. Squeeze lime juice over fruit.

SNACK
⅔ cup low-fat granola cereal
¾ cup calcium-fortified skim milk

CALORIES: 1349
SATURATED FAT: 8%
SODIUM: 1979MG
DIETARY FIBER: 25G
CALCIUM: 1595MG

Day 6

BREAKFAST
Honey oatmeal

Cook ½ cup quick-cooking oats with 1 cup calcium-fortified skim milk. Stir in 1 teaspoon honey.

1 apricot

LUNCH
Cobb salad

Arrange 3 ounces chopped cooked chicken or turkey breast, 1 chopped hard-cooked egg, 1 cup grape tomatoes, ½ cup grated carrot, and ½ cup grated zucchini in rows over 2 cups mixed salad greens. Sprinkle with 1 crumbled cooked turkey bacon slice. Serve with 2 tablespoons fat-free blue cheese dressing.

1 medium apple or pear

DINNER
Triple Cheese Pizza
(See recipe on page 106.)

Crunchy vegetable and bean salad

Combine ½ cup canned three-bean salad with 2 tablespoons diced carrot, 2 tablespoons diced green pepper, and 1 tablespoon chopped onion. Serve on a lettuce leaf.

SNACK
1 plum
¼ cup unsalted mixed nuts

CALORIES: 1317
SATURATED FAT: 9%
SODIUM: 1781MG
DIETARY FIBER: 26G
CALCIUM: 1193MG

Day 7

BREAKFAST
Vegetable-cheese scramble

Melt 2 teaspoons light butter in a nonstick skillet coated with vegetable cooking spray. Sauté 1 chopped green onion and 2 tablespoons chopped sweet red pepper in skillet. Beat 1 egg, 1 egg white and 1 tablespoon water. Pour egg mixture over vegetables. Cook, stirring frequently until eggs are set. Sprinkle with 3 tablespoons shredded reduced-fat Cheddar cheese.

1 slice turkey bacon
½ grapefruit

LUNCH
Opened-faced peanut butter and banana sandwich

Spread 1 ½ tablespoons reduced-fat peanut butter on one half of a whole wheat English muffin. Slice 1 small banana; arrange banana slices over peanut butter. Drizzle with 1 teaspoon honey

1 cup calcium-fortified skim milk

DINNER
Spaghetti squash with mushroom marinara

Sauté 1½ cups sliced mushrooms, 2 tablespoons chopped onion, ¼ teaspoon minced garlic, and ⅛ teaspoon crushed fennel seeds in 2 teaspoons olive oil in a nonstick skillet coated with vegetable cooking spray. Stir in ¾ cup low-sodium pasta sauce. Serve over cooked spaghetti squash strands removed from one half of a cooked spaghetti squash. Top with 1 tablespoon shredded Parmesan cheese.

Spinach-Orange Salad

Toss together 1 cup baby spinach leaves, ½ cup orange segments, ¼ cup red onion, and 1 tablespoon crumbled feta cheese. Drizzle with 1 tablespoon fat-free raspberry vinaigrette.

SNACK
1 cup raspberries or blueberries

CALORIES: 1268
SATURATED FAT: 10%
SODIUM: 1371MG
DIETARY FIBER: 31G
CALCIUM: 1124MG

got milk?®

Don't skimp on it if you're looking to up your calcium intake. As well as building strong bones and teeth, this essential mineral helps your muscles contract, your heart beat, and your blood clot. Use milk when making soups, oatmeal, and casseroles. You won't know it's there — but your body will. If you just can't face donning a milk moustache, there are other options. Cheese and yogurt (choose lower fat versions, if possible) as well as green leafy vegetables, sardines, and salmon are all calcium rich. You can even find calcium-fortified orange juice and tofu.

diet plan Week

Day 1

BREAKFAST

1 cup bran flakes

1 cup calcium-fortified skim milk

½ cup raspberries

LUNCH

Tomato, mozzarella, and white bean salad

Combine ½ cup cannellini beans, 1 tablespoon chopped red onion, 1½ teaspoons chopped fresh basil, and 1 tablespoon fat-free balsamic vinaigrette. Arrange 1 sliced tomato and 2 ounces sliced part-skim mozzarella cheese on a plate. Mound bean mixture in center of plate. Drizzle with 1 tablespoon fat-free balsamic vinaigrette; sprinkle with chopped fresh basil and freshly ground pepper.

1 small whole wheat roll or **6 whole wheat crackers**

DINNER

Spicy catfish

Combine 1 teaspoon paprika, ¼ teaspoon dried thyme, ¼ teaspoon garlic salt, ⅛ teaspoon black pepper, and ⅛ teaspoon ground red pepper. Coat 5 ounces catfish with vegetable cooking spray. Sprinkle paprika mixture over fish before grilling or broiling.

Parmesan corn on the cob

Combine 1 tablespoon grated Parmesan cheese, 2 teaspoons light butter, 1 teaspoon fresh oregano, and dash of black pepper. Spread cheese mixture over 1 ear cooked corn.

Sweet and tangy broccoli slaw with apple

Combine 2 tablespoons apple cider vinegar, 1 tablespoon plus 1 teaspoon sugar, 2¼ teaspoons apple juice or water, dash each of mustard seeds and celery seeds. Heat vinegar mixture in microwave or small saucepan until sugar dissolves. Pour over 1½ cups broccoli slaw mix. Stir in ¼ cup chopped apple. Serve 1 cup slaw with dinner. Reserve remaining slaw for lunch on day 3.

SNACK

2 cups watermelon or **other muskmelon**

CALORIES:	1267
SATURATED FAT:	10%
SODIUM:	1926MG
DIETARY FIBER:	28G
CALCIUM:	1190MG

Day 2

BREAKFAST

Honey oatmeal

Cook ½ cup quick-cooking oats with 1 cup calcium-fortified skim milk. Stir in 1 teaspoon honey.

1 small banana

LUNCH

Carrot-Fennel Soup

(See recipe on page 108.)

Tossed salad with summer squash

Toss together 1½ cups mixed salad greens, ½ cup chopped tomato, ¼ cup sliced zucchini, and ¼ cup sliced yellow squash. Drizzle with 2 tablespoons fat-free Italian dressing and ½ ounce shaved Parmesan cheese.

¼ medium cantaloupe or **Persian melon**

DINNER

Cranberry-orange turkey cutlets

Sprinkle cutlets with ⅛ teaspoon each salt and pepper. Cook in a nonstick skillet coated with vegetable cooking spray until done. Remove turkey from skillet. Add ¼ cup whole-berry cranberry sauce, 1 tablespoon orange juice, ⅛ teaspoon crystallized ginger, and ⅛ teaspoon grated fresh orange rind (optional). Cook until heated. Spoon sauce over warm turkey.

Hazelnut Brussels sprouts

Steam Brussels sprouts. Melt 1 teaspoon light butter in a small nonstick skillet. Add ⅛ teaspoon minced garlic. Sauté until fragrant. Add Brussels sprouts, tossing to coat. Sprinkle with 1 tablespoon chopped hazelnuts or pecans.

Brown rice with green onions

Stir 1 tablespoon sliced green onions into ½ cup cooked quick-cooking brown rice.

SNACK

½ cup vanilla or **fruit-flavored low-fat yogurt**

1 cup blackberries

CALORIES:	1204
SATURATED FAT:	6%
SODIUM:	1402MG
DIETARY FIBER:	29G
CALCIUM:	1310MG

Day 3

BREAKFAST

Pineapple smoothie

Combine ½ cup chopped fresh pineapple, ½ cup sliced banana, ½ cup lemon or pineapple low-fat yogurt, and 2 tablespoons apple juice in blender. Process until blended.

½ whole wheat English muffin

1 teaspoon light butter

LUNCH

Turkey-slaw wrap

Spoon ½ cup broccoli slaw (from day 1) onto a whole wheat tortilla. Top with 2 ounces thinly sliced smoked turkey and 1 ounce sliced part-skim mozzarella. Roll up.

1 cup blackberries

DINNER

½ of a single serving frozen reduced-fat macaroni and cheese dinner

Lima beans with bacon

Chop 1 slice Canadian bacon. Sauté bacon, 1 tablespoon chopped onion, and ⅛ teaspoon minced garlic in 1 teaspoon light butter in small skillet. Stir in ½ cup cooked fresh or frozen lima beans and ½ teaspoon fresh thyme.

Crumb-topped broiled tomato

Spread 1 teaspoon Dijon mustard over cut side of one half of a tomato. Combine 2 tablespoons dry bread crumbs, 1 tablespoon Parmesan cheese, ⅛ teaspoon dried Italian seasoning, and a dash of pepper. Spoon crumb mixture on tomato. Spray lightly with olive oil-flavored cooking spray. Broil 2 to 3 minutes or until golden.

¼ Persian melon or cantaloupe

SNACK

1 cup toasted oat O-shaped cereal

1 cup calcium-fortified skim milk

CALORIES:	1350
SATURATED FAT:	8%
SODIUM:	2261MG
DIETARY FIBER:	27G
CALCIUM:	1352MG

Day 4

BREAKFAST

Oatmeal with honey, dates, and walnuts

Cook ½ cup quick-cooking oats in 1 cup calcium-fortified skim milk. Stir in 1½ tablespoons chopped dates, 2 teaspoons chopped walnuts or pecans, and 1 teaspoon honey.

1 small banana

LUNCH

Open-faced tuna melt

Combine ⅓ cup canned white tuna in water drained with 1½ tablespoons fat-free mayonnaise, 1 teaspoon mustard, 1 teaspoon pickle relish, ½ teaspoon small capers, and ⅛ teaspoon pepper. Place 1 tomato slice on half of a toasted whole wheat English muffin. Top with tuna mixture. Broil 1 minute. Top with 3 tablespoons shredded reduced-fat Cheddar cheese. Broil until cheese melts.

Cucumber, radish, and onion salad

Toss together ½ cup sliced or chopped cucumber, ¼ cup sliced radish, 1 tablespoon coarsely chopped red onion, and 1 tablespoon chopped fresh parsley. Combine 1 tablespoon red wine vinegar, 1 teaspoon olive oil, ¼ teaspoon sugar, and a dash of salt and pepper. Pour over cucumber mixture; toss.

DINNER

Garlic Scallops over Pasta

(See recipe on page 108.)

Mixed greens with arugula and grapefruit

Arrange ½ cup grapefruit sections over 1 cup mixed greens and ¼ cup arugula. Sprinkle with 1 tablespoon pine nuts. Combine 1 tablespoon fat-free Italian dressing, 1 teaspoon red wine vinegar, and ½ teaspoon Dijon mustard. Drizzle over salad.

SNACK

Pineapple ambrosia

Combine ¾ cup chopped pineapple, ½ cup orange sections, 1 tablespoon orange juice, 1 teaspoon honey, and 2 or 3 drops coconut extract. Sprinkle with 2 teaspoons toasted coconut.

CALORIES:	1341
SATURATED FAT:	5%
SODIUM:	2105MG
DIETARY FIBER:	25G
CALCIUM:	1101MG

Day 5

BREAKFAST

Cheese grits

Stir 2 tablespoons shredded reduced-fat Cheddar cheese into ½ cup cooked quick-cooking grits.

1 link turkey breakfast sausage

Broiled grapefruit

Combine 1 tablespoon no-sugar-added orange marmalade, 1 teaspoon honey, and a dash of ground ginger. Spread over cut side of half a grapefruit.

LUNCH

Spinach salad with apples, bacon, and cheese

Chop 2 slices Canadian bacon. Arrange 6 apple slices, chopped bacon, and 1 ounce cubed Edam cheese over 2 cups baby spinach leaves. Drizzle with 2 tablespoons fat-free balsamic vinaigrette.

1 cup Carrot-Fennel Soup
(leftover from day 2 lunch)

SNACK

1 cup blackberries

DINNER

Beef and Couscous Stuffed Peppers
(See recipe on page 110.)

Roasted green beans

Toss 1 cup green beans with 1 teaspoon olive oil. Roast at 425°F until tender.

SNACK

¾ cup toasted oat O-shaped cereal

¾ cup calcium-fortified skim milk

CALORIES: 1351
SATURATED FAT: 11%
SODIUM: 2323MG
DIETARY FIBER: 34G
CALCIUM: 1401MG

Day 6

BREAKFAST

1 cup crispy wheat cereal squares or other unsweetened whole grain cereal with **1 cup calcium-fortified skim milk**

½ cup blueberries

LUNCH

Turkey-cranberry sandwich

Spread 2 slices whole wheat bread each with 1 tablespoon fat-free cream cheese. Spoon ¼ cup whole-berry cranberry sauce over 1 slice of bread. Top with 2 ounces thinly sliced turkey and 5 baby spinach leaves. Top with remaining bread slice, cream cheese side down.

1 orange

DINNER

Cumin-scented pork tenderloin

Combine 1½ teaspoons ground cumin, 1 teaspoon ground coriander, ¼ teaspoon salt, and ¼ teaspoon ground red pepper. Rub mixture onto ¾ pound pork tenderloin coated with cooking spray. Grill, bake, or broil. Enjoy 3 ounces cooked pork. Reserve 2 ounces for day 7.

Roasted spiced rutabaga

Combine 2 teaspoons melted light butter, 2 teaspoons brown sugar, ⅛ teaspoon ground nutmeg, and a dash of salt and red pepper. Toss with 1 cup cubed rutabaga. Roast at 400°F until tender, stirring frequently.

Sautéed zucchini, yellow squash, and onion

Sauté ½ cup zucchini slices, ½ cup yellow squash slices, and ¼ cup coarsely chopped onion in a nonstick skillet coated with vegetable cooking spray and 1 teaspoon olive oil. Sprinkle with fresh or dried marjoram.

SNACK

1 medium apple

1 ounce thinly sliced Edam cheese

CALORIES: 1347
SATURATED FAT: 8%
SODIUM: 1892MG
DIETARY FIBER: 25G
CALCIUM: 1034MG

Day 7

BREAKFAST

½ cup low-fat granola

1 cup calcium-fortified skim milk

½ cup blueberries

LUNCH

Mexican pork and bean topped potato

Combine 2 ounces cubed Cumin-Scented Pork Tenderloin (leftover from day 6), ½ cup pinto beans, and ⅓ cup salsa. Split a medium baked potato and top with bean mixture. Dollop with 1 tablespoon fat-free sour cream, and sprinkle with 2 tablespoons reduced-fat Monterey Jack or Cheddar cheese.

1 orange

DINNER

Garden Frittata
(See recipe on page 108.)

1 link cooked turkey breakfast sausage

1 cup mixed fruit such as cubed pineapple, blackberries, and cantaloupe

SNACK

Lemon yogurt with raspberries

Spoon one half cup low-fat lemon yogurt over ½ cup raspberries. Sprinkle with 2 teaspoons toasted slivered almonds.

CALORIES: 1358
SATURATED FAT: 9%
SODIUM: 2155MG
DIETARY FIBER: 32G
CALCIUM: 1351MG

---

essential fatty acids like omega-3s are just that: essential

As well as lowering cholesterol and triglyceride levels, naturally thinning the blood to decrease the risk of clots and strokes, and even reducing hypertension, omega-3s are also beneficial to brain growth and development. So how to add more of them into your diet? Key omega-3s eicosapentaenoic acid (EPA) and docosahexaenoic acid (DHA) occur in cold-water fish like sardines, herring, mackerel, albacore tuna, and salmon. Not a seafood fan? Add a daily dose of flaxseed, canola oil, walnuts, or dark green leafy vegetables, all of which are rich in alpha-linolenic acid (ALA). And be on the lookout for eggs fortified with omega-3s; they're increasingly common in supermarket aisles.

exercise:
the key to permanent
weight loss

The U.S. Department of Agriculture's Dietary Guidelines for Americans recommends that adults engage in at least 30 minutes of moderate-intensity activity most days of the week; more if they are trying to lose weight.

Exercise is the not-so-secret tool of successful "losers," people who not only lose weight, but also maintain the loss long term. Regular exercise is not only essential to permanent weight loss, it also promotes good health. It helps reduce the risk of cardiovascular disease, hypertension, osteoporosis, diabetes, and certain forms of cancer; promotes psychological well-being; and may also help prevent age-related cognitive decline. Plus, exercise combats stress, anxiety, and sleeplessness.

THE BEST EXERCISE
Any activity you will do consistently is the "best" exercise for you, so find something you love and make it part of your daily life. Think of exercise as recreational fun, rather than something on the to-do list, and you'll be more likely to stick with it. Walking is easy, and it burns almost as many calories as jogging. Or try biking, aerobic dance, tennis, hiking, swimming, jumping rope, boxing, yoga—anything to get moving.

GET STARTED
Start slow, especially if you aren't used to exercising. Walking is one of the easiest forms of exercise, and just about anyone can do it. For the first two weeks of an exercise program, concentrate mainly on stretching and limbering up forgotten muscles. Focus on consistency and length of exercise time instead of intensity, and build up gradually. If you have sciatica, arthritis, or foot problems, try swimming, water aerobics, or bicycling instead of walking.

WARM UP, COOL DOWN, AND STRETCH
Begin each session with 5 minutes of slow activity to warm up the muscles and help prevent injury. Cool down at the end of your workout by exercising gently for 5 minutes or so until your heart rate and breathing return to normal. Gently stretch, focusing on the areas such as the calf, Achilles tendon, bottom of the foot, hamstrings, and lower back.

BUILD INTENSITY AND INCREASE TIME
When you first begin walking, start with a 10-minute walk at a moderate pace in which your heart rate increases and your breathing becomes faster, but you are still able to carry on a conversation. Notice what parts of your body are tired and aching afterward. Focus on those areas when you stretch the next day.

Build to 20 minutes a day in the first few weeks. As you become more fit, increase to 30 minutes or more most days. As you walk farther and faster, you will notice your heart doesn't beat as fast and you don't breathe as hard as you did a few weeks before. You'll also be surprised to find that you are enjoying yourself and looking forward to your daily exercise. These are all signs that you are getting in shape. After two weeks of walking gently, pick up the pace. You should be breathing harder, and it should be more difficult to hold a conversation. After a month or so, you can lengthen your walk or start to jog, trot up stairs, or power walk to burn more calories.

STRIVE FOR VARIETY
Consider a mix of activities that combine endurance, strength, and flexibility. Endurance activities, such as walking or biking, build stamina and strengthen the cardiovascular system. Weight-bearing exercise, such as lifting weights or jogging, builds both muscle (which revs up your metabolism) and bone mass (which can help prevent osteoporosis). Aim for lifting weights two to three times a week. Stretching maintains flexibility, especially in the joints.

SECRETS TO SUCCESS

Break it up. If you don't have time for one long exercise session, break it up into smaller sessions.

Mix it up. Vary activities or intensity to work different muscles and prevent boredom.

Buddy up. Find a friend to exercise with. You can help each other stick to a plan and stay motivated.

Make an appointment. Pick a realistic time to exercise that regularly fits your schedule, and then keep the appointment. If you're not a morning person, don't promise yourself you'll get up an hour early to exercise. You probably won't.

Practice stealth exercise. Keep moving throughout the day by parking at the far end of the lot or taking the stairs. Do bicep curls with bags of groceries, pace while talking on the phone, or walk the length of the mall before hitting any of the shops. It all adds up.

Make it a family affair.
Get everyone involved in a game of softball, or take a bike ride together. Childhood obesity is a growing problem in America. Be a role model and an advocate for an active lifestyle. To meet your own fitness goals, you may need to also exercise on your own. If a 5-foot tall person tries to walk with a 6-footer, the taller person will get little benefit, while the shorter person may have to walk fast enough to risk injury or burnout.

Expect the unexpected. Create a plan that allows you to exercise while traveling, meeting work deadlines, caring for sick children, or dealing with any other curveballs life throws your way.

Set goals. Write down specific, measurable goals like walking 30 minutes every day or eating five servings of fruit and vegetables; they are easier to meet than the vague "eat healthier" or "exercise more" type.

Keep a record. It's easy to underestimate how much you are eating and to overestimate how much you are exercising. An exercise log and food diary keeps you honest. See the journal on pages 18 to 21.

Reward success. Track your progress and treat yourself to a healthy nonfood reward such as a book or a bouquet of flowers every time you reach a goal.

WHAT'S YOUR EXERCISE PERSONALITY?

Finding an exercise program that fits your personality and interests can mean the difference between success and failure.

- Love music? Take a hip-hop, Latin dance, ballet, or aerobic dance class.
- Enjoy the outdoors? Try hiking, canoeing, swimming, or cycling.
- Prefer structure? Take classes such as spinning, kickboxing, or circuit training.
- Need calm and serenity? Try tai chi, yoga, or Pilates.
- Enjoy time alone? Try solitary exercise like swimming, walking, or exercising to a videotape.
- Prefer social events and group activities? Join a cycling or running club, or play pickup basketball.
- Crave variety? Find several activities you enjoy and mix things up.

burn baby burn

CALORIES BURNED IN 30 MINUTES (150-POUND PERSON)	
Walking 3 mph	160
Walking 4.5 mph	220
Bicycling 6 mph	120
Bicycling 12 mph	205
Tennis, singles	200
Swimming, 25 yards per minute	138
Swimming, 50 yards per minute	250
Hiking and backpacking	204
Cross-country skiing	350
Jumping rope	375
Jogging, 5.5 mph	370
Jogging, 7 mph	460

Healthy weights can only be achieved by proper nutrition and exercise. Consult your physician before starting a new exercise or nutrition program, especially if you suffer from any medical condition or regularly use prescription or over-the-counter medications.

daily journal

Recording what you eat and how you exercise is a highly effective weight-loss tool recommended by most dieticians. Studies show that most successful "losers" — those who lost weight and maintained the loss — keep journals. Tracking your progress helps keep you honest and reminds you to drink enough water, eat enough fruits and vegetables, get enough exercise and sleep, and more.

journal Week 1

Healthy Basics

	DAY 1	DAY 2	DAY 3	DAY 4	DAY 5	DAY 6	DAY 7
SLEEP (Box = 1 hour)	☐☐☐☐ ☐☐☐☐	☐☐☐☐ ☐☐☐☐	☐☐☐☐ ☐☐☐☐	☐☐☐☐ ☐☐☐☐	☐☐☐☐ ☐☐☐☐	☐☐☐☐ ☐☐☐☐	☐☐☐☐ ☐☐☐☐
EXERCISE (Box = 30 minutes)	☐☐☐☐	☐☐☐☐	☐☐☐☐	☐☐☐☐	☐☐☐☐	☐☐☐☐	☐☐☐☐
RELAXATION (Box = 15 minutes)	☐☐☐☐	☐☐☐☐	☐☐☐☐	☐☐☐☐	☐☐☐☐	☐☐☐☐	☐☐☐☐
WATER (Box = 8 oz. glass)	☐☐☐☐ ☐☐☐☐	☐☐☐☐ ☐☐☐☐	☐☐☐☐ ☐☐☐☐	☐☐☐☐ ☐☐☐☐	☐☐☐☐ ☐☐☐☐	☐☐☐☐ ☐☐☐☐	☐☐☐☐ ☐☐☐☐
FRUIT (Box = 1 serving)	☐☐☐☐☐	☐☐☐☐☐	☐☐☐☐☐	☐☐☐☐☐	☐☐☐☐☐	☐☐☐☐☐	☐☐☐☐☐
VEGETABLES (Box = 1 serving)	☐☐☐☐☐	☐☐☐☐☐	☐☐☐☐☐	☐☐☐☐☐	☐☐☐☐☐	☐☐☐☐☐	☐☐☐☐☐

Meal Journal

	DAY 1	DAY 2	DAY 3	DAY 4	DAY 5	DAY 6	DAY 7
BREAKFAST							
LUNCH							
SNACKS							
DINNER							

journal Week ❷

Healthy Basics

	DAY 1	DAY 2	DAY 3	DAY 4	DAY 5	DAY 6	DAY 7
SLEEP (Box = 1 hour)	☐☐☐☐ ☐☐☐☐	☐☐☐☐ ☐☐☐☐	☐☐☐☐ ☐☐☐☐	☐☐☐☐ ☐☐☐☐	☐☐☐☐ ☐☐☐☐	☐☐☐☐ ☐☐☐☐	☐☐☐☐ ☐☐☐☐
EXERCISE (Box = 30 minutes)	☐☐☐☐	☐☐☐☐	☐☐☐☐	☐☐☐☐	☐☐☐☐	☐☐☐☐	☐☐☐☐
RELAXATION (Box = 15 minutes)	☐☐☐☐	☐☐☐☐	☐☐☐☐	☐☐☐☐	☐☐☐☐	☐☐☐☐	☐☐☐☐
WATER (Box = 8 oz. glass)	☐☐☐☐ ☐☐☐☐	☐☐☐☐ ☐☐☐☐	☐☐☐☐ ☐☐☐☐	☐☐☐☐ ☐☐☐☐	☐☐☐☐ ☐☐☐☐	☐☐☐☐ ☐☐☐☐	☐☐☐☐ ☐☐☐☐
FRUIT (Box = 1 serving)	☐☐☐☐☐	☐☐☐☐☐	☐☐☐☐☐	☐☐☐☐☐	☐☐☐☐☐	☐☐☐☐☐	☐☐☐☐☐
VEGETABLES (Box = 1 serving)	☐☐☐☐☐	☐☐☐☐☐	☐☐☐☐☐	☐☐☐☐☐	☐☐☐☐☐	☐☐☐☐☐	☐☐☐☐☐

Meal Journal

	DAY 1	DAY 2	DAY 3	DAY 4	DAY 5	DAY 6	DAY 7
BREAKFAST							
LUNCH							
SNACKS							
DINNER							

journal Week ❸

Healthy Basics

	DAY 1	DAY 2	DAY 3	DAY 4	DAY 5	DAY 6	DAY 7
SLEEP (Box = 1 hour)	☐☐☐☐ ☐☐☐☐	☐☐☐☐ ☐☐☐☐	☐☐☐☐ ☐☐☐☐	☐☐☐☐ ☐☐☐☐	☐☐☐☐ ☐☐☐☐	☐☐☐☐ ☐☐☐☐	☐☐☐☐ ☐☐☐☐
EXERCISE (Box = 30 minutes)	☐☐☐☐	☐☐☐☐	☐☐☐☐	☐☐☐☐	☐☐☐☐	☐☐☐☐	☐☐☐☐
RELAXATION (Box = 15 minutes)	☐☐☐☐	☐☐☐☐	☐☐☐☐	☐☐☐☐	☐☐☐☐	☐☐☐☐	☐☐☐☐
WATER (Box = 8 oz. glass)	☐☐☐☐ ☐☐☐☐	☐☐☐☐ ☐☐☐☐	☐☐☐☐ ☐☐☐☐	☐☐☐☐ ☐☐☐☐	☐☐☐☐ ☐☐☐☐	☐☐☐☐ ☐☐☐☐	☐☐☐☐ ☐☐☐☐
FRUIT (Box = 1 serving)	☐☐☐☐☐	☐☐☐☐☐	☐☐☐☐☐	☐☐☐☐☐	☐☐☐☐☐	☐☐☐☐☐	☐☐☐☐☐
VEGETABLES (Box = 1 serving)	☐☐☐☐☐	☐☐☐☐☐	☐☐☐☐☐	☐☐☐☐☐	☐☐☐☐☐	☐☐☐☐☐	☐☐☐☐☐

Meal Journal

	DAY 1	DAY 2	DAY 3	DAY 4	DAY 5	DAY 6	DAY 7
BREAKFAST							
LUNCH							
SNACKS							
DINNER							

journal Week ❹

Healthy Basics

	DAY 1	DAY 2	DAY 3	DAY 4	DAY 5	DAY 6	DAY 7
SLEEP (Box = 1 hour)	☐☐☐☐ ☐☐☐☐	☐☐☐☐ ☐☐☐☐	☐☐☐☐ ☐☐☐☐	☐☐☐☐ ☐☐☐☐	☐☐☐☐ ☐☐☐☐	☐☐☐☐ ☐☐☐☐	☐☐☐☐ ☐☐☐☐
EXERCISE (Box = 30 minutes)	☐☐☐☐	☐☐☐☐	☐☐☐☐	☐☐☐☐	☐☐☐☐	☐☐☐☐	☐☐☐☐
RELAXATION (Box = 15 minutes)	☐☐☐☐	☐☐☐☐	☐☐☐☐	☐☐☐☐	☐☐☐☐	☐☐☐☐	☐☐☐☐
WATER (Box = 8 oz. glass)	☐☐☐ ☐☐☐	☐☐☐ ☐☐☐	☐☐☐ ☐☐☐	☐☐☐ ☐☐☐	☐☐☐ ☐☐☐	☐☐☐ ☐☐☐	☐☐☐ ☐☐☐
FRUIT (Box = 1 serving)	☐☐☐☐☐	☐☐☐☐☐	☐☐☐☐☐	☐☐☐☐☐	☐☐☐☐☐	☐☐☐☐☐	☐☐☐☐☐
VEGETABLES (Box = 1 serving)	☐☐☐☐☐	☐☐☐☐☐	☐☐☐☐☐	☐☐☐☐☐	☐☐☐☐☐	☐☐☐☐☐	☐☐☐☐☐

Meal Journal

	DAY 1	DAY 2	DAY 3	DAY 4	DAY 5	DAY 6	DAY 7
BREAKFAST							
LUNCH							
SNACKS							
DINNER							

healthy
how-to

So you've filled the shopping cart with lots of fresh healthy produce. Wondering what to do with it all once you get home? Here's the scoop on how to store, handle, and prepare fresh fruit and vegetables for maximum flavor, plus easy ways to sneak more into your diet.

STORE

Most fruit and vegetables should be stored unwashed, because water encourages bacterial growth and speeds deterioration. Wash fresh produce immediately prior to use. Any produce that's already been cut, peeled, chopped, or broken apart should be wrapped in plastic and refrigerated.

RIPEN

Stone fruit, pears, bananas, avocados, and many tropical fruit will continue ripening or maturing after being picked. Store them at room temperature. Put them in a paper bag to accelerate the process; adding an apple makes these fruit ripen even faster. Check the fruit every day, and refrigerate when ripe.

WASH

Wash your hands with hot water and soap for at least 20 seconds before handling fresh produce. Then rinse produce in warm water (do not use soap or detergents). Use a scrub brush to remove any surface dirt. Be sure to wash produce even if you plan to discard the skin or rind; bacteria on the surface can be transferred to the flesh by peeling or cutting.

on good terms

You're starting with healthy ingredients. Check out the following glossary of cooking terms to keep the integrity of your fresh fare:

SAUTÉ

To sauté means to cook food quickly in a small amount of fat over direct heat. Try cooking with olive oil or butter to add flavor, but add as little as possible or use a nonstick pan to reduce the amount needed.

STEAM

Lightly steaming fresh produce helps preserve nutrients, flavor, color, texture, and shape. It's also fat free. To steam-cook vegetables like broccoli or sugar snap peas, place on a rack or steamer basket over boiling water, cover pan, and cook until tender but still firm.

STIR-FRY

In this Asian cooking method, small pieces of food are quickly fried in a large pan over high heat. Little fat is used, and the food is constantly stirred until it is crisp-tender.

ROAST

Vegetables such as squash, sweet potatoes, leeks, and asparagus can be roasted in the oven. Brush them with olive oil, mix with herbs or other seasonings, and then slowly cook.

GRILL

Grilling adds a smoky sweetness to vegetables like eggplant, sweet peppers, and corn, but can also be used to cook peaches, pineapple, and other fruit.

sneaky additions

Adding fruit and vegetables to each meal and snack is an easy way to get at least five servings a day. Here are a dozen clever ideas:

1. Add dried apricots or cranberries to oatmeal, or top cereal with berries.

2. Dried fruit make a tasty and portable snack. Combine with unsalted nuts for extra protein and staying power.

3. Try sliced zucchini or cucumbers on sandwiches along with the staple lettuce and tomato.

4. Try mashed cauliflower, parsnips, or celery root instead of traditional potatoes.

5. Top meat, potatoes, or eggs with fresh salsa instead of a fat-based condiment.

6. Purée fresh fruit to make a sauce for meat, poultry, seafood, pancakes, waffles, or French toast.

7. Add chopped apples or grapes to chicken or tuna salad.

8. Blend cooked carrots into fruit smoothies.

9. Add fresh veggies such as mushrooms, sweet peppers, broccoli, or spinach to frozen pizzas before baking.

10. Add fresh, sliced mushrooms or grated carrots and zucchini to bottled marinara sauce, or mix frozen peas or lima beans into canned soups.

11. Try adding fresh strawberries or oranges or a sprinkle of dried blueberries or cherries to a green salad.

12. Defrost a bag of frozen peas with a quick soak in some hot water. Then simply pour into salads.

Fruit

Nothing beats the goodness of fresh fruit ripe with natural sweetness. Fruit is perfect for dessert, a snack, or even to accompany meats and vegetables. The variety of fresh fruit available year-round makes it easier than ever to indulge your sweet tooth without loading up on calories and fat. Discover new flavors from around the globe or enjoy traditional favorites. The rainbow of colorful, tasty fruit in the market also offers an array of vital nutrients and phytochemicals that help fight disease. But best of all, it tastes great!

This indispensable guide tells you how to select, store, prepare, and use fresh fruit. You'll find information on familiar fruit like apples and watermelons, as well as ethnic fruit from breadfruit to sapote and more. So, savor the flavor of good health by treating yourself to the fabulous taste of fresh fruit!

Apples

Apples are one of nature's great nutritional gifts, and even the wrapping is edible. They are low in calories; are fat-, sodium-, and cholesterol-free; an excellent source of fiber; and contain many of the phytochemicals that research shows may play an important role in preventing disease.

Ongoing research indicates that apples may reduce LDL cholesterol (the bad kind), lower the risk of stroke, improve lung function, and reduce the risk of certain types of cancer. Apples are also a good source of the mineral boron, which may promote bone health.

Some studies also indicate that eating apples and other high-fiber fruit may help you lose weight. It's thought that the fiber makes you feel full and slows down the rate at which the fruit's natural sugar is released into the blood stream, which helps to keep blood sugar levels steady.

Look for firm, well-colored apples with a fresh fragrance and a smooth skin free of bruises and gouges. A tan or brown area, called scald, does not affect the taste. Store apples in the refrigerator away from strong-smelling foods to prevent them from absorbing odors. Properly stored apples have a shelf life of up to ninety days. Some types of apples will naturally brown when cut and exposed to air. To slow this process, dip cut apples in a mixture of one part lemon juice to three parts water or in vitamin C-fortified 100% apple juice.

1 Braeburn

This crisp and juicy apple varies in color from orange to red with a yellow background. Its spicy-sweet, rich flavor makes it a good multipurpose eating apple that's delicious by itself as a snack or served with cheese.

2 Cameo

Cameo® apples, which were discovered in Washington State in the late 1980s, have red stripes over a creamy background. Cameos resist browning and have a sweet-tart flavor and extra crispy texture that make them perfect for snacks, salads, and fruit trays. Cameos are denser than some apples and so take a little longer to cook, but they hold their shape well during baking.

3 Cortland

The Cortland is a McIntosh cross, and it's a little sweeter than its McIntosh parent, with only a hint of tartness. Cortland has snowy white flesh that resists browning, making it a good choice for salads, fruit kabobs, and garnishes.

4 Crispin/Mutsu

The Crispin apple originated in Japan, where it is called Mutsu. Similar in appearance to a Golden Delicious, the Crispin is sweet, yet refreshing and juicy. It has a super crisp texture that is appealing for snacking, baking, and making applesauce.

5 Empire

The Empire, a cross between the McIntosh and Red Delicious varieties, is a good all-purpose apple. It's crisp and juicy with a sweet-tart flavor and creamy white flesh. Empires are great eaten out of hand or in salads.

6 Fuji

Fuji apples originated in Japan in the 1930s and are now one of the top-selling apples in the United States. This fragrant, sweet, crisp, juicy apple is bicolored, usually striped with red and green to yellow. It makes a great snack and a fine addition to salads.

7 Gala

The extra-sweet Gala is crisp and juicy with a slightly spicy flavor that makes it a wonderful apple for snacking, sauces, and salads. Galas have a mottled skin and vary in color from cream to red- and yellow-striped.

8 Golden Delicious

This sweet and mellow all-purpose apple is good for baking, sauces, or eating fresh. It has a pale yellow skin, sometimes with a red blush, and crisp, pale yellow flesh that resists browning, so it's a good choice for salads. If you use Golden Delicious apples for pies, you can reduce the amount of added sugar.

9 Granny Smith

The Granny Smith apple has a bright green skin and a distinctive greenish flesh, which is sometimes blushed with red. Its tart, full-bodied flavor and crisp texture make it a great choice for pies, as well as snacks and sauces. Many apple pie recipes call for Granny Smith apples because the flesh holds its shape when cooked.

Nutrition Facts

Apples

SOURCE: USDA

Braeburn
Serving Size: 1 medium (154g)

Calories	80	
Total Fat	0g	0%
Saturated Fat	0g	0%
Trans Fat	0g	
Cholesterol	0mg	0%
Sodium	0mg	0%
Potassium	170mg	
Total Carbohydrate	21g	7%
Dietary Fiber	4g	16%
Sugar	16g	
Protein	0g	
Vitamin A		2%
Vitamin C		10%
Calcium		0%
Iron		2%

Fuji
Serving Size: 1 medium (154g)

Calories	80	
Total Fat	0g	0%
Saturated Fat	0g	0%
Trans Fat	0g	
Cholesterol	0mg	0%
Sodium	0mg	0%
Potassium	170mg	
Total Carbohydrate	21g	7%
Dietary Fiber	4g	16%
Sugar	16g	
Protein	0g	
Vitamin A		2%
Vitamin C		10%
Calcium		0%
Iron		2%

Cameo
Serving Size: 1 medium (154g)

Calories	80	
Total Fat	0g	0%
Saturated Fat	0g	0%
Trans Fat	0g	
Cholesterol	0mg	0%
Sodium	0mg	0%
Potassium	170mg	
Total Carbohydrate	22g	7%
Dietary Fiber	5g	20%
Sugar	16g	
Protein	0g	
Vitamin A		2%
Vitamin C		8%
Calcium		0%
Iron		2%

Gala
Serving Size: 1 medium (154g)

Calories	80	
Total Fat	0g	0%
Saturated Fat	0g	0%
Trans Fat	0g	
Cholesterol	0mg	0%
Sodium	0mg	0%
Potassium	170mg	
Total Carbohydrate	21g	7%
Dietary Fiber	4g	16%
Sugar	16g	
Protein	0g	
Vitamin A		2%
Vitamin C		10%
Calcium		0%
Iron		2%

Cortland
Serving Size: 1 medium (138g)

Calories	80	
Total Fat	0g	0%
Saturated Fat	0g	0%
Trans Fat	0g	
Cholesterol	0mg	0%
Sodium	0mg	0%
Potassium	160mg	
Total Carbohydrate	21g	7%
Dietary Fiber	3g	12%
Sugar	18g	
Protein	0g	
Vitamin A		2%
Vitamin C		15%
Calcium		0%
Iron		2%

Golden Delicious
Serving Size: 1 medium (138g)

Calories	60	
Total Fat	0g	0%
Saturated Fat	0g	0%
Trans Fat	0g	
Cholesterol	0mg	0%
Sodium	0mg	0%
Potassium	103mg	
Total Carbohydrate	17g	6%
Dietary Fiber	2g	8%
Sugar	14g	
Protein	0g	
Vitamin A		0%
Vitamin C		10%
Calcium		0%
Iron		2%

Crispin/Mutsu
Serving Size: 1 medium (154g)

Calories	80	
Total Fat	0g	0%
Saturated Fat	0g	0%
Trans Fat	0g	
Cholesterol	0mg	0%
Sodium	0mg	0%
Potassium	170mg	
Total Carbohydrate	21g	7%
Dietary Fiber	4g	16%
Sugar	16g	
Protein	0g	
Vitamin A		2%
Vitamin C		10%
Calcium		0%
Iron		2%

Granny Smith
Serving Size: 1 medium (154g)

Calories	70	
Total Fat	0g	0%
Saturated Fat	0g	0%
Trans Fat	0g	
Cholesterol	0mg	0%
Sodium	0mg	0%
Potassium	170mg	
Total Carbohydrate	19g	6%
Dietary Fiber	3g	12%
Sugar	16g	
Protein	0g	
Vitamin A		0%
Vitamin C		15%
Calcium		0%
Iron		2%

Empire
Serving Size: 1 medium (154g)

Calories	80	
Total Fat	0g	0%
Saturated Fat	0g	0%
Trans Fat	0g	
Cholesterol	0mg	0%
Sodium	0mg	0%
Potassium	170mg	
Total Carbohydrate	21g	7%
Dietary Fiber	4g	16%
Sugar	16g	
Protein	0g	
Vitamin A		2%
Vitamin C		10%
Calcium		0%
Iron		2%

Apples

Pick the Best

Snacking: Braeburn, Cameo, Cortland, Crispin/Mutsu, Empire, Fuji, Gala, Golden Delicious, Granny Smith, Honeycrisp, Jonagold, McIntosh, Northern Spy, Pink Lady, Red Delicious, Winesap

Salad: Cameo, Cortland, Empire, Fuji, Gala, Golden Delicious, Granny Smith, Honeycrisp, Jonagold, Pink Lady, Red Delicious, Winesap

Pie: Cameo, Cortland, Golden Delicious, Granny Smith, Idared, Jonathan, McIntosh, Pink Lady, Rome Beauty, Winesap

Sauce: Cameo, Cortland, Crispin/Mutsu, Gala, Golden Delicious, Granny Smith, Honeycrisp, Idared, Jonagold, McIntosh, Pink Lady, Rome Beauty, Winesap

Baking: Cameo, Cortland, Crispin/Mutsu, Golden Delicious, Granny Smith, Idared, Jonagold, Jonathan, Northern Spy, Rome Beauty, Winesap

Honeycrisp

The Honeycrisp apple is aptly named for its mild, honey flavor. Honeycrisps have distinctive mottled red skin over a yellow background. Their flesh is coarse and very crisp, some say explosive. Honeycrisps are excellent for snacking, salads, and sauces. This is a relatively new apple, but supplies are growing.

Image Courtesy of New York Apple Association
©New York Apple Association

Idared

The Idared is a large Jonathan cross, and, like the Jonathan, it has a tangy flavor and bright red skin. The firm-textured flesh holds its shape well when cooked, making it a good choice for baking and pies. It's also great when used for making applesauce.

Jonagold

The Jonagold is a cross between two great apples: Jonathan and Golden Delicious. Its yellow-green skin is often mottled with red and orange, and its flesh is almost yellow. This juicy apple has a honey-tart flavor and crisp texture and is excellent for both eating out of hand and cooking.

Jonathan

The Jonathan apple has a crimson color with occasional touches of green and is often used in pies and other baking. Its spicy fragrance and juicy, sweet-tart flavor also blends well with other apples when making apple cider or sauce.

McIntosh

McIntosh apples are deep red and sometimes tinged with green. The tangy and tart flavor works well for snacks or applesauce and gives a pleasant sharpness to pies. However, the McIntosh's tender white flesh cooks down quite a bit, so cut bigger slices or add a thickener when using this apple in pie recipes.

Northern Spy

The Northern Spy has a red skin that's streaked with yellow. It is a hard apple that ripens late and stores well. Its tart acidity makes it excellent for cooking and baking.

Pink Lady

The aptly named Pink Lady® apple has a pink skin and very white flesh. This apple, a Golden Delicious cross, has a sweet-tart flavor and crunchy texture that makes it great for snacking, salads, pies, and sauces.

Red Delicious

The Red Delicious is probably the best-known apple in the United States. Its color varies from a striped red to a solid, deep red. Red Delicious apples grown in the western United States have an elongated shape with pronounced "feet" (the five knobs at the bottom of the apple). Those grown in the East are rounder. Both are sweet and juicy and make tasty snacks and salads.

Rome Beauty

The Rome Beauty has a deep red skin, streaked with yellow. This apple is mildly tart, and works so well for cooking that it is sometimes called the "baker's buddy." It is especially good baked whole or sautéed.

Winesap

The Winesap has a thick, deep red skin and a crisp, yellowish flesh. Its sweet-tart flavor has an appropriately winey aftertaste. This all-purpose apple keeps well and works well for snacking, salads, sauces, and pies.

Nutrition Facts

SOURCE: USDA

Apples

Honeycrisp
Serving Size: 1 medium (154g)

Calories	80
Total Fat	0g 0%
Saturated Fat	0g 0%
Trans Fat	0g
Cholesterol	0mg 0%
Sodium	0mg 0%
Potassium	170mg
Total Carbohydrate	21g 7%
Dietary Fiber	4g 16%
Sugar	16g
Protein	0g
Vitamin A	2%
Vitamin C	10%
Calcium	0%
Iron	2%

Northern Spy
Serving Size: 1 medium (154g)

Calories	80
Total Fat	0g 0%
Saturated Fat	0g 0%
Trans Fat	0g
Cholesterol	0mg 0%
Sodium	0mg 0%
Potassium	170mg
Total Carbohydrate	21g 7%
Dietary Fiber	4g 16%
Sugar	16g
Protein	0g
Vitamin A	2%
Vitamin C	10%
Calcium	0%
Iron	2%

Idared
Serving Size: 1 medium (154g)

Calories	80
Total Fat	0g 0%
Saturated Fat	0g 0%
Trans Fat	0g
Cholesterol	0mg 0%
Sodium	0mg 0%
Potassium	170mg
Total Carbohydrate	21g 7%
Dietary Fiber	4g 16%
Sugar	16g
Protein	0g
Vitamin A	2%
Vitamin C	10%
Calcium	0%
Iron	2%

Pink Lady
Serving Size: 1 medium (154g)

Calories	80
Total Fat	0g 0%
Saturated Fat	0g 0%
Trans Fat	0g
Cholesterol	0mg 0%
Sodium	0mg 0%
Potassium	170mg
Total Carbohydrate	21g 7%
Dietary Fiber	4g 16%
Sugar	16g
Protein	0g
Vitamin A	2%
Vitamin C	10%
Calcium	0%
Iron	2%

Jonagold
Serving Size: 1 medium (154g)

Calories	80
Total Fat	0g 0%
Saturated Fat	0g 0%
Trans Fat	0g
Cholesterol	0mg 0%
Sodium	0mg 0%
Potassium	170mg
Total Carbohydrate	21g 7%
Dietary Fiber	4g 16%
Sugar	16g
Protein	0g
Vitamin A	2%
Vitamin C	10%
Calcium	0%
Iron	2%

Red Delicious
Serving Size: 1 medium (154g)

Calories	80
Total Fat	0g 0%
Saturated Fat	0g 0%
Trans Fat	0g
Cholesterol	0mg 0%
Sodium	0mg 0%
Potassium	170mg
Total Carbohydrate	21g 7%
Dietary Fiber	4g 16%
Sugar	16g
Protein	0g
Vitamin A	2%
Vitamin C	10%
Calcium	0%
Iron	2%

Jonathan
Serving Size: 1 medium (154g)

Calories	80
Total Fat	0g 0%
Saturated Fat	0g 0%
Trans Fat	0g
Cholesterol	0mg 0%
Sodium	0mg 0%
Potassium	170mg
Total Carbohydrate	21g 7%
Dietary Fiber	4g 16%
Sugar	16g
Protein	0g
Vitamin A	2%
Vitamin C	10%
Calcium	0%
Iron	2%

Rome Beauty
Serving Size: 1 medium (154g)

Calories	80
Total Fat	0g 0%
Saturated Fat	0g 0%
Trans Fat	0g
Cholesterol	0mg 0%
Sodium	0mg 0%
Potassium	170mg
Total Carbohydrate	21g 7%
Dietary Fiber	4g 16%
Sugar	16g
Protein	0g
Vitamin A	2%
Vitamin C	10%
Calcium	0%
Iron	2%

McIntosh
Serving Size: 1 medium (154g)

Calories	80
Total Fat	0g 0%
Saturated Fat	0g 0%
Trans Fat	0g
Cholesterol	0mg 0%
Sodium	0mg 0%
Potassium	170mg
Total Carbohydrate	21g 7%
Dietary Fiber	4g 16%
Sugar	16g
Protein	0g
Vitamin A	2%
Vitamin C	10%
Calcium	0%
Iron	2%

Winesap
Serving Size: 1 medium (154g)

Calories	80
Total Fat	0g 0%
Saturated Fat	0g 0%
Trans Fat	0g
Cholesterol	0mg 0%
Sodium	0mg 0%
Potassium	170mg
Total Carbohydrate	21g 7%
Dietary Fiber	4g 16%
Sugar	16g
Protein	0g
Vitamin A	2%
Vitamin C	10%
Calcium	0%
Iron	2%

Bananas

Bananas are a top-selling fruit in the United States. They have no fat, cholesterol, or sodium, and are a good source of vitamins C and B6, potassium, and dietary fiber. Bananas are extremely versatile and can be eaten raw or cooked.

Mix fresh bananas into yogurt or smoothies, add them to fruit salads or cereal, or eat them out of hand. Bananas can also be baked, fried, boiled, steamed, or sautéed, and when cooked, they add a sweet flavor and chewy texture to a variety of dishes. Drier bananas such as plantains are used as a vegetable.

Burro

The Burro banana is thicker and shorter than a Cavendish banana and is sometimes called a chunky banana. It has creamy white flesh that yellows as it ripens, and a flavor that is an intriguing mix of banana and lemon. Burro bananas ripen more quickly than the common variety and develop black spots along the ribs when ripe. They are excellent to eat out of hand or add to fruit salads, and they can also be dried for banana chips.

Cavendish

The Cavendish banana is the most widely available and most familiar to North American consumers. Bananas are one of the most popular fruits in the United States and Canada and are available year-round. They're great as a snack, sliced into cereal, added to fruit smoothies, or even peeled and frozen for a cool ice cream-like summer dessert.

Selecting Bananas

Bananas are one of the few fruits that develop a better flavor when they ripen off the plant. They are often harvested green. When stored at room temperature, they will continue ripening and the skin will turn black, yellow, red, or brown, depending on the variety.

Look for plump, evenly colored bananas with no bruises or splits in the skin. Solid green bananas are unripe and must ripen some before using. Bananas with a bit of green on their tips are best for cooking, because they are firm enough to hold their shape. Riper yellow bananas with a few specks of black or brown are best for desserts, baking, or snacking.

Manzano

Manzano bananas are smaller than regular bananas, with a slightly sweeter strawberry-apple taste and drier texture. The yellow skin turns completely black when ripe. The Manzano banana is delicious eaten out of hand and also cooks well.

Niño

The Niño banana, also called finger banana or baby banana, is usually no more than three inches long—the perfect size for a child's lunch box. It has a bright yellow skin and cream-colored flesh. Sweeter than the Cavendish banana, the Niño is also excellent in fruit salad, baked into bread, or sliced to top pancakes, waffles, or yogurt. For a low-fat, naturally sweet dessert, brush a Niño banana with honey or fruit juice, and bake for fifteen minutes at 350°F.

Plantain

The plantain is a cooking banana with a firm texture and mild flavor that's sometimes compared to squash. It has thick skin that varies in color from green to yellow to brownish black, and the flesh ranges from white to salmon pink, depending on ripeness. Unlike most bananas, plantains are often cooked before they are ripe and can be fried, braised, mashed, sautéed, or stewed. Plantains have more starch than sugar. They are often used as a savory side dish in Latin cuisine. As plantains ripen, they become sweeter and can be used in desserts.

Red

The red banana has a reddish purple skin and a creamy to light pink flesh. It is firmer and sweeter than the Cavendish banana, as well as plumper and shorter. The flesh becomes rather soft when the banana is ripe, making it better for baking than eating out of hand.

In the Kitchen

Storing bananas in the refrigerator will slow the ripening process. This will cause the skin to darken, but the flesh will be fine. To speed ripening, place bananas in a perforated bag with a ripe apple and store the bag at room temperature for a few days. Cut bananas will turn brown when exposed to air. To slow this process, toss them with a little lemon, lime, or orange juice.

Overripe bananas can be used to make muffins, breads, or other baked goods. They can also be peeled, tightly wrapped, and frozen for up to six months. Another option is to mash them, add a teaspoon of lemon juice for each banana, and freeze in an airtight container. Firm bananas can also be peeled, wrapped, and frozen, then later sliced while still slightly frozen for fruit salads.

Nutrition Facts

SOURCE: USDA

Bananas

Burro
Serving Size: 1 medium (85g)

Calories		80
Total Fat	0g	0%
Saturated Fat	0g	0%
Trans Fat		0g
Cholesterol	0mg	0%
Sodium	0mg	0%
Potassium		304mg
Total Carbohydrate	20g	7%
Dietary Fiber	1g	4%
Sugar		13g
Protein		1g
Vitamin A		0%
Vitamin C		15%
Calcium		0%
Iron		0%

Niño
Serving Size: 1 medium (85g)

Calories		80
Total Fat	0g	0%
Saturated Fat	0g	0%
Trans Fat		0g
Cholesterol	0mg	0%
Sodium	0mg	0%
Potassium		350mg
Total Carbohydrate	20g	7%
Dietary Fiber	1g	4%
Sugar		13g
Protein		1g
Vitamin A		0%
Vitamin C		15%
Calcium		0%
Iron		0%

Cavendish
Serving Size: 1 small (101g)

Calories		90
Total Fat	0g	0%
Saturated Fat	0g	0%
Trans Fat		0g
Cholesterol	0mg	0%
Sodium	0mg	0%
Potassium		360mg
Total Carbohydrate	23g	8%
Dietary Fiber	3g	12%
Sugar		12g
Protein		1g
Vitamin A		2%
Vitamin C		15%
Calcium		0%
Iron		2%

Plantain
Serving Size: 1 small (89.5g)

Calories		110
Total Fat	0g	0%
Saturated Fat	0g	0%
Trans Fat		0g
Cholesterol	0mg	0%
Sodium	0mg	0%
Potassium		450mg
Total Carbohydrate	29g	10%
Dietary Fiber	2g	8%
Sugar		13g
Protein		1g
Vitamin A		20%
Vitamin C		25%
Calcium		0%
Iron		2%

Manzano
Serving Size: 1 small (73g)

Calories		70
Total Fat	0g	0%
Saturated Fat	0g	0%
Trans Fat		0g
Cholesterol	0mg	0%
Sodium	0mg	0%
Potassium		290mg
Total Carbohydrate	17g	6%
Dietary Fiber	1g	4%
Sugar		15g
Protein		1g
Vitamin A		2%
Vitamin C		10%
Calcium		0%
Iron		2%

Red
Serving Size: 1 small (99g)

Calories		90
Total Fat	0g	0%
Saturated Fat	0g	0%
Trans Fat		0g
Cholesterol	0mg	0%
Sodium	0mg	0%
Potassium		366mg
Total Carbohydrate	23g	8%
Dietary Fiber	1g	4%
Sugar		16g
Protein		1g
Vitamin A		2%
Vitamin C		15%
Calcium		0%
Iron		2%

Berries

Berries, the jewels of the produce department, add beauty and flavor across the menu. A bowl of unadorned, ripe berries makes a perfect snack or ending to a meal. But don't stop there. Berries can be added to sauces, used to top cereal, mixed into yogurt or smoothies, layered over salads, served with ice cream or frozen yogurt, or baked into pies and desserts.

Select vividly colored berries that are uniform in size. Strawberries should have a fresh, green cap, or hull. Other berries should not have a hull; if they do, it means they were picked before ripening and could taste tart.

Discard any moldy, shriveled, or discolored berries. Do not wash berries until you are ready to use them. Refrigerate berries in an airtight container, preferably in a single layer.

Blackberry

Blackberries are found in the wild and are also widely cultivated throughout the United States. The largest of the wild berries, blackberries are purplish-black, sweet, and juicy. Store them, unwashed, in the refrigerator for one to two days. They're delicious cooked, which intensifies their flavor, or eaten as a snack.

Blueberry

Blueberries should have smooth, silver frosted blue-black skins bursting with sweet juice. They are delicious eaten alone, mixed into smoothies or yogurt, as a topping for cereal or pancakes, or mixed into baked goods. Look for plump, uniformly sized berries, and store them in the refrigerator, unwashed, for up to five days.

Health Benefits

Berries are low-calorie, high-fiber treats with almost no fat, and many (especially blueberries) are filled with antioxidants. These compounds may help prevent cell damage that can lead to some types of cancer and heart disease. Some studies also show that antioxidants in berries may slow age-related declines in cognitive function, memory, and vision.

Berries are also loaded with natural compounds called phytochemicals that are partly responsible for their bright color. Scientists are studying how phytochemicals such as anthocyanins can ward off disease and promote good health. Some berries even have an added nutritional punch: cranberries contain bacteria-fighting compounds that may help prevent urinary tract infections, ulcers, and gum disease, and the folate in strawberries may reduce the risk of cardiovascular disease and some birth defects.

Boysenberry

The boysenberry is a cross between the blackberry, raspberry, and loganberry. It looks like a large, purple-red raspberry and has a tart-sweet flavor that combines its predecessors' best attributes. Store boysenberries in the refrigerator, unwashed, for two to three days. Use them in pies, on top of yogurt or cereal, mixed into fresh fruit salad, or as an ice cream topping.

Cranberry

Cranberries are scarlet red, tart, and firm. They are usually sold in 12-ounce plastic bags and, if tightly wrapped, can be stored in the refrigerator for up to two months or frozen for up to a year. Cranberries are traditionally served with a holiday turkey dinner, but they're also excellent in muffins, sauces, chutneys, and relishes. You can make an uncooked cranberry sauce by grinding berries in a food processor with apples, oranges, or dried apricots. Sweetened, dried cranberries are great for sprinkling on top of salads, or substitute them for raisins when baking.

Tasty Idea

For a low-calorie Italian-style treat with a surprisingly delectable flavor, marinate halved strawberries in two to three tablespoons each of sugar and good-quality balsamic vinegar.

Currants (Red, Black, and White)

Currants are tiny berries that are related to the gooseberry. The white and red varieties are delicious eaten out of hand, served with cream or milk and sugar, or made into jams, jellies, and sauces. Black currants are usually used in preserves, syrups, and liqueurs like crème de cassis. Don't confuse these fresh berries with dried currants, which look like miniature raisins—those "currants" are actually dried Zante grapes. Fresh currants can be stored in the refrigerator for up to four days.

Gooseberry

The tart gooseberry can be as small as a blueberry or as big as a cherry tomato. Gooseberries also come in a variety of colors (green is the most common) and can have a smooth or fuzzy skin. Store them in the refrigerator for up to a week, and use them in pies, jellies, and sauces.

Loganberry

There is some dispute over the loganberry's identity: some botanists say it is a cross between a blackberry and red raspberry, while others believe it's a separate species. Whatever its origins, the ruby red, blackberry-shaped berry is delicious cooked or fresh. Use loganberries in jams or preserves, add them to fruit salads, or top yogurt or ice cream with them. Store them, unwashed, in the refrigerator and use within a few days.

Nutrition Facts

SOURCE: USDA

Berries

Blackberry
Serving Size: 1/2 cup/125ml (72g)

Calories	30	
Total Fat	0g	0%
Saturated Fat	0g	0%
Trans Fat	0g	
Cholesterol	0mg	0%
Sodium	0mg	0%
Potassium	115mg	
Total Carbohydrate	7g	2%
Dietary Fiber	4g	16%
Sugar	3g	
Protein	1g	
Vitamin A		4%
Vitamin C		25%
Calcium		2%
Iron		2%

Blueberry
Serving Size: 1/2 cup/125ml (75g)

Calories	40	
Total Fat	0g	0%
Saturated Fat	0g	0%
Trans Fat	0g	
Cholesterol	0mg	0%
Sodium	0mg	0%
Potassium	55mg	
Total Carbohydrate	11g	4%
Dietary Fiber	2g	8%
Sugar	7g	
Protein	1g	
Vitamin A		0%
Vitamin C		10%
Calcium		0%
Iron		2%

Boysenberry
Serving Size: 1/2 cup/125ml (72g)

Calories	30	
Total Fat	0g	0%
Saturated Fat	0g	0%
Trans Fat	0g	
Cholesterol	0mg	0%
Sodium	0mg	0%
Potassium	115mg	
Total Carbohydrate	7g	2%
Dietary Fiber	4g	16%
Sugar	3g	
Protein	1g	
Vitamin A		4%
Vitamin C		25%
Calcium		2%
Iron		2%

Cranberry
Serving Size: 1/2 cup/125ml (55g)

Calories	30	
Total Fat	0g	0%
Saturated Fat	0g	0%
Trans Fat	0g	
Cholesterol	0mg	0%
Sodium	0mg	0%
Potassium	18mg	
Total Carbohydrate	7g	2%
Dietary Fiber	2g	8%
Sugar	5g	
Protein	0g	
Vitamin A		0%
Vitamin C		10%
Calcium		0%
Iron		0%

Currants
Serving Size: 1/2 cup/125ml (56g)

Calories	30	
Total Fat	0g	0%
Saturated Fat	0g	0%
Trans Fat	0g	
Cholesterol	0mg	0%
Sodium	0mg	0%
Potassium	154mg	
Total Carbohydrate	8g	3%
Dietary Fiber	2g	8%
Sugar	4g	
Protein	1g	
Vitamin A		0%
Vitamin C		40%
Calcium		2%
Iron		4%

Gooseberry
Serving Size: 1/2 cup/125ml (75g)

Calories	35	
Total Fat	0g	0%
Saturated Fat	0g	0%
Trans Fat	0g	
Cholesterol	0mg	0%
Sodium	0mg	0%
Potassium	159mg	
Total Carbohydrate	8g	3%
Dietary Fiber	3g	12%
Sugar	4g	
Protein	1g	
Vitamin A		4%
Vitamin C		35%
Calcium		2%
Iron		2%

Loganberry
Serving Size: 1/2 cup/125ml (72g)

Calories	30	
Total Fat	0g	0%
Saturated Fat	0g	0%
Trans Fat	0g	
Cholesterol	0mg	0%
Sodium	0mg	0%
Potassium	120mg	
Total Carbohydrate	7g	2%
Dietary Fiber	4g	16%
Sugar	3g	
Protein	1g	
Vitamin A		4%
Vitamin C		25%
Calcium		2%
Iron		2%

Berries

Raspberry

Raspberries come in three main varieties: black, golden, and red. These intensely flavored berries can be stored, unwashed, in the refrigerator for two to three days. They are fragile, and so are best served fresh with a touch of cream or on top of a salad or ice cream. To make a fresh raspberry sauce: purée the berries and then force them through a strainer. Add a tablespoon each of confectioner's sugar and orange juice or an orange or raspberry liqueur. Serve the sauce over poached pears, pancakes or waffles, or frozen desserts.

Strawberry

Strawberries vary in size, color, and shape, depending on the variety. The smaller varieties are usually the sweetest. Store strawberries, unwashed, in the refrigerator for two to three days. Be sure to wash strawberries before hulling them, as once they are hulled, they soak up a lot of moisture. Use a sharp knife to remove the hull. Strawberries are delicious on their own, or added to salad, baked into pie, sliced and served on top of pancakes or cereal, blended into smoothies or yogurt, or made into soufflés, sauces or frozen confections.

Citrus

Research indicates that eating citrus may help lower cholesterol and blood pressure, fight cancer, reduce the risk of cataracts, and aid the body's healing process. Why? Citrus fruit are packed with nutrients that contribute to good health, including folate, potassium, vitamin B6, thiamine, and niacin, plus fiber and a host of disease-fighting phytonutrients and other antioxidants. Citrus is also an excellent source of vitamin C (one navel orange provides 140% of the minimum daily requirement). Vitamin C may help prevent infection and some forms of cancer and makes it easier for the body to absorb iron.

Select fruit that are firm and heavy for their size. They should be evenly colored, but don't worry if a ripe orange has a bit of green on it. Oranges turn orange as they ripen, but in warm weather, the skins of some varieties may reabsorb chlorophyll and become slightly green. Some other citrus fruit may have small brown patches, called russeting, that do not affect the flavor.

Grapefruit

Grapefruit, so named because the fruit grows in clusters like grapes, come in white, pink, and red varieties. All three have a yellow skin, which is sometimes blushed with pink. Grapefruit will keep in the refrigerator for up to two weeks. The best way to eat a grapefruit is to cut one in half, and then scoop out the flavorful fruit with a serrated spoon. Or try adding peeled segments to a fruit salad, or sprinkle halves with a little brown sugar and broil.

Kumquat

The kumquat looks like a miniature orange with a round or slightly oval shape. Although they're not much bigger than a cherry tomato, kumquats pack a lot of flavor. Their rind is sweet and edible, and they are usually eaten unpeeled. The fruit inside is dry and tart with hints of tangerine and orange flavors. Store them in the refrigerator for up to a month. Slice raw kumquats and serve on salad, or cook them to make marmalade or as a sauce or relish for meat, fish, or poultry.

Lemon

Lemons vary in size and can have thick or thin peels, depending on the variety. Look for firm, plump lemons that are brightly colored with no tinges of green, which indicates they may not be ripe. Store them in the refrigerator for two to three weeks. Lemons add zing to lots of dishes. Try squeezing lemon juice over vegetables, or freshen the flavor of tap water by adding a lemon twist. Use lemon juice to add flavor to soups, stews, salad dressings, and marinades instead of using salt or butter.

Lemon, Meyer

Meyer lemons are thought to be a cross between a lemon and an orange. They're sweeter and less acidic than regular lemons, with a rounder shape and smoother skin. Store them in the refrigerator for up to two weeks. They can be used in any recipe that calls for lemon.

Lime

Limes are green-skinned, with pale green pulp and a shape like a lemon. The Persian lime is the most widely available variety in the United States; it tastes tart and sour, but is more aromatic than a lemon. Select heavy limes with a smooth skin and refrigerate for up to ten days. Limes are often used in Asian and Central American cuisines and in marinades.

Lime, Key

Key limes are a diminutive variety of lime that originated in Florida. Key limes have a tangy, tart flavor and are round and yellowish. Their most famous use is Key lime pie, but Key limes can also be substituted for Persian limes.

Nutrition Facts
SOURCE: USDA

Berries

Raspberry

Serving Size: 1/2 cup/125ml (60g)

Calories		30
Total Fat	0g	0%
Saturated Fat	0g	0%
Trans Fat		0g
Cholesterol	0mg	0%
Sodium	0mg	0%
Potassium		90mg
Total Carbohydrate	7g	2%
Dietary Fiber	4g	16%
Sugar		3g
Protein		1g
Vitamin A		0%
Vitamin C		25%
Calcium		2%
Iron		2%

Strawberry

Serving Size: 1/2 cup/125ml (72g)

Calories		25
Total Fat	0g	0%
Saturated Fat	0g	0%
Trans Fat		0g
Cholesterol	0mg	0%
Sodium	0mg	0%
Potassium		110mg
Total Carbohydrate	6g	2%
Dietary Fiber	1g	4%
Sugar		3g
Protein		0g
Vitamin A		0%
Vitamin C		70%
Calcium		2%
Iron		2%

Citrus

Grapefruit

Serving Size: 1 medium (256g)

Calories		80
Total Fat	0g	0%
Saturated Fat	0g	0%
Trans Fat		0g
Cholesterol	0mg	0%
Sodium	0mg	0%
Potassium		355mg
Total Carbohydrate	21g	7%
Dietary Fiber	3g	12%
Sugar		18g
Protein		2g
Vitamin A		45%
Vitamin C		150%
Calcium		4%
Iron		2%

Kumquat

Serving Size: 1 medium (19g)

Calories		15
Total Fat	0g	0%
Saturated Fat	0g	0%
Trans Fat		0g
Cholesterol	0mg	0%
Sodium	0mg	0%
Potassium		35mg
Total Carbohydrate	3g	1%
Dietary Fiber	1g	4%
Sugar		2g
Protein		0g
Vitamin A		2%
Vitamin C		15%
Calcium		2%
Iron		0%

Citrus

Lemon

Serving Size: 1 medium (84g)

Calories		25
Total Fat	0g	0%
Saturated Fat	0g	0%
Trans Fat		0g
Cholesterol	0mg	0%
Sodium	0mg	0%
Potassium		115mg
Total Carbohydrate	8g	3%
Dietary Fiber	2g	8%
Sugar		2g
Protein		1g
Vitamin A		0%
Vitamin C		70%
Calcium		2%
Iron		2%

Lemon, Meyer

Serving Size: 1 medium (58g)

Calories		15
Total Fat	0g	0%
Saturated Fat	0g	0%
Trans Fat		0g
Cholesterol	0mg	0%
Sodium	0mg	0%
Potassium		80mg
Total Carbohydrate	5g	2%
Dietary Fiber	1g	4%
Sugar		2g
Protein		1g
Vitamin A		0%
Vitamin C		50%
Calcium		2%
Iron		2%

Lime

Serving Size: 1 medium (67g)

Calories		20
Total Fat	0g	0%
Saturated Fat	0g	0%
Trans Fat		0g
Cholesterol	0mg	0%
Sodium	0mg	0%
Potassium		75mg
Total Carbohydrate	7g	2%
Dietary Fiber	2g	8%
Sugar		0g
Protein		0g
Vitamin A		0%
Vitamin C		35%
Calcium		0%
Iron		0%

Lime, Key

Serving Size: 1 medium (67g)

Calories		15
Total Fat	0g	0%
Saturated Fat	0g	0%
Trans Fat		0g
Cholesterol	0mg	0%
Sodium	0mg	0%
Potassium		65mg
Total Carbohydrate	5g	2%
Dietary Fiber	2g	8%
Sugar		1g
Protein		0g
Vitamin A		0%
Vitamin C		30%
Calcium		0%
Iron		0%

1

2

3

4

5

6

7

8

9

1 | Orange, Blood

Blood oranges can have bright red to maroon flesh, or white flesh streaked with red. Their flavor is deliciously sweet-tart, and they have a thinner skin and less acidity than navel oranges. Blood oranges can be eaten fresh or tossed in salads or salsas, where their vivid color adds eye appeal. For a quick sauce that goes well with grilled meat or poultry: melt two tablespoons of orange marmalade in the microwave, and then mix with a peeled, chopped blood orange.

2 | Orange, Juice

"Juice orange" is a generic term, as many varieties can be used. Two excellent and very juicy oranges are Hamlin, which is seedless, and Valencia, which has few seeds.

3 | Orange, Navel

The navel orange is one of the best varieties for eating out of hand. They have a medium-thick peel with a distinctive bump on the blossom end. These oranges are usually seedless and are easy to peel and section, making them perfect for adding to fruit salads or serving with a chocolate-flavored yogurt dip.

4 | Orange, Temple

Often considered Florida's finest eating orange, temple oranges have a pebbly peel and deep orange color. They are a cross between a tangerine and an orange, and they have a flavor all their own. Temple oranges are easy to peel, fragrant, sweet, and juicy—delectable when eaten raw, served with pancakes or waffles, or mixed with other fruits.

5 | Orange, Valencia

Valencias can be medium to large in size, round to oval in shape, and yellow to orange in color, with the occasional green tinge. They are tasty when eaten fresh, but a thin skin also means they're also great for juicing. Try adding the juice to marinades for meat, poultry, or fish.

6 | Pomelo

Pomelos can be about the size of a cantaloupe, or as big as twenty-five pounds and a foot across. Varieties of this Malaysian native differ in other ways, too. The thick, soft rind may be yellow, yellow-brown, or pink, and the flesh ranges from light yellow to coral pink. Pomelos can be juicy or a bit dry, with a flavor that might be spicy-sweet or tangy and tart. They are believed to be the ancestor of the grapefruit and can be used in the same way. Store them in the refrigerator for up to a week.

7 | Tangelo

Tangelos are an orange-grapefruit hybrid that comes in different sizes and colors. They can be as small as an orange or as large as a grapefruit, with a smooth or rough skin and yellow-orange to deep orange color. The Minneola tangelo, also called Honeybell, is the most widely available. Sweet and juicy, the tangelo is delicious eaten out of hand or added to salads or desserts.

8 | Tangerine/Mandarin

The tangerine is the most common Mandarin orange sold in the United States, a category that also includes clementines, dancy oranges, and satsumas. Tangerines are easy to peel and section and taste quite sweet. Eat them fresh or add to salads.

9 | Ugli Fruit

The Ugli® fruit, also known as uniq fruit, is a tangerine-grapefruit cross from Jamaica. Its thick, bumpy, yellow-green skin is easy to peel. The flesh is yellow-orange, very juicy, and sweeter than a grapefruit, with a hint of tangerine to the flavor. They are delicious halved and eaten like a grapefruit or added to fruit or vegetable salads. Store Ugli fruit at room temperature for up to five days or in the refrigerator for up to three weeks.

Nutrition Facts
SOURCE: USDA

Citrus

Orange, Blood
Serving Size: 1 medium (140g)

Calories		70
Total Fat	0g	0%
Saturated Fat	0g	0%
Trans Fat	0g	
Cholesterol	0mg	0%
Sodium	0mg	0%
Potassium	240mg	
Total Carbohydrate	16g	5%
Dietary Fiber	3g	12%
Sugar	12g	
Protein	1g	
Vitamin A		6%
Vitamin C		120%
Calcium		6%
Iron		0%

Orange, Juice
Serving Size: 1 medium (151g)

Calories		70
Total Fat	0g	0%
Saturated Fat	0g	0%
Trans Fat	0g	
Cholesterol	0mg	0%
Sodium	0.8mg	0%
Potassium	255mg	
Total Carbohydrate	17g	6%
Dietary Fiber	4g	16%
Sugar	11g	
Protein	1g	
Vitamin A		6%
Vitamin C		110%
Calcium		6%
Iron		0%

Orange, Navel
Serving Size: 1 medium (140g)

Calories		70
Total Fat	0g	0%
Saturated Fat	0g	0%
Trans Fat	0g	
Cholesterol	0mg	0%
Sodium	0mg	0%
Potassium	240mg	
Total Carbohydrate	18g	6%
Dietary Fiber	3g	12%
Sugar	12g	
Protein	1g	
Vitamin A		6%
Vitamin C		140%
Calcium		6%
Iron		2%

Orange, Temple
Serving Size: 1 medium (154g)

Calories		70
Total Fat	0g	0%
Saturated Fat	0g	0%
Trans Fat	0g	
Cholesterol	0mg	0%
Sodium	0mg	0%
Potassium	260mg	
Total Carbohydrate	21g	7%
Dietary Fiber	7g	28%
Sugar	14g	
Protein	1g	
Vitamin A		2%
Vitamin C		130%
Calcium		6%
Iron		2%

Orange, Valencia
Serving Size: 1 medium (120g)

Calories		60
Total Fat	0g	0%
Saturated Fat	0g	0%
Trans Fat	0g	
Cholesterol	0mg	0%
Sodium	0mg	0%
Potassium	220mg	
Total Carbohydrate	14g	5%
Dietary Fiber	3g	12%
Sugar	11g	
Protein	1g	
Vitamin A		6%
Vitamin C		100%
Calcium		4%
Iron		0%

Pomelo
Serving Size: 1 medium (609g)

Calories		230
Total Fat	0g	0%
Saturated Fat	0g	0%
Trans Fat	0g	
Cholesterol	0mg	0%
Sodium	5mg	0%
Potassium	1315mg	
Total Carbohydrate	59g	20%
Dietary Fiber	6g	24%
Sugar	8g	
Protein	5g	
Vitamin A		0%
Vitamin C		620%
Calcium		2%
Iron		4%

Tangelo
Serving Size: 1 medium (96g)

Calories		45
Total Fat	0g	0%
Saturated Fat	0g	0%
Trans Fat	0g	
Cholesterol	0mg	0%
Sodium	0mg	0%
Potassium	170mg	
Total Carbohydrate	11g	4%
Dietary Fiber	2g	8%
Sugar	9g	
Protein	1g	
Vitamin A		4%
Vitamin C		90%
Calcium		4%
Iron		0%

Tangerine/Mandarin
Serving Size: 1 medium (84g)

Calories		45
Total Fat	0g	0%
Saturated Fat	0g	0%
Trans Fat	0g	
Cholesterol	0mg	0%
Sodium	0mg	0%
Potassium	140mg	
Total Carbohydrate	11g	4%
Dietary Fiber	2g	8%
Sugar	9g	
Protein	1g	
Vitamin A		10%
Vitamin C		35%
Calcium		4%
Iron		0%

Ugli Fruit
Serving Size: 1 medium (156g)

Calories		40
Total Fat	0g	0%
Saturated Fat	0g	0%
Trans Fat	0g	
Cholesterol	0mg	0%
Sodium	0mg	0%
Potassium		n/a
Total Carbohydrate	8g	3%
Dietary Fiber	1g	4%
Sugar	6g	
Protein	2g	
Vitamin A		n/a
Vitamin C		n/a
Calcium		n/a
Iron		n/a

Grapes

The grape is actually a berry, and thousands of different varieties are grown around the world. Some are grown for making wine, some for table grapes, and others for producing commercial products such as raisins, jams, or jellies. Grapes can be classified by color: black (sometimes called purple), red, and white (also called green). Black and red grapes range in color from light red to purple to purple-black, while white grapes vary from pale yellow-green to light green. Some have seeds; some are seedless.

Preliminary studies show that eating grapes and other foods that are high in phytochemicals like quercetin, anthocyanin, and catechin may help protect against heart disease and certain cancers. Another phytochemical called resveratrol found in the skin of grapes (especially black grapes) may have anti-inflammatory properties and help fight breast, colon, and liver cancers. A ½-cup serving of seedless grapes has only 60 calories and supplies 15% of the RDA for vitamin C, making it a ready-to-eat low-calorie treat that's available year-round.

Black/Purple

Black seeded grapes include perennial favorites such as Ribier, Concord, and Niabell. Ribiers originated in France and have a firm skin and a mild, sweet, juicy flesh. Concord grapes are mild tasting and have a skin that slips off easily; it's also the most important juice and jelly variety. Niabell is a Concord-type grape with a rich, earthy flavor.

Red

There are several well-known varieties of red seeded grapes. Red Globe has plum-sized berries, a crisp texture, and sweet flavor. Emperor grapes have large, deep red clusters and a lasting flavor. Christmas Rose, created by crossing four older grape varieties, is tart-sweet. Rouge grapes are dark red with a thick skin, crisp texture, and mildly sweet, earthy taste. The super-sweet Cardinal is another favorite seeded variety.

When purchasing table grapes, look for plump, full-colored grapes still attached to the stem. White grapes that are fully ripe will have a pale yellow tinge. Ripe black grapes will have a deep, rich color, with no green. Avoid grapes with brown areas at the stem connections or that are withered. Some varieties of grapes, especially darker ones, have a dusting of silvery-white "bloom." This is perfectly normal and indicates ripeness. Store grapes, unwashed, in a perforated plastic bag for up to a week in the refrigerator.

Grapes are delicious when eaten out of hand; added to fruit salads, yogurt, or smoothies; or tossed in vegetable salads. They also make a beautiful, edible garnish. Grapes can be mixed into chicken or tuna salad or sauces for meat, poultry, and seafood. To make a refreshing summer treat, freeze grapes in a single layer on a baking sheet until they are hard. Transfer them to a resealable plastic bag and return them to the freezer.

A word of caution: Whole grapes are not an appropriate snack for babies or toddlers because they pose a significant choking hazard. Cut grapes into quarters before serving them to young children.

Seedless

Thompson seedless is the most popular grape variety in the United States, and its light green, oblong berries are sweet, mild, and juicy. Next is Flame seedless, a Thompson seedless cross that is red, round, crunchy, and sweet. Perlette and champagne grapes are also popular. Perlette means "little pearl" in French, and these round grapes have a mild and sweet to slightly tart taste. Champagne grapes, also known as Black Corinth, are no bigger than a pea. They have an exceedingly sweet, mild, wine-like flavor. Black beauty, also called beauty seedless, is one of the few seedless black grapes. Ruby seedless and crimson seedless also sometimes appear in the market.

White/Green

Some of the most popular white seeded table grapes include Calmeria and Muscat. Calmeria grapes, sometimes called "lady fingers" because of their elongated shape, are mild, yet tangy and sweet. Muscat grapes are plump and juicy with a rich perfume and an intense sweetness. They are often used for wine, but are also excellent as a table grape.

Nutrition Facts
SOURCE: USDA

Grapes

Black/Purple
Serving Size: 1/2 cup/125ml (80g)

Calories	50
Total Fat	0g 0%
Saturated Fat	0g 0%
Trans Fat	0g
Cholesterol	0mg 0%
Sodium	0mg 0%
Potassium	130mg
Total Carbohydrate	13g 4%
Dietary Fiber	1g 4%
Sugar	12g
Protein	1g
Vitamin A	2%
Vitamin C	8%
Calcium	0%
Iron	0%

Seedless
Serving Size: 1/2 cup/125ml (85g)

Calories	60
Total Fat	0g 0%
Saturated Fat	0g 0%
Trans Fat	0g
Cholesterol	0mg 0%
Sodium	0mg 0%
Potassium	160mg
Total Carbohydrate	15g 5%
Dietary Fiber	1g 4%
Sugar	13g
Protein	1g
Vitamin A	2%
Vitamin C	15%
Calcium	0%
Iron	2%

Red
Serving Size: 1/2 cup/125ml (85g)

Calories	60
Total Fat	0g 0%
Saturated Fat	0g 0%
Trans Fat	0g
Cholesterol	0mg 0%
Sodium	0mg 0%
Potassium	160mg
Total Carbohydrate	14g 5%
Dietary Fiber	1g 4%
Sugar	12g
Protein	1g
Vitamin A	2%
Vitamin C	15%
Calcium	0%
Iron	2%

White/Green
Serving Size: 1/2 cup/125ml (80g)

Calories	60
Total Fat	0g 0%
Saturated Fat	0g 0%
Trans Fat	0g
Cholesterol	0mg 0%
Sodium	0mg 0%
Potassium	160mg
Total Carbohydrate	14g 5%
Dietary Fiber	1g 4%
Sugar	12g
Protein	1g
Vitamin A	2%
Vitamin C	15%
Calcium	0%
Iron	2%

Melons

Melons fall into two general categories: muskmelon and watermelon. There are two types of muskmelon — those with a netted skin, like cantaloupe, and those with a smooth rind, like casaba.

Orange, yellow, and red fruit such as melons are a good source of vitamin A and antioxidants. They also contain phytochemicals like carotenoids and bioflavonoids, two types of plant chemicals that research suggests foster heart health and good vision, boost the immune system, and reduce the risk of some cancers. Honeydew melon, cantaloupe, and watermelon are also good sources of vitamin C.

Select muskmelons that are heavy for their size. Ripe muskmelons will yield to slight pressure at the blossom end and have a fruity fragrance. If it smells good, it will usually taste good. The skin should feel springy, not mushy. Melons will continue to ripen at room temperature, but they won't get any sweeter. Refrigerate most ripe melons for up to five days (pepinos can be refrigerated for three).

Watermelons should also be heavy and firm, and symmetrical in shape. Avoid those with bruises or cuts, but don't worry about the creamy yellow spot on the bottom — that's where it sat on the ground, ripening in the sun. Uncut watermelons can be stored at room temperature for seven to ten days. Refrigerate after cutting.

Cantaloupe

A perfectly ripe cantaloupe has a raised netting on a pale gold or gray-green background, and the flesh is bright orange, juicy, and sweet. Cantaloupe is delicious enough on its own, but it can also be added to fruit salads and smoothies. Or, for an appetizer, try wrapping cantaloupe balls in paper-thin slices of prosciutto.

Casaba

Casabas are round with a thick yellow furrowed rind. The flesh is cream to pale green in color, and extremely juicy. It is delicately sweet, with hints of cucumber. Serve casaba slices unadorned or top them with sorbet or yogurt. For a low-fat dessert, drizzle casaba chunks or balls with a fruit-flavored liqueur.

Crenshaw

Crenshaw melons are considered one of the sweetest muskmelons. They are thought to be a casaba-Persian melon cross, and they can weigh from five to nine pounds. The rind is slightly ribbed, and it turns golden green at peak ripeness. The flesh is salmon-orange and has a sweet, yet spicy, flavor. Serve a Crenshaw on its own or with a squeeze of lime to complement its spiciness, or add to salads, smoothies, or sorbet.

Pepino

Pepino melons can be as small as a plum or as big as a papaya. The entire melon is edible—from the smooth, ivory or light green skin with violet streaks to the yellow-gold flesh. (Peel the melon before eating out of hand if the skin seems tough.) When ripe, it is sweetly aromatic, with a mild cantaloupe flavor and hints of banana and pear that are enhanced by a sprinkling of lemon, lime, salt, pepper, or fresh basil.

Honeydew

Honeydew melons have a smooth, creamy yellow rind and tender, sweet, pale green flesh. Honeydews weigh from four to eight pounds and are rather oval in shape. They are extremely succulent and mix well with other fruits. Try topping honeydew melon with yogurt and a sprinkle of granola or use it to make a refreshing, cold fruit soup.

Persian

Persian melons are close cousins to the cantaloupe, but the netting on their pale gray-green rind is finer and the salmon-colored flesh is firmer. Try matching their delicious sweetness with thinly sliced prosciutto for an appetizer, or use Persian melons in smoothies and summer salads.

Juan Canary

Juan Canary melons, sometimes simply called Canary melons, are somewhat oval shaped and have a bright canary yellow, smooth, slightly ridged rind. The flesh is pale green to cream in color, with a pinkish tinge around the seed cavity. The taste is delicate, but the texture is crisp and firm. Add slices or chunks to fruit salads or platters or freeze melon balls to make edible "ice cubes" for fruit drinks.

Watermelon

Most watermelon varieties are large (some weigh up to thirty-five pounds) and have an elongated, oval shape, although some are smaller or rounder. The rind ranges from pale to dark green in color and can be solid or striped. Red or deep pink flesh is typical, though there are also white, yellow, and pale pink watermelons. Some are considered "seedless" because they have very few seeds, or those that are present are tiny, soft, and edible. Chilled, sweetly moist watermelon wedges are the quintessential summer picnic dessert. Watermelon balls brighten fruit salads, while a hollowed-out watermelon makes an attractive "basket" for serving it.

Nutrition Facts
SOURCE: USDA

Melons

Cantaloupe
Serving Size: 1/2 cup/125ml (80g)

Calories	25
Total Fat	0g 0%
Saturated Fat	0g 0%
Trans Fat	0g
Cholesterol	0mg 0%
Sodium	15mg 1%
Potassium	220mg
Total Carbohydrate	7g 2%
Dietary Fiber	1g 4%
Sugar	6g
Protein	1g
Vitamin A	50%
Vitamin C	50%
Calcium	0%
Iron	0%

Juan Canary
Serving Size: 1/2 cup/125ml (89g)

Calories	30
Total Fat	0g 0%
Saturated Fat	0g 0%
Trans Fat	0g
Cholesterol	0mg 0%
Sodium	15mg 1%
Potassium	240mg
Total Carbohydrate	7g 2%
Dietary Fiber	1g 4%
Sugar	6g
Protein	1g
Vitamin A	60%
Vitamin C	50%
Calcium	0%
Iron	2%

Casaba
Serving Size: 1/2 cup/125ml (85g)

Calories	90
Total Fat	0g 0%
Saturated Fat	0g 0%
Trans Fat	0g
Cholesterol	0mg 0%
Sodium	10mg 0%
Potassium	180mg
Total Carbohydrate	5g 2%
Dietary Fiber	1g 4%
Sugar	5g
Protein	1g
Vitamin A	0%
Vitamin C	25%
Calcium	0%
Iron	2%

Pepino
Serving Size: 1/2 cup/125ml (71g)

Calories	25
Total Fat	0g 0%
Saturated Fat	0g 0%
Trans Fat	0g
Cholesterol	0mg 0%
Sodium	10mg 0%
Potassium	190mg
Total Carbohydrate	6g 2%
Dietary Fiber	1g 4%
Sugar	5g
Protein	1g
Vitamin A	50%
Vitamin C	45%
Calcium	0%
Iron	0%

Crenshaw
Serving Size: 1/2 cup/125ml (85g)

Calories	25
Total Fat	0g 0%
Saturated Fat	0g 0%
Trans Fat	0g
Cholesterol	0mg 0%
Sodium	10mg 0%
Potassium	160mg
Total Carbohydrate	6g 2%
Dietary Fiber	1g 4%
Sugar	5g
Protein	1g
Vitamin A	0%
Vitamin C	30%
Calcium	0%
Iron	2%

Persian
Serving Size: 1/2 cup/125ml (85g)

Calories	30
Total Fat	0g 0%
Saturated Fat	0g 0%
Trans Fat	0g
Cholesterol	0mg 0%
Sodium	15mg 1%
Potassium	200mg
Total Carbohydrate	8g 3%
Dietary Fiber	1g 4%
Sugar	7g
Protein	0g
Vitamin A	0%
Vitamin C	25%
Calcium	0%
Iron	0%

Honeydew
Serving Size: 1/2 cup/125ml (85g)

Calories	30
Total Fat	0g 0%
Saturated Fat	0g 0%
Trans Fat	0g
Cholesterol	0mg 0%
Sodium	15mg 1%
Potassium	190mg
Total Carbohydrate	8g 3%
Dietary Fiber	1g 4%
Sugar	7g
Protein	0g
Vitamin A	0%
Vitamin C	25%
Calcium	0%
Iron	0%

Watermelon
Serving Size: 1/2 cup/125ml (76g)

Calories	25
Total Fat	0g 0%
Saturated Fat	0g 0%
Trans Fat	0g
Cholesterol	0mg 0%
Sodium	0mg 0%
Potassium	85mg
Total Carbohydrate	6g 2%
Dietary Fiber	0g 0%
Sugar	5g
Protein	0g
Vitamin A	8%
Vitamin C	10%
Calcium	0%
Iron	2%

Pears

Pears are refreshingly sweet and loaded with nutrients. A medium pear has fewer than 100 calories, and no fat, cholesterol, or sodium. What pears do have is plenty of fiber, vitamins, minerals, and phytochemicals to help maintain health and fight disease.

Pears are high in pectin and lignan, two soluble fibers that research shows lower cholesterol and may prevent heart disease. Fiber promotes healthy digestion, and pectin in particular, may protect against colon cancer. The high fiber content in pears also slows the rate at which sugar enters the bloodstream, avoiding the blood sugar spike you get from lower-fiber, simple carbohydrates.

Enjoy pears any time of day, from a French toast breakfast to an afternoon snack or evening cheese course. Underripe pears can be substituted for apples in recipes for pies, muffins, or other treats. Overripe pears can be puréed for smoothies, sauces, and soups.

Anjou

There are both green and red Anjou pears, and both varieties are very sweet and juicy. The pale green Anjous do not change color as they ripen. These pears are delicious eaten out of hand or sliced for salads. Underripe Anjous are excellent for poaching, roasting, and baking.

Asian

There are more than 100 varieties of Asian pears, which are also called apple pears or Chinese pears. They range in color from golden brown to pale yellow green. Asian pears have a crisp texture and a round, apple-like shape. Their sweet crunchiness makes them tasty on their own, in sandwiches, or grilled and served with pork.

Ripening Pears

Pears are picked when they are mature, but not yet fully ripe. They will continue to ripen at room temperature. You'll know when they're ready to eat when the neck yields slightly to pressure. To speed the ripening process, place pears in a perforated paper bag with an apple or banana. Be sure to check them daily, and then refrigerate when ripe. Don't go by color; with most varieties, it doesn't change much as the pears ripen.

Bartlett

Yellow Bartletts, which change from green to bright yellow as they ripen, possess the quintessential pear aroma and flavor. They make a succulent, fresh snack and are good for canning and cooking. Red Bartletts are bright red, but otherwise have the same characteristics and uses as the yellow variety.

Bosc

Bosc pears are brown and often russeted. They are highly aromatic and have a firm, yet tender flesh, and a sweet spiced flavor. Boscs are ideal for poaching or making tarts.

Comice

Comice pears are bursting with sweet juice. They are often very large, with a red blush on their green skin. Comice pears are refreshing to eat on their own, or serve with blue cheese as a simple dessert. They are too juicy for cooking.

Forelle

The Forelle is a small pear that turns from green to bright yellow with crimson freckles as it ripens. Forelles are slightly crisp, very sweet, and juicy. They're the perfect size for snacking or tucking into a lunch box.

Packham

The Packham is a Bartlett cross with a bumpy, pale green skin and white flesh. Packhams are sweet and fragrant. Eat them fresh, add them to a salad, or poach them in red wine. **Note:** Packhams must be peeled before cooking because their skin discolors and darkens when heated.

Seckel

Seckels, also called sugar pears, are tiny and ultra-sweet. Their maroon and olive skin does not change color while ripening. Seckels are an excellent choice for children's snacks, or they can be pickled whole or in halves and used as a garnish.

Preparing Fresh Pears

Pear flesh naturally turns brown when exposed to air. To prevent this, coat cut pears with ingredients that contain acid, like salad dressing, or dip them in acidulated water or an anti-browning agent sold in grocery stores. (To make acidulated water, combine 3 tablespoons of lemon juice with 1 quart of cold water.) Poaching, or gently cooking in liquid at just under the boiling point, also preserves pears' fresh color and enhances their delicate flavor. Common poaching liquids include vanilla sugar syrup and red or white wine.

Nutrition Facts

SOURCE: USDA

Pears

Anjou
Serving Size: 1 medium (125g)

Calories		70
Total Fat	0g	0%
Saturated Fat	0g	0%
Trans Fat		0g
Cholesterol	0mg	0%
Sodium	0mg	0%
Potassium		150mg
Total Carbohydrate	19g	6%
Dietary Fiber	4g	16%
Sugar		12g
Protein		0g
Vitamin A		0%
Vitamin C		8%
Calcium		2%
Iron		2%

Asian
Serving Size: 1 medium (125g)

Calories		50
Total Fat	0g	0%
Saturated Fat	0g	0%
Trans Fat		0g
Cholesterol	0mg	0%
Sodium	0mg	0%
Potassium		150mg
Total Carbohydrate	13g	4%
Dietary Fiber	4g	16%
Sugar		9g
Protein		1g
Vitamin A		0%
Vitamin C		8%
Calcium		0%
Iron		0%

Bartlett
Serving Size: 1 medium (125g)

Calories		70
Total Fat	0g	0%
Saturated Fat	0g	0%
Trans Fat		0g
Cholesterol	0mg	0%
Sodium	0mg	0%
Potassium		150mg
Total Carbohydrate	19g	6%
Dietary Fiber	4g	16%
Sugar		12g
Protein		0g
Vitamin A		0%
Vitamin C		8%
Calcium		2%
Iron		2%

Bosc
Serving Size: 1 medium (125g)

Calories		70
Total Fat	0g	0%
Saturated Fat	0g	0%
Trans Fat		0g
Cholesterol	0mg	0%
Sodium	0mg	0%
Potassium		150mg
Total Carbohydrate	19g	6%
Dietary Fiber	4g	16%
Sugar		12g
Protein		0g
Vitamin A		0%
Vitamin C		8%
Calcium		2%
Iron		2%

Comice
Serving Size: 1 medium (166g)

Calories		100
Total Fat	0g	0%
Saturated Fat	0g	0%
Trans Fat		0g
Cholesterol	0mg	0%
Sodium	0mg	0%
Potassium		200mg
Total Carbohydrate	26g	9%
Dietary Fiber	5g	20%
Sugar		16g
Protein		1g
Vitamin A		0%
Vitamin C		10%
Calcium		2%
Iron		2%

Forelle
Serving Size: 1 medium (139g)

Calories		80
Total Fat	0g	0%
Saturated Fat	0g	0%
Trans Fat		0g
Cholesterol	0mg	0%
Sodium	0mg	0%
Potassium		170mg
Total Carbohydrate	21g	7%
Dietary Fiber	4g	16%
Sugar		14g
Protein		1g
Vitamin A		0%
Vitamin C		10%
Calcium		2%
Iron		2%

Packham
Serving Size: 1 medium (185g)

Calories		80
Total Fat	0g	0%
Saturated Fat	0g	0%
Trans Fat		0g
Cholesterol	0mg	0%
Sodium	0mg	0%
Potassium		160mg
Total Carbohydrate	23g	8%
Dietary Fiber	6g	24%
Sugar		17g
Protein		1g
Vitamin A		6%
Vitamin C		0%
Calcium		16%
Iron		2%

Seckel
Serving Size: 1 medium (166g)

Calories		100
Total Fat	1g	2%
Saturated Fat	0g	0%
Trans Fat		0g
Cholesterol	0mg	0%
Sodium	0mg	0%
Potassium		200mg
Total Carbohydrate	25g	8%
Dietary Fiber	4g	16%
Sugar		14g
Protein		1g
Vitamin A		0%
Vitamin C		10%
Calcium		2%
Iron		2%

Pears

Starkrimson

The Starkrimson is a sweet, mild red pear variety that's sometimes called "early red." They are excellent for eating out of hand; they also add a vibrant color to salads or other dishes.

Taylor's Gold

Taylor's Gold pears have a cinnamon-colored skin and creamy, tender flesh. These delicately perfumed pears are delicious alone, or use them to make a conserve for spreading on waffles or toast.

Stone Fruit

Stone fruit are truly the taste of summer. Consumers eagerly anticipate the first handful of cherries and juicy plums of the season, and one bite of a plump peach easily demonstrates why the expression "peachy" means "unusually fine." Rapid shipping and advanced harvesting and storage techniques have extended the season, so stone fruit can now be a great source of nutrition throughout the year.

Here are some of the health highlights:

Apricots are an excellent source of beta-carotene, a nutrient the body converts to vitamin A and uses to fight disease and infection and maintain healthy vision. Apricots also provide vitamin C, fiber, and potassium.

Cherries provide potassium, B vitamins, and vitamin C, as well as phytochemicals that research shows may prevent heart disease, reduce inflammation and pain, fight cancer, and improve bone health.

One medium **peach** has about 40 calories and provides fiber, vitamins A and C, and beta-carotene, as well as phytochemicals that may help prevent age-related vision loss.

Prunes are high in antioxidants and provide potassium, vitamin A, magnesium, and iron. Prunes are also high in fiber, which promotes good digestion.

Apricot

Apricots originated in China and are related to peaches. Their skin color ranges from pale yellow to deep orange, and their flesh can be anywhere from a golden cream to bright orange. Select plump, firm (but not hard) apricots that are uniformly colored. Refrigerate ripe apricots in a plastic bag for three to five days. Fresh apricots make a great snack, or serve dried apricots and fresh goat cheese as an hors d'oeuvre.

Cherry, Bing

Bing cherries are large, sweet, and juicy. Their color ranges from deep garnet to almost black. Look for plump, bright fruit with the stems attached. Store cherries, unwashed, in a plastic bag in the refrigerator for two to three days. Bing cherries are excellent for cooking or snacking. Dried, they can be sprinkled on salads, or substituted for raisins in breads, cookies, and muffins.

Cherry, Rainier

Rainier cherries have a golden-pink blush to their skin; a finely textured, firm, clear flesh; and colorless juice. They are highly perishable, so store them unwashed in the refrigerator and consume soon after purchase. This cherry is so sweet that you can reduce the amount of sugar in recipes when cooking with it.

Nectarine

Nectarines have a smooth, brilliantly golden-yellow skin that's blushed with red. They taste similar to peaches, but nectarines are a separate and distinct fruit. When ripe, they are fragrant and will yield slightly to pressure. Store underripe nectarines at room temperature. Once ripe, they will keep in the refrigerator for a week or more. Eat nectarines alone, or use them to make fruit salads.

Peach

Peaches have a fuzzy skin that can be pinkish white to red-tinged gold in color, with white to golden yellow flesh. Peaches fall into two categories: clingstone and freestone. Clingstone peaches have a pit that "clings" to the flesh, while freestone peach pits pull away easily. Use freestone peaches when uniform slices are desired for a tart or composed salad. Underripe peaches will soften and become juicier and more flavorful when stored at room temperature for one or two days. They won't get any sweeter, however, so avoid fruit that is hard or tinged with green. Refrigerate ripe peaches for up to five days. Peaches are wonderful on their own, or they can be mixed with pancake batter or cottage cheese. Try grilling them over hot coals and serving with ice cream for a summer dessert.

Peach, Donut

This flat, round, donut-shaped peach is originally from China. It is exceptionally sweet and low in acid. Ripen donut peaches at room temperature for two to three days, and then store in the refrigerator for a day or two. Donut peaches are excellent for eating out of hand, or add them to sauces or salsas for meat and poultry.

Nutrition Facts
SOURCE: USDA

Pears

Starkrimson
Serving Size: 1 medium (166g)

Calories		100
Total Fat	0g	0%
Saturated Fat	0g	0%
Trans Fat		0g
Cholesterol	0mg	0%
Sodium	0mg	0%
Potassium	200mg	
Total Carbohydrate	26g	9%
Dietary Fiber	5g	20%
Sugar	16g	
Protein		1g
Vitamin A		0%
Vitamin C		10%
Calcium		2%
Iron		2%

Taylor's Gold
Serving Size: 1 medium (166g)

Calories		100
Total Fat	0g	0%
Saturated Fat	0g	0%
Trans Fat		0g
Cholesterol	0mg	0%
Sodium	0mg	0%
Potassium	200mg	
Total Carbohydrate	26g	9%
Dietary Fiber	5g	20%
Sugar	16g	
Protein		1g
Vitamin A		0%
Vitamin C		10%
Calcium		2%
Iron		2%

Stone Fruit

Apricot
Serving Size: 1 medium (35g)

Calories		15
Total Fat	0g	0%
Saturated Fat	0g	0%
Trans Fat		0g
Cholesterol	0mg	0%
Sodium	0mg	0%
Potassium	90mg	
Total Carbohydrate	4g	1%
Dietary Fiber	1g	4%
Sugar	3g	
Protein		0g
Vitamin A		15%
Vitamin C		6%
Calcium		0%
Iron		0%

Cherry, Bing
Serving Size: 1/2 cup/125ml (70g)

Calories		45
Total Fat	0g	0%
Saturated Fat	0g	0%
Trans Fat		0g
Cholesterol	0mg	0%
Sodium	0mg	0%
Potassium	160mg	
Total Carbohydrate	12g	4%
Dietary Fiber	2g	8%
Sugar	9g	
Protein		1g
Vitamin A		0%
Vitamin C		8%
Calcium		0%
Iron		2%

Stone Fruit

Cherry, Rainier
Serving Size: 1/2 cup/125ml (70g)

Calories		45
Total Fat	0g	0%
Saturated Fat	0g	0%
Trans Fat		0g
Cholesterol	0mg	0%
Sodium	0mg	0%
Potassium	135mg	
Total Carbohydrate	10g	3%
Dietary Fiber	2g	8%
Sugar	8g	
Protein		1g
Vitamin A		2%
Vitamin C		6%
Calcium		2%
Iron		2%

Nectarine
Serving Size: 1 medium (140g)

Calories		70
Total Fat	0.5g	1%
Saturated Fat	0g	0%
Trans Fat		0g
Cholesterol	0mg	0%
Sodium	0mg	0%
Potassium	300mg	
Total Carbohydrate	16g	5%
Dietary Fiber	2g	8%
Sugar	12g	
Protein		1g
Vitamin A		4%
Vitamin C		15%
Calcium		0%
Iron		2%

Peach
Serving Size: 1 medium (98g)

Calories		40
Total Fat	0g	0%
Saturated Fat	0g	0%
Trans Fat		0g
Cholesterol	0mg	0%
Sodium	0mg	0%
Potassium	190mg	
Total Carbohydrate	11g	4%
Dietary Fiber	2g	8%
Sugar	9g	
Protein		1g
Vitamin A		2%
Vitamin C		10%
Calcium		0%
Iron		0%

Peach, Donut
Serving Size: 1 medium (47g)

Calories		20
Total Fat	0g	0%
Saturated Fat	0g	0%
Trans Fat		0g
Cholesterol	0mg	0%
Sodium	0mg	0%
Potassium	90mg	
Total Carbohydrate	5g	2%
Dietary Fiber	1g	4%
Sugar	4g	
Protein		0g
Vitamin A		0%
Vitamin C		4%
Calcium		0%
Iron		0%

Stone Fruit

Plum

There are hundreds of varieties of plums that range from sweet to tart in flavor and come in yellows, greens, reds, purples, blues, and everything in between. There are two main varieties: Japanese and European. Japanese plums are larger and juicier than European plums, and they have a softer flesh. Both are great for eating fresh, but European plums are better for cooking and drying. Ripe plums are firm, but yield to gentle pressure. Look for plums with a smooth skin that is free of blemishes or cracks. Store ripe plums in the refrigerator for up to four days.

Pluot

Pluots® are a plum-apricot hybrid that are sometimes marketed as "dinosaur eggs." They have a plum-like shape and a smooth skin that ranges from yellowish green to speckled red to deep purple, depending on the variety. Pluots contain more sugar than plums and have a firmer texture and longer shelf life than apricots. With their intensely sweet blend of flavors, pluots make a wonderful snack and work well in any recipe calling for plums.

Prune

All prunes are plums, but not all plums can be prunes. Prune plums, unlike other varieties, have a high sugar content and can be dried with the pits without fermenting. Look for slightly soft, somewhat flexible fruit with a blemish-free, bluish-black skin. They can be enjoyed fresh, cooked into sauces, or added to sweet or savory dishes.

Tropical Fruit

Tropical fruit such as papaya, kiwifruit, and carambola were, until recently, only available in specialty produce markets. But today, these and others are sold in most grocery stores alongside familiar offerings such as bananas and apples. These luscious fruit offer more than a taste of paradise: They are low calorie, cholesterol free, and nutritious.

Many tropical fruit continue ripening or softening after harvest, and so can be purchased while still firm and slightly green. Most should be kept at room temperature as they ripen, and then later refrigerated, unless otherwise noted.

Carambola/Star Fruit

Carambolas are typically three to five inches long, with five distinct ribs running lengthwise. They are also called star fruit, because cutting the fruit crosswise produces crisp, star-shaped slices. The flavor may be very sweet to slightly tart. Select firm, shiny carambolas that are mostly yellow. Store ripe carambolas in the refrigerator, tightly wrapped in a plastic bag for up to a week. Carambolas are a good source of vitamin C. Slice them for snacks or salads or juice them to add to fruit drinks; don't worry about peeling them first. Their distinctive shape makes them a beautiful garnish.

Cherimoya

The cherimoya, sometimes called a custard apple, tastes like pineapple, papaya, and banana combined. It has a thin, green, and often scaly skin and can be round, oval, or heart shaped. Cherimoyas are a fair source of vitamin C. Select fruit that is firm and heavy for its size and free of brown blotches. Wrap and refrigerate ripe cherimoyas for up to four days. Cut in half and serve fresh (remove the seeds first), or freeze for thirty minutes and eat like sorbet.

Coconut

Coconuts have three layers: a hard, brown, hairy husk (which is usually removed before consumers see it) over a thin, brown skin that protects the creamy, white meat. Select heavy coconuts that sound full of liquid and avoid those with weeping "eyes." Fresh coconuts provide iron, potassium, and protein. Whole, unopened coconuts can be stored at room temperature for up to six months. Fresh, grated coconut meat should be tightly covered and stored in the refrigerator for up to four days. Coconuts are high in saturated fat, but small amounts add a nutty, candy-like natural sweetness to fruit salads, whole-grain cereals, and desserts.

Feijoa

The feijoa is sometimes called a pineapple guava, but it's not a true guava. It's an egg-shaped fruit with a thin, bitter, lime- to olive-green skin (which should be removed before use). The cream-colored flesh is strong tasting, with hints of quince, pineapple, and mint. The jelly-like center has edible seeds. Ripe feijoas are fragrant and yield slightly to the touch; refrigerate them for three to five days. Try feijoas in fruit compotes, or make them into a sauce for roasted meat.

Guava

There are many guava varieties. Some are as small as an egg, others as large as an apple. Their skin might be red, yellow, or purplish-black, while their flesh ranges from pale yellow to vivid red. Fresh guavas are an excellent source of vitamin C. Look for firm guavas that yield to gentle pressure. Avoid bruised guavas, or unripe ones (they are mouth-puckeringly tart). Ripe guavas smell fragrant and fruity and can be stored in the refrigerator for up to four days. Puréed guavas make a tasty beverage base, while the flesh can be made into jam, jelly, sauces, or preserves.

Kiwano

The kiwano, also called a horned melon or horned cucumber, has short "horns" on its bright yellow or orange skin. Kiwanos are about the size of a large pear with a pale yellow-green, soft pulp and edible seeds. Select kiwanos with intact horns and no soft spots or bruises. Store at room temperature. Unripe kiwanos will keep for up to two weeks; ripe ones are good for three to four days. The sweet-tart flavor with hints of bananas and cucumbers is a welcome addition to fruit salads and even roasted meats.

Nutrition Facts

SOURCE: USDA

Stone Fruit

Plum
Serving Size: 1 medium (66g)

Calories		40
Total Fat	0.5g	1%
Saturated Fat	0g	0%
Trans Fat	0g	
Cholesterol	0mg	0%
Sodium	0mg	0%
Potassium	110mg	
Total Carbohydrate	10g	3%
Dietary Fiber	1g	4%
Sugar	5g	
Protein	1g	
Vitamin A		4%
Vitamin C		10%
Calcium		0%
Iron		0%

Pluot
Serving Size: 1 medium (106g)

Calories		35
Total Fat	0g	0%
Saturated Fat	0g	0%
Trans Fat	0g	
Cholesterol	0mg	0%
Sodium	0mg	0%
Potassium	153mg	
Total Carbohydrate	9g	3%
Dietary Fiber	2g	8%
Sugar	7g	
Protein	1g	
Vitamin A		n/a
Vitamin C		8%
Calcium		n/a
Iron		n/a

Prune
Serving Size: 1/4 cup/50ml (40g)

Calories		110
Total Fat	0g	0%
Saturated Fat	0g	0%
Trans Fat	0g	
Cholesterol	0mg	0%
Sodium	5mg	0%
Potassium	290mg	
Total Carbohydrate	26g	9%
Dietary Fiber	2g	8%
Sugar	13g	
Protein	1g	
Vitamin A		10%
Vitamin C		4%
Calcium		0%
Iron		4%

Tropical Fruit

Carambola/Star Fruit
Serving Size: 1 medium (91g)

Calories		30
Total Fat	0g	0%
Saturated Fat	0g	0%
Trans Fat	0g	
Cholesterol	0mg	0%
Sodium	0mg	0%
Potassium	120mg	
Total Carbohydrate	6g	2%
Dietary Fiber	3g	12%
Sugar	4g	
Protein	1g	
Vitamin A		2%
Vitamin C		50%
Calcium		0%
Iron		0%

Cherimoya
Serving Size: 1/2 cup/125ml (125g)

Calories		90
Total Fat	1g	2%
Saturated Fat	0g	0%
Trans Fat	0g	
Cholesterol	0mg	0%
Sodium	0mg	0%
Potassium	340mg	
Total Carbohydrate	22g	7%
Dietary Fiber	3g	12%
Sugar	0g	
Protein	2g	
Vitamin A		0%
Vitamin C		25%
Calcium		2%
Iron		2%

Tropical Fruit

Coconut
Serving Size: 1/2 cup/125ml (40g)

Calories		140
Total Fat	13g	20%
Saturated Fat	12g	60%
Trans Fat	0g	
Cholesterol	0mg	0%
Sodium	10mg	0%
Potassium	150mg	
Total Carbohydrate	6g	2%
Dietary Fiber	4g	16%
Sugar	2g	
Protein	1g	
Vitamin A		0%
Vitamin C		2%
Calcium		0%
Iron		6%

Feijoa
Serving Size: 1 medium (50g)

Calories		25
Total Fat	0g	0%
Saturated Fat	0g	0%
Trans Fat	0g	
Cholesterol	0mg	0%
Sodium	0mg	0%
Potassium	80mg	
Total Carbohydrate	5g	2%
Dietary Fiber	2g	8%
Sugar	3g	
Protein	1g	
Vitamin A		0%
Vitamin C		15%
Calcium		0%
Iron		0%

Guava
Serving Size: 1 medium (90g)

Calories		60
Total Fat	1g	2%
Saturated Fat	0g	0%
Trans Fat	0g	
Cholesterol	0mg	0%
Sodium	0mg	0%
Potassium	380mg	
Total Carbohydrate	13g	4%
Dietary Fiber	5g	20%
Sugar	8g	
Protein	1g	
Vitamin A		10%
Vitamin C		340%
Calcium		2%
Iron		2%

Kiwano
Serving Size: 1 medium (100g)

Calories		25
Total Fat	0g	0%
Saturated Fat	0g	0%
Trans Fat	0g	
Cholesterol	0mg	0%
Sodium	1mg	0%
Potassium		n/a
Total Carbohydrate	3g	1%
Dietary Fiber	1g	4%
Sugar	0g	
Protein	1g	
Vitamin A		6%
Vitamin C		40%
Calcium		2%
Iron		6%

Tropical Fruit

Kiwifruit, Gold

Gold kiwifruit has yellow flesh and tiny, edible seeds. The skin is bronze colored, smooth, and edible. Buy firm kiwifruit and allow them to ripen at home. Ripe kiwifruit will yield to gentle pressure and can be refrigerated for up to one week. At fewer than 50 calories, kiwifruit is a good nutritional bargain: It supplies magnesium and fiber and is a good source of vitamin C and potassium.

Kiwifruit, Green

The green kiwifruit's brown skin is edible, though it's fuzzy enough that few people actually eat it. The green flesh has tiny, edible black seeds. Refrigerate ripe kiwifruit for up to three weeks. Kiwifruit can be cooked, but heat turns the vibrant flesh an unappetizing shade of drab green. So, slice raw, ripe kiwifruit in half and scoop the flesh out with a spoon. Or peel, slice, and add to salads or mix with yogurt.

Mango

Mangos can be round, oblong, or kidney shaped and have a single, large seed. Their thin, tough skin is green at first, then turns a greenish yellow to bright yellow with red mottling as they ripen. Store at room temperature until ripe, and then refrigerate for up to five days. The golden-orange flesh is juicy, sweet-tart, and high in vitamins A, C, and D. Mangos make a tasty treat when peeled and served plain, combined with jalapeños and red onions for a spicy chutney, or puréed to make a sauce for French toast, pancakes, or waffles.

Papaya

Papayas can weigh from one to twenty pounds and are oval, with a mostly yellow skin. They contain papain, a digestive enzyme, and are a good source of vitamins A and C. Look for papayas with richly colored skins free of dark spots. Refrigerate ripe papayas and use as soon as possible. Try making salsa with fresh papaya, dessert sauces with puréed papaya, or a salad dressing with the edible seeds.

Passion Fruit

Passion fruit are egg-shaped and about three inches long. The most common variety has a dimpled, brownish-purple skin and soft, golden flesh with edible seeds. The intense, sweetly tart flavor is described variously as lemon-jasmine-honey or jasmine-banana-lime. Choose deeply colored fruit that's heavy for its size and store refrigerated for up to five days. Passion fruit purée adds a tropical flavor to drinks, vinaigrettes, sauces, syrups, and sorbets.

Pineapple

Ripe pineapples are juicy and sweetly tangy, with rough, diamond-patterned skins. They are a good source of vitamin C, as well as other natural substances that studies indicate relieve indigestion, promote healing, and build bone. Ripe pineapples are slightly soft to the touch, with bright leaves and a rich color that shows no sign of green. Underripe pineapples are firmer; they will soften and become less acidic after picking, but will not get any sweeter. Tightly wrap and refrigerate ripe fruit for up to three days. Try fresh pineapple for a snack, or sauté, broil, or grill fresh slices and serve with vanilla ice cream for dessert.

Sapote

There are many varieties of sapote; the white sapote is the most common. It's about the size of an orange, with a creamy, custard-like flesh surrounding three to five seeds. The skin ranges from chartreuse to yellow in color. Its sweet flavor has notes of peach, avocado, and vanilla. Sapotes are a good source of potassium, vitamin C, iron, and dietary fiber. Store ripe sapotes in the refrigerator for up to three days. They aren't used in cooking, but are delicious eaten out of hand. They can also be puréed and added to fruit drinks or sauces (discard seeds first).

Sapote, Mamey

The mamey sapote is football shaped, with a thick, rough, russet rind and a single, large pit. The sweet flesh is salmon pink to golden red in color, and tastes something like apricots and almonds. They are high in fiber, and also provide moderate amounts of vitamins A and C. Store at room temperature for up to a week. Eat mamey sapotes fresh, turn them into jam, or purée for sauces and beverages.

Other Fruit

Fruit is an essential part of a healthy diet and naturally satisfies your sweet tooth without adding extra calories or fat. Different fruit provide a range of vitamins, minerals, fiber, and phytochemicals that give you an energy boost while reducing the risk of disease and protecting against the effects of aging. Most are cholesterol free and contain little, if any, fat or sodium. Be sure to eat a variety of fresh fruit every day to take advantage of the full spectrum of benefits!

Avocado, Florida and Haas

Avocados all have a buttery, nutty flavor, but their appearance varies greatly depending on whether it's a Haas, Fuerte, or other favorite. They can be round or pear shaped and weigh between three ounces and four pounds. The skin can be pebbly and almost black, or smooth and green, usually with a pale green or greenish-gold flesh. Avocados ripen best after picking, a process that is accelerated by placing several avocados in a paper bag. When they yield to gentle pressure, transfer them to the refrigerator. Avocados are a good source of heart-healthy monounsaturated fats, folate, potassium, vitamin E, and phytochemicals that may protect against eye disease and high cholesterol. Eat avocados with a sprinkling of sea salt, top with chicken or tuna salad, or toss one in the blender with peaches, yogurt, blueberries, and crushed ice for a power-packed smoothie.

Date

Dates are typically one to two inches long, with an oval shape, papery skin and single, narrow seed. They might be yellow, golden brown, black, or mahogany. Fresh dates should be plump, soft, and shiny. Avoid those that are shriveled, moldy, or encrusted with sugar crystals. Wrap them in plastic and refrigerate for up to two weeks. Dates are a good source of dietary fiber, potassium, B-complex vitamins, magnesium, and iron. Dates—fresh or dried—make a high-energy snack. They're also delicious in salads, compotes, baked goods, or served with fresh goat cheese.

Nutrition Facts
SOURCE: USDA

Tropical Fruit

Kiwifruit, Gold
Serving Size: 1 medium peeled (76g)

Calories	45	
Total Fat	0g	0%
Saturated Fat	0g	0%
Trans Fat	0g	
Cholesterol	0mg	0%
Sodium	0mg	0%
Potassium	210mg	
Total Carbohydrate	11g	4%
Dietary Fiber	3g	12%
Sugar	8g	
Protein	1g	
Vitamin A		2%
Vitamin C		90%
Calcium		2%
Iron		2%

Kiwifruit, Green
Serving Size: 1 medium peeled (76g)

Calories	45	
Total Fat	0g	0%
Saturated Fat	0g	0%
Trans Fat	0g	
Cholesterol	0mg	0%
Sodium	0mg	0%
Potassium	240mg	
Total Carbohydrate	11g	4%
Dietary Fiber	2g	8%
Sugar	7g	
Protein	1g	
Vitamin A		2%
Vitamin C		120%
Calcium		2%
Iron		2%

Mango
Serving Size: 1 medium (207g)

Calories	130	
Total Fat	0.5g	1%
Saturated Fat	0g	0%
Trans Fat	0g	
Cholesterol	0mg	0%
Sodium	0mg	0%
Potassium	330mg	
Total Carbohydrate	35g	12%
Dietary Fiber	4g	16%
Sugar	31g	
Protein	1g	
Vitamin A		30%
Vitamin C		100%
Calcium		2%
Iron		2%

Papaya
Serving Size: 1 medium (304g)

Calories	120	
Total Fat	0g	0%
Saturated Fat	0g	0%
Trans Fat	0g	
Cholesterol	0mg	0%
Sodium	10mg	0%
Potassium	780mg	
Total Carbohydrate	30g	10%
Dietary Fiber	5g	20%
Sugar	18g	
Protein	2g	
Vitamin A		70%
Vitamin C		310%
Calcium		8%
Iron		2%

Passion Fruit
Serving Size: 1/2 cup/125ml (125g)

Calories	120	
Total Fat	1g	2%
Saturated Fat	0g	0%
Trans Fat	0g	
Cholesterol	0mg	0%
Sodium	35mg	1%
Potassium	435mg	
Total Carbohydrate	29g	10%
Dietary Fiber	13g	52%
Sugar	14g	
Protein	3g	
Vitamin A		30%
Vitamin C		60%
Calcium		2%
Iron		10%

Pineapple
Serving Size: 1/2 cup/125ml (125g)

Calories	60	
Total Fat	0g	0%
Saturated Fat	0g	0%
Trans Fat	0g	
Cholesterol	0mg	0%
Sodium	0mg	0%
Potassium	145mg	
Total Carbohydrate	16g	5%
Dietary Fiber	2g	8%
Sugar	12g	
Protein	1g	
Vitamin A		2%
Vitamin C		80%
Calcium		2%
Iron		2%

Sapote
Serving Size: 1 medium (225g)

Calories	300	
Total Fat	1.5g	2%
Saturated Fat	0g	0%
Trans Fat	0g	
Cholesterol	0mg	0%
Sodium	20mg	1%
Potassium	770mg	
Total Carbohydrate	76g	25%
Dietary Fiber	6g	24%
Sugar	47g	
Protein	5g	
Vitamin A		20%
Vitamin C		70%
Calcium		8%
Iron		10%

Sapote, Mamey
Serving Size: 1 medium (170g)

Calories	140	
Total Fat	2g	3%
Saturated Fat	0g	0%
Trans Fat	0g	
Cholesterol	0mg	0%
Sodium	20mg	1%
Potassium	330mg	
Total Carbohydrate	34g	11%
Dietary Fiber	9g	36%
Sugar	23g	
Protein	1g	
Vitamin A		2%
Vitamin C		40%
Calcium		4%
Iron		8%

Other Fruit

Avocado, Florida and Haas
Serving Size: 1 medium (201g)

Calories	320	
Total Fat	29g	45%
Saturated Fat	4.5g	23%
Trans Fat	0g	
Cholesterol	0mg	0%
Sodium	15mg	1%
Potassium	980mg	
Total Carbohydrate	17g	6%
Dietary Fiber	13g	52%
Sugar	1g	
Protein	4g	
Vitamin A		6%
Vitamin C		35%
Calcium		2%
Iron		6%

Date
Serving Size: 1/2 cup/125ml (125g)

Calories	350	
Total Fat	0g	0%
Saturated Fat	0g	0%
Trans Fat	0g	
Cholesterol	0mg	0%
Sodium	0mg	0%
Potassium	820mg	
Total Carbohydrate	94g	31%
Dietary Fiber	10g	40%
Sugar	79g	
Protein	3g	
Vitamin A		0%
Vitamin C		0%
Calcium		4%
Iron		8%

Other Fruit

Fig

There are hundreds of fig varieties, and Calimyrna, Mission, Kadota, and Adriatic are among the most popular. They range from white to green to purplish-black in color. The white, pinkish-yellow, or green flesh is soft and speckled with edible seeds. Both fresh and dried figs provide antioxidants, potassium, calcium, and iron. Fresh figs are highly perishable and should be refrigerated for just two or three days. Cut into quarters and serve for a quick snack (the skin is edible), or pair with cheese or cured meats.

Persimmon

Persimmons are yellow-orange to pumpkin in color and are a source of vitamin C. Fuyu persimmons are tomato-shaped and have a spicy and sweet flavor that's reminiscent of mango and papaya. Fuyus remain firm when ripe and so can be used in fruit salads. The Hachiya persimmon (also called Japanese persimmon) is large and round, with a slightly elongated base. Ripe Hachiyas are almost mushy and very sweet, but unripe ones are unpleasantly astringent. Ripen them at room temperature, then refrigerate for up to three days. Persimmons are excellent eaten out of hand (peel them first), or use a purée as a sauce for desserts.

Quince

Quinces have yellow skin and yellowish-white flesh. This aromatic fruit looks and tastes like an apple-pear cross, but it is drier and more tart than either. Look for large, firm, brightly colored quinces with little greening. Wrap in plastic and store in the refrigerator for up to two months. Quinces are high in pectin and are excellent for making preserves, jams, and jellies. They can also be stewed, combined with apples in pies or other desserts, or added to meat stews.

Pomegranate

The pomegranate's leathery, red (or sometimes pinkish yellow) skin encases hundreds of edible seeds, each surrounded by a translucent sac filled with brilliant red, sweet-tart juice. Pomegranates are rich in potassium and are a source of vitamin C. Select fruit that are heavy for their size, with bright, unblemished skins. Store in a dark, cool place for a month or in the refrigerator for up to two months. To serve, cut pomegranates in half and scoop the juice sacs away from the tough, white membranes that separate them. Eat them fresh, use a sprinkling to garnish salads or dips, or add them to fish or poultry dishes.

Prickly Pear/Cactus Pear

Prickly pears are about the size and shape of a regular pear, but they grow on a cactus. Their prickly skin can be green or red; the flesh of green varieties is yellowish to gold, while that of the red variety is magenta. Regardless of color, prickly pears have a soft texture, are scattered with black seeds, and taste of watermelon. Ripe prickly pears are evenly colored and yield slightly to pressure. Store in the refrigerator for up to a week, and peel and remove seeds before using. Prickly pears can be chilled and eaten, blended into tropical drinks, or puréed and used to glaze a pork roast.

Nutrition Facts

SOURCE: USDA

Other Fruit

Fig
Serving Size: 1 medium (50g)

Calories		35
Total Fat	0g	0%
Saturated Fat	0g	0%
Trans Fat	0g	
Cholesterol	0mg	0%
Sodium	0mg	0%
Potassium	120mg	
Total Carbohydrate	10g	3%
Dietary Fiber	1g	4%
Sugar	8g	
Protein	0g	
Vitamin A		2%
Vitamin C		2%
Calcium		2%
Iron		2%

Persimmon
Serving Size: 1 medium (25g)

Calories		30
Total Fat	0g	0%
Saturated Fat	0g	0%
Trans Fat	0g	
Cholesterol	0mg	0%
Sodium	0mg	0%
Potassium	80mg	
Total Carbohydrate	8g	3%
Dietary Fiber	0g	0%
Sugar	0g	
Protein	0g	
Vitamin A		0%
Vitamin C		25%
Calcium		0%
Iron		4%

Pomegranate
Serving Size: 1 medium (155g)

Calories		100
Total Fat	0g	0%
Saturated Fat	0g	0%
Trans Fat	0g	
Cholesterol	0mg	0%
Sodium	0mg	0%
Potassium	400mg	
Total Carbohydrate	26g	9%
Dietary Fiber	1g	4%
Sugar	26g	
Protein	1g	
Vitamin A		4%
Vitamin C		15%
Calcium		0%
Iron		2%

Prickly Pear/Cactus Pear
Serving Size: 1 medium (103g)

Calories		4
Total Fat	0.5g	1%
Saturated Fat	0g	0
Trans Fat	0	
Cholesterol	0mg	0%
Sodium	5mg	0%
Potassium	230m	
Total Carbohydrate	10g	0%
Dietary Fiber	4g	16%
Sugar	0%	
Protein	1	
Vitamin A		0%
Vitamin C		25%
Calcium		6%
Iron		2%

Quince
Serving Size: 1 medium (92g)

Calories		5
Total Fat	0g	0%
Saturated Fat	0g	0%
Trans Fat	0	
Cholesterol	0mg	0%
Sodium	0mg	0%
Potassium	180m	
Total Carbohydrate	14g	5%
Dietary Fiber	2g	8%
Sugar	12	
Protein	0	
Vitamin A		0%
Vitamin C		25%
Calcium		2%
Iron		4%

Vegetables

An incredible array of fresh vegetables is now available in supermarkets, gourmet groceries, and produce markets. Many varieties were once virtually unknown, but today's advanced storage and shipping technology means fresh produce from across the globe is now available year-round. The selection has never been better; there is a world of flavor and nutrition at your fingertips. But questions certainly come with the bounty. What's the difference between white and green asparagus? How do you cook a malanga? What's a good substitute for boniato?

This essential kitchen companion will answer such questions and help you make smart selections for your family's menu. It includes nutritional information, selection and storage guidelines, and preparation and serving tips on both familiar vegetables like cucumbers and some less familiar ethnic vegetables like fresh bamboo shoots and yuca. In short, these pages provide everything you need to enjoy a flavorful variety of veggies and reap the healthy rewards of a diet rich in produce!

Beans and Peas (Legumes)

Legumes are the edible seeds of pods that split in half on both sides when ripe. They can be used fresh, dried, sprouted, or ground into flour. They are a staple food throughout much of the world.

Tasty and low fat, legumes are a healthy addition to any meal. They are high in protein and are perfect for meatless entrées as well as salads, soups, stews, casseroles, and purées. Most are an excellent source of folic acid, a B vitamin that may reduce the risk of stroke, heart disease, certain types of cancer, and birth defects. Dried beans are especially high in fiber and help reduce cholesterol, improve digestion, and can aid in weight loss.

Many legumes are sold either fresh or dried. When buying fresh, look for plump and firm pods or beans that are evenly colored. Most should be stored in their pods in the refrigerator for no more than three days. Fresh beans and peas can be steamed, sautéed, stir-fried, lightly boiled, baked, or even served raw.

Dried, canned, and frozen beans and peas are a good alternative when fresh go out of season. In fact, some legumes are almost always sold dried. Dried beans can be stored for up to a year. To prepare, soak them overnight in water (use ten cups of cold water per two cups of dry beans), drain, and then cook according to package or recipe directions. To quick-soak: boil the beans in water (use the same ratio as for overnight soaking) for two to three minutes, turn off heat, cover, set aside for one to four hours, drain, and proceed with recipe.

1 Black Beans

Black beans, or turtle beans, are black with cream-colored flesh. They're popular in Latin and Caribbean dishes such as Cuban black bean soup and are delicious in a Southwestern-style salad made with corn, red sweet peppers, and vinaigrette.

2 Black-Eyed Peas

Black-eyed peas are beige with a black dot or "eye" at their inner curve. They're used in Southern specialties like "Hoppin' John," a dish of seasoned black-eyed peas, rice, and salt pork or bacon that is traditionally served on New Year's Day for good luck. Try them in a bean salad made with tomatoes, sliced green onions, and lemon vinaigrette.

3 Cranberry Beans

Cranberry beans, also called borlotti or Roman beans, are tan and mottled with red. These tender beans have a nutlike flavor and absorb spices well. They're popular in Italian cooking. Mix them with bitter greens for an interesting salad, or use them in succotash instead of lima beans.

4 Fava Beans

Fava beans are pale green when fresh, and tan and flat like a lima bean when dried. They're popular in Mediterranean and Middle Eastern cooking and also make a tasty addition to soups. Serve tender, young fava beans (slip the tough outer skin off first) with an aged pecorino, or purée and add to vegetable dips.

5 Garbanzo Beans

Garbanzo beans, or chickpeas, are round, buff colored, and firm textured. They are often used in Mediterranean, Indian, and Middle Eastern cooking and are the main ingredient in hummus and falafel. Add them to soups, salads, casseroles, and dishes made with couscous.

6 Green Peas

"English pea" is the proper name for what is often called a green or garden pea. Fresh green peas are sweet and work well in a variety of recipes. Try dressing cooked peas with butter, mint, salt, and pepper, or add them to salads, soups, and other side dishes.

7 Lima Beans

Lima beans are green and kidney shaped, and the two most popular varieties are Fordhook and baby lima. Fordhooks are plumper and more flavorful. Baby limas are fully mature, but naturally petite. With their creamy, sweet taste, lima beans can stand on their own as a side dish. Along with corn and red or green sweet peppers, lima beans are also a classic ingredient in succotash, and they are also delectable when puréed with a little olive oil, garlic, and lemon juice.

8 Pinto Beans

Pinto beans are oval and beige with streaks of red; they turn brown when cooked. These beans are a staple in Latin American and Southwestern cooking and are often used to make refried beans, burritos, and tacos.

Nutrition Facts

SOURCE: USDA

Beans and Peas (Legumes)

Black Beans
Serving Size: 1/2 cup/125ml (97g)

Calories		330
Total Fat	1.5g	2%
Saturated Fat	0g	0%
Trans Fat	0g	
Cholesterol	0mg	0%
Sodium	0mg	0%
Potassium	1440mg	
Total Carbohydrate	60g	20%
Dietary Fiber	13g	52%
Sugar	2g	
Protein	21g	
Vitamin A		0%
Vitamin C		0%
Calcium		10%
Iron		25%

Garbanzo Beans
Serving Size: 1/2 cup/125ml (100g)

Calories		360
Total Fat	6g	9%
Saturated Fat	0.5g	3%
Trans Fat	0g	
Cholesterol	0mg	0%
Sodium	25mg	1%
Potassium	880mg	
Total Carbohydrate	61g	20%
Dietary Fiber	10g	40%
Sugar	11g	
Protein	19g	
Vitamin A		2%
Vitamin C		6%
Calcium		10%
Iron		35%

Black-Eyed Peas
Serving Size: 1/2 cup/125ml (73g)

Calories		70
Total Fat	0g	0%
Saturated Fat	0g	0%
Trans Fat	0g	
Cholesterol	0mg	0%
Sodium		0%
Potassium	320mg	
Total Carbohydrate	14g	5%
Dietary Fiber	4g	16%
Sugar	2g	
Protein	2g	
Vitamin A		0%
Vitamin C		4%
Calcium		10%
Iron		4%

Green Peas
Serving Size: 1/2 cup/125ml (73g)

Calories		60
Total Fat	0g	0%
Saturated Fat	0g	0%
Trans Fat	0g	
Cholesterol	0mg	0%
Sodium	0mg	0%
Potassium	180mg	
Total Carbohydrate	10g	3%
Dietary Fiber	4g	16%
Sugar	4g	
Protein	4g	
Vitamin A		10%
Vitamin C		15%
Calcium		2%
Iron		6%

Cranberry Beans
Serving Size: 1/2 cup/125ml (89ml)

Calories		330
Total Fat	1g	2%
Saturated Fat	0g	0%
Trans Fat	0g	
Cholesterol	0mg	0%
Sodium	5mg	0%
Potassium	1300mg	
Total Carbohydrate	59g	20%
Dietary Fiber	24g	96%
Sugar	n/a	
Protein	22g	
Vitamin A		0%
Vitamin C		0%
Calcium		10%
Iron		25%

Lima Beans
Serving Size: 1/2 cup/125ml (78g)

Calories		90
Total Fat	0.5g	1%
Saturated Fat	0g	0%
Trans Fat	0g	
Cholesterol	0mg	0%
Sodium	5mg	0%
Potassium	370mg	
Total Carbohydrate	16g	5%
Dietary Fiber	4g	16%
Sugar	1g	
Protein	5g	
Vitamin A		4%
Vitamin C		30%
Calcium		2%
Iron		15%

Fava Beans
Serving Size: 1/2 cup/125ml (39g)

Calories		40
Total Fat	0g	0%
Saturated Fat	0g	0%
Trans Fat	0g	
Cholesterol	0mg	0%
Sodium	25mg	1%
Potassium	140mg	
Total Carbohydrate	6g	2%
Dietary Fiber	2g	8%
Sugar	3g	
Protein	3g	
Vitamin A		4%
Vitamin C		30%
Calcium		2%
Iron		6%

Pinto Beans
Serving Size: 1/2 cup/125ml (97g)

Calories		330
Total Fat	1g	2%
Saturated Fat	0g	0%
Trans Fat	0g	
Cholesterol	0mg	0%
Sodium	10mg	0%
Potassium	1290mg	
Total Carbohydrate	61g	20%
Dietary Fiber	6g	20%
Sugar	2g	
Protein	20g	
Vitamin A		0%
Vitamin C		10%
Calcium		10%
Iron		30%

Beans and Peas

Red Beans

"Red bean" is a broad category that includes kidney beans of different colors and sizes. They range from light, brownish red to crimson and are cream colored inside. Red beans hold their shape and texture when cooked and so are perfect for *chili con carne* and Louisiana-style dishes such as red beans and rice.

Snow Peas

Snow peas are thin and crisp, with an edible green pod that encases tiny, tender peas. They are a common addition to Chinese-style stir-fries and salads.

Soybeans/Edamame

Edamame is the Japanese name for green soybeans. They are picked when fully grown but not yet mature and are usually sold while still in their bright green pods. Edamame are easy to digest and are an excellent source of protein and fiber. Steam the pods for twenty minutes, and then serve warm or refrigerate until ready to use. Sprinkle with sea salt and serve as a snack or appetizer, allowing people to shell them like peanuts.

Sugar Snap Peas

Sugar snap peas are a cross between English and snow peas. The plump, bright green pods are entirely edible and have a pleasing sweetness and crunch. Serve them raw in salads or dress sautéed sugar snap peas with soy sauce, rice vinegar, and toasted sesame seeds.

Beans,
Green and Yellow

Green beans have tender pods with immature seeds, and the entire bean is eaten. They are also called snap beans or string beans, although modern varieties no longer have the stringy fiber along the side that earned the name. Wax beans are a pale yellow type of green bean; there are also purple varieties that turn green when cooked.

Green beans are a fair source of vitamins A and C. Look for bright, slender beans that are free of blemishes. Wrap them in plastic, and store refrigerated for up to five days. To prepare, snap off the stem end and cook until just crisp-tender.

Chinese Long

These pencil-thin green beans are also called yard-long beans because they can grow up to three feet in length. They are usually shorter than that in the market. Chinese long beans are related to black-eyed peas, but they taste more like green beans. Cut into two-inch pieces and add to stir-fries or sauté in sesame oil.

French Green

French green beans are tiny, slender, young green beans with a delicate flavor. They are also called *haricot vert* (French for "green bean"), but are not the same as French-cut or "frenched" green beans—terms referring to any green bean cut lengthwise into thin strips. Try tossing these tender beans with tomatoes, garlic, and olive oil.

Flat

Flat beans are larger and flatter than other green beans and have a stronger flavor. They are also called Italian, Romano or Roma beans, or pole beans, because of how some varieties are grown. Flat beans seasoned with bacon are popular in the South. Or, lightly steam flat beans and then sauté with olive oil and garlic, and top with chopped hazelnuts.

Snap/String

These familiar green beans can be steamed, sautéed, lightly boiled, microwaved, or even roasted or pickled. Serve them simply with butter or olive oil; toss them with lemon zest or toasted pine nuts; or add them to potato, pasta, or green salads.

Yellow Wax

Wax beans can be light to deep yellow, and they have a subtle flavor. Try sautéing wax beans with mushrooms, or use them in any recipe calling for green beans.

Nutrition Facts

SOURCE: USDA

Beans and Peas (Legumes)

Red Beans
Serving Size: 1/2 cup/125ml (92g)

Calories	310
Total Fat	1g 2%
Saturated Fat	0g 0%
Trans Fat	0g
Cholesterol	0mg 0%
Sodium	10mg 0%
Potassium	1300mg
Total Carbohydrate	56g 19%
Dietary Fiber	13g 52%
Sugar	2g
Protein	21g
Vitamin A	0%
Vitamin C	6%
Calcium	8%
Iron	35%

Snow Peas
Serving Size: 1/2 cup/125ml (73g)

Calories	30
Total Fat	0g 0%
Saturated Fat	0g 0%
Trans Fat	0g
Cholesterol	0mg 0%
Sodium	0mg 0%
Potassium	200mg
Total Carbohydrate	5g 2%
Dietary Fiber	1g 4%
Sugar	3g
Protein	2g
Vitamin A	2%
Vitamin C	70%
Calcium	4%
Iron	8%

Soybeans/Edamame
Serving Size: 1/2 cup/125ml (90g)

Calories	190
Total Fat	9g 14%
Saturated Fat	1g 5%
Trans Fat	0g
Cholesterol	0mg 0%
Sodium	20mg 1%
Potassium	800mg
Total Carbohydrate	14g 5%
Dietary Fiber	5g 20%
Sugar	8g
Protein	17g
Vitamin A	0%
Vitamin C	60%
Calcium	25%
Iron	25%

Sugar Snap Peas
Serving Size: 1/2 cup/125ml (53g)

Calories	25
Total Fat	0g 0%
Saturated Fat	0g 0%
Trans Fat	0g
Cholesterol	0mg 0%
Sodium	0mg 0%
Potassium	n/a
Total Carbohydrate	5g 2%
Dietary Fiber	2g 8%
Sugar	2g
Protein	1g
Vitamin A	4%
Vitamin C	6%
Calcium	4%
Iron	2%

Beans, Green and Yellow

French Green
Serving Size: 1/2 cup/125ml (92g)

Calories	320
Total Fat	2g 3%
Saturated Fat	0g 0%
Trans Fat	0g
Cholesterol	0mg 0%
Sodium	15mg 1%
Potassium	1210mg
Total Carbohydrate	59g 20%
Dietary Fiber	23g 92%
Sugar	n/a
Protein	17g
Vitamin A	0%
Vitamin C	8%
Calcium	15%
Iron	15%

Flat
Serving Size: 1/2 cup/125ml (55ml)

Calories	15
Total Fat	0g 0%
Saturated Fat	0g 0%
Trans Fat	0g
Cholesterol	0mg 0%
Sodium	0mg 0%
Potassium	115mg
Total Carbohydrate	4g 1%
Dietary Fiber	2g 8%
Sugar	1g
Protein	1g
Vitamin A	8%
Vitamin C	15%
Calcium	2%
Iron	4%

Snap/String
Serving Size: 1/2 cup/125ml (55g)

Calories	15
Total Fat	0g 0%
Saturated Fat	0g 0%
Trans Fat	0g
Cholesterol	0mg 0%
Sodium	0mg 0%
Potassium	115mg
Total Carbohydrate	4g 1%
Dietary Fiber	2g 8%
Sugar	1g
Protein	1g
Vitamin A	8%
Vitamin C	15%
Calcium	2%
Iron	4%

Yellow Wax
Serving Size: 1/2 cup/125ml (62g)

Calories	15
Total Fat	0g 0%
Saturated Fat	0g 0%
Trans Fat	0g
Cholesterol	0mg 0%
Sodium	0mg 0%
Potassium	115mg
Total Carbohydrate	4g 1%
Dietary Fiber	2g 8%
Sugar	1g
Protein	1g
Vitamin A	2%
Vitamin C	15%
Calcium	2%
Iron	4%

Beans, Green and Yellow

Chinese Long
Serving Size: 1/2 cup/125ml (46g)

Calories	20
Total Fat	0g 0%
Saturated Fat	0g 0%
Trans Fat	0g
Cholesterol	0mg 0%
Sodium	0mg 0%
Potassium	110mg
Total Carbohydrate	4g 1%
Dietary Fiber	2g 8%
Sugar	n/a
Protein	1g
Vitamin A	8%
Vitamin C	15%
Calcium	2%
Iron	2%

Cabbages

Cabbage is versatile, flavorful, a good value, and good for you. The many varieties come in different shapes and sizes with curly or plain leaves in a range of whites, reds, purples, and greens. This low-calorie vegetable contains fiber, folate, calcium, and iron. Cabbage is also an excellent source of vitamin K, which helps prevent clotting disorders and may reduce the risk of osteoporosis, and contains phytochemicals that may help prevent some forms of cancer.

Choose firm cabbages that are heavy for their size, with crisp leaves and no sign of browning. Wrap heads tightly in plastic and refrigerate for up to a week. Discard the outer leaves and core before using. Serve raw in salads; add to side dishes, stews, and stir-fries; or boil and serve with butter or a light white sauce.

Green

This familiar, round, compact cabbage is traditionally used in coleslaw or cooked with corned beef, but it can also be braised with onions and apples, stuffed with sausage, or turned into a hearty stew with beans, tomatoes, and sliced turkey kielbasa.

Napa

Napa cabbage is cylindrical in shape, with pale green leaves and white ribs. It's crisp, with a mild and delicate sweetness. Napa cabbage is commonly used in Asian cooking; try shredding it and combining with soy sauce, sesame oil, rice vinegar, and sugar for an Asian-style coleslaw.

Red

Red cabbage is firm and round, with shiny, dark red or purple leaves. It has a peppery taste and is a colorful addition to salads. Red cabbage is often called for in German and Swedish recipes.

Savoy

Savoy cabbage forms a loose head of crinkly, crisply succulent leaves. It has a mild, mellow flavor that makes it a favorite for Italian and other cuisines. Try substituting it for lettuce on tacos, braising and serving with fish, or using in a spicy coleslaw.

Nutrition Facts

SOURCE: USDA

Cabbages

Green		
Serving Size: 1 cup/250ml (70g)		
Calories		15
Total Fat	0g	0%
Saturated Fat	0g	0%
Trans Fat		0g
Cholesterol	0mg	0%
Sodium	15mg	1%
Potassium	175mg	
Total Carbohydrate	4g	1%
Dietary Fiber	2g	8%
Sugar		2g
Protein		1g
Vitamin A		2%
Vitamin C		60%
Calcium		4%
Iron		2%

Red		
Serving Size: 1 cup/250ml (89g)		
Calories		30
Total Fat	0g	0%
Saturated Fat	0g	0%
Trans Fat		0g
Cholesterol	0mg	0%
Sodium	25mg	1%
Potassium	220mg	
Total Carbohydrate	7g	2%
Dietary Fiber	2g	8%
Sugar		3g
Protein		1g
Vitamin A		20%
Vitamin C		80%
Calcium		4%
Iron		4%

Napa		
Serving Size: 1 cup/250ml (85g)		
Calories		15
Total Fat	0g	0%
Saturated Fat	0g	0%
Trans Fat		0g
Cholesterol	0mg	0%
Sodium	10mg	0%
Potassium	21mg	
Total Carbohydrate	3g	1%
Dietary Fiber	1g	4%
Sugar		1g
Protein		1g
Vitamin A		20%
Vitamin C		40%
Calcium		6%
Iron		0%

Savoy		
Serving Size: 1 cup/250ml (70g)		
Calories		20
Total Fat	0g	0%
Saturated Fat	0g	0%
Trans Fat		0g
Cholesterol	0mg	0%
Sodium	20mg	1%
Potassium	160mg	
Total Carbohydrate	4g	1%
Dietary Fiber	2g	8%
Sugar		2g
Protein		1g
Vitamin A		15%
Vitamin C		35%
Calcium		2%
Iron		2%

Cucumbers

Cucumbers belong to the gourd family and are botanically a fruit, even though they are used as a vegetable. Cucumbers are long and round, with green skin and pale greenish-white flesh. The seeds are edible, but those of more mature cucumbers may taste bitter and should be removed. Cucumbers are low in calories and a source of vitamins A and C.

Look for firm cucumbers with unblemished, brightly colored skins. Don't just pick the shiny ones, though. Some cucumbers are coated with wax to prevent moisture loss; these should be washed thoroughly before using. Wrap unwashed cucumbers in plastic and refrigerate for up to ten days.

Cucumbers

Armenian

Armenian cucumbers are also called Turkish or Syrian cucumbers. They have corduroy-like ribs and thin skin (no peeling required) and grow into long, twisted shapes. Add sliced Armenian cucumbers to stir-fries, or steam and top with butter.

Common

Common cucumbers are available year-round. Serve them sliced with a sprinkle of salt and fresh-cracked pepper, or make a Greek-style sauce by mixing cucumbers with plain yogurt, garlic, and fresh mint.

English/Burpless

English cucumbers, also called hothouse or burpless cucumbers, are virtually seedless. They can grow up to two feet long and are usually sold shrink-wrapped in plastic. They add extra crunch to salads and sandwiches and can be used in any recipe that calls for cucumbers.

Japanese

Japanese cucumbers have tiny, white bumps on their thin, green skin. They are crisp, mild, and sweet, with fewer seeds than the common cucumber. Add them to salads, or make quick pickles by brining them overnight.

Kirby

Kirby cucumbers are small and perfect for pickling. They are firm and crunchy, with a waxy, green skin and tart flavor. Use Kirby cucumbers in homemade pickle or other recipes.

Eggplants

Eggplants come in a range of whites, mauves, and purples, although there are also yellow and green varieties. Eggplants can be striped or solid-colored, fat or sleek, diminutive or up to a foot long. This so-called vegetable (it's botanically a fruit) is a source of fiber and contains trace amounts of vitamin C.

Choose firm, unblemished eggplants that are heavy for their size. They are highly perishable and grow bitter with age. Store them in a cool, dry place and use within a few days of purchase. Eggplants are common in Mediterranean, Indian, Asian, Italian, and Middle Eastern dishes, and they can be baked, broiled, or grilled. Eggplants are also tasty when fried, but be warned — they absorb more fat during cooking than most other vegetables.

Chinese

Chinese eggplants are long and slim, and they may be white to lavender in color. They are delicately flavored, with a meaty flesh and tender skin. Chinese eggplant is a good choice for stir-fries and sautéed dishes.

Japanese

Japanese eggplants are long and thin, with a light purple skin that darkens as it matures. They resemble Chinese eggplants in texture and flavor and can be used interchangeably with them. Try sliced Japanese eggplant braised in curry sauce.

Italian

Italian eggplants, sometimes called baby eggplants, look like smaller versions of common purple, mauve, and white varieties. They are also slightly sweeter. Try substituting Italian eggplant for pasta in lasagna or grilling over charcoal.

Purple

Purple eggplant, sometimes called American eggplant, is the most common variety. Its dark purple skin is smooth and glossy, and it is typically large and pear shaped. Try adding slices to pizza or combining it with tomatoes, onions, sweet peppers, garlic, zucchini, and herbs in a traditional French ratatouille.

White

White eggplant is egg shaped, and the white skin is thick and tough. The flesh is firm, with a delicate taste. It can be prepared in the same way as other varieties, but may require less cooking time.

Nutrition Facts
SOURCE: USDA

Cucumbers

Armenian
Serving Size: 1 medium (300g)

Calories	40
Total Fat	0g 0%
Saturated Fat	0g 0%
Trans Fat	0g
Cholesterol	0mg 0%
Sodium	5mg 0%
Potassium	423mg
Total Carbohydrate	8g 3%
Dietary Fiber	2g 8%
Sugar	7g
Protein	2g
Vitamin A	15%
Vitamin C	25%
Calcium	4%
Iron	4%

Common
Serving Size: 1/2 cup/125ml (52g)

Calories	10
Total Fat	0g 0%
Saturated Fat	0g 0%
Trans Fat	0g
Cholesterol	0mg 0%
Sodium	0mg 0%
Potassium	75mg
Total Carbohydrate	2g 1%
Dietary Fiber	0g 0%
Sugar	1g
Protein	0g
Vitamin A	2%
Vitamin C	2%
Calcium	0%
Iron	0%

English/Burpless
Serving Size: 1/2 cup/125ml (65g)

Calories	10
Total Fat	0g 0%
Saturated Fat	0g 0%
Trans Fat	0g
Cholesterol	0mg 0%
Sodium	0mg 0%
Potassium	95mg
Total Carbohydrate	2g 1%
Dietary Fiber	1g 4%
Sugar	1g
Protein	1g
Vitamin A	4%
Vitamin C	6%
Calcium	0%
Iron	0%

Japanese
Serving Size: 1/2 cup/125ml (65g)

Calories	10
Total Fat	0g 0%
Saturated Fat	0g 0%
Trans Fat	0g
Cholesterol	0mg 0%
Sodium	0mg 0%
Potassium	75mg
Total Carbohydrate	2g 1%
Dietary Fiber	1g 4%
Sugar	1g
Protein	1g
Vitamin A	4%
Vitamin C	6%
Calcium	0%
Iron	0%

Kirby
Serving Size: 1 medium (225g)

Calories	35
Total Fat	0g 0%
Saturated Fat	0g 0%
Trans Fat	0g
Cholesterol	0mg 0%
Sodium	0mg 0%
Potassium	330mg
Total Carbohydrate	8g 3%
Dietary Fiber	1g 4%
Sugar	4g
Protein	1g
Vitamin A	4%
Vitamin C	10%
Calcium	4%
Iron	4%

Eggplants

Chinese
Serving Size: 1/2 cup/125ml (41g)

Calories	10
Total Fat	0g 0%
Saturated Fat	0g 0%
Trans Fat	0g
Cholesterol	0mg 0%
Sodium	0mg 0%
Potassium	95mg
Total Carbohydrate	2g 1%
Dietary Fiber	1g 4%
Sugar	1g
Protein	0g
Vitamin A	0%
Vitamin C	2%
Calcium	0%
Iron	0%

Italian
Serving Size: 1/2 cup/125ml (41g)

Calories	10
Total Fat	0g 0%
Saturated Fat	0g 0%
Trans Fat	0g
Cholesterol	0mg 0%
Sodium	0mg 0%
Potassium	95mg
Total Carbohydrate	2g 1%
Dietary Fiber	1g 4%
Sugar	1g
Protein	0g
Vitamin A	0%
Vitamin C	2%
Calcium	0%
Iron	0%

Japanese
Serving Size: 1/2 cup/125ml (458g)

Calories	110
Total Fat	1g 2%
Saturated Fat	0g 0%
Trans Fat	0g
Cholesterol	0mg 0%
Sodium	10mg 0%
Potassium	1053mg
Total Carbohydrate	26g 9%
Dietary Fiber	2g 8%
Sugar	16g
Protein	5g
Vitamin A	2%
Vitamin C	15%
Calcium	4%
Iron	6%

Purple
Serving Size: 1/2 cup/125ml (41g)

Calories	10
Total Fat	0g 0%
Saturated Fat	0g 0%
Trans Fat	0g
Cholesterol	0mg 0%
Sodium	0mg 0%
Potassium	95mg
Total Carbohydrate	2g 1%
Dietary Fiber	1g 2%
Sugar	1g
Protein	0g
Vitamin A	0%
Vitamin C	2%
Calcium	0%
Iron	0%

White
Serving Size: 1/2 cup/125ml (41g)

Calories	10
Total Fat	0g 0%
Saturated Fat	0g 0%
Trans Fat	0g
Cholesterol	0mg 0%
Sodium	0mg 0%
Potassium	95mg
Total Carbohydrate	2g 1%
Dietary Fiber	1g 2%
Sugar	1g
Protein	0g
Vitamin A	0%
Vitamin C	2%
Calcium	0%
Iron	0%

Greens

Leafy greens are an important addition to a healthy diet. They contain few calories, little fat, and no cholesterol, plus they taste great. Many are high in vitamins A, C, and E; beta-carotene; calcium; iron; and fiber. Some are also considered cruciferous vegetables, which research shows may reduce the risk of various types of cancer.

Tender, young greens can be added to salads. Mature greens can be wilted, braised, or steamed, or added to soups or side dishes. Be sure to buy plenty if you plan to use them this way, as greens lose a lot of volume when cooked. Select greens with firm stalks and crisp leaves that are brightly colored and show no signs of wilting, yellowing, or insect damage. Wash all greens thoroughly just before using.

Arugula

Arugula is a tender, peppery green that's long been used by Italian cooks. Wrap in plastic (put a damp paper towel around the roots first), refrigerate, and use within two days. Arugula makes a tasty grilled steak salad, pizza topping, or addition to pasta sauces.

Belgian Endive

Belgian endive should be crisp, with tightly furled heads tipped in a pale greenish yellow (it's grown in the dark to keep it from turning green). Wrap in plastic and refrigerate for no more than a day. Combine Belgian endive with Roquefort cheese and walnuts for an elegant first course. It can also be steamed, braised, sautéed, roasted, or grilled.

Bok Choy

Bok choy has a bulb-like base and crunchy white stalks with large, dark green leaves. Its mild, slightly peppery flavor is similar to that of cabbage, and it's often added to stir-fries and soups. Refrigerate for up to four days.

Baby Bok Choy/Shanghai

Baby bok choy, sometimes called Shanghai bok choy, is small (less than ten inches long), with a delicate flavor reminiscent of spinach. Wrap in plastic and refrigerate for three days. The raw stalks make a crunchy snack, or dress sautéed baby bok choy with soy sauce, sesame seed oil, and rice vinegar.

Chicory

Chicory is related to endive and radicchio. It has curly, green leaves with pale centers and is sometimes mistakenly called curly endive. Refrigerate unwashed chicory for up to three days. Its bitter flavor is a refreshing addition to salads; try it with tangerines or blood oranges in a light vinaigrette.

Tasty Idea

Try a typical Italian-style preparation for spinach. Sauté minced garlic in a little olive oil. Add spinach; cover and cook until leaves are wilted (about five minutes). Remove the cover and add a few tablespoons each of raisins and toasted pine nuts. Cook a few minutes more until liquid evaporates.

Nutrition Facts
SOURCE: USDA

Greens

Arugula
Serving Size: 1 cup/250ml (20g)

Calories	5
Total Fat	0g 0%
Saturated Fat	0g 0%
Trans Fat	0g
Cholesterol	0mg 0%
Sodium	5mg 0%
Potassium	75mg
Total Carbohydrate	1g 0%
Dietary Fiber	0g 0%
Sugar	0g
Protein	1g
Vitamin A	10%
Vitamin C	6%
Calcium	4%
Iron	2%

Belgian Endive
Serving Size: 1 cup/250ml (90g)

Calories	15
Total Fat	0g 0%
Saturated Fat	0g 0%
Trans Fat	0g
Cholesterol	0mg 0%
Sodium	0mg 0%
Potassium	190mg
Total Carbohydrate	4g 1%
Dietary Fiber	3g 12%
Sugar	0g
Protein	1g
Vitamin A	0%
Vitamin C	4%
Calcium	2%
Iron	2%

Bok Choy
Serving Size: 1 cup/250ml (70g)

Calories	10
Total Fat	0g 0%
Saturated Fat	0g 0%
Trans Fat	0g
Cholesterol	0mg 0%
Sodium	45mg 2%
Potassium	180mg
Total Carbohydrate	2g 1%
Dietary Fiber	1g 4%
Sugar	1g
Protein	1g
Vitamin A	60%
Vitamin C	50%
Calcium	8%
Iron	4%

Baby Bok Choy/Shanghai
Serving Size: 1/2 cup/125ml (35g)

Calories	5
Total Fat	0g 0%
Saturated Fat	0g 0%
Trans Fat	0g
Cholesterol	0mg 0%
Sodium	25mg 1%
Potassium	90mg
Total Carbohydrate	1g 0%
Dietary Fiber	0g 0%
Sugar	0g
Protein	1g
Vitamin A	30%
Vitamin C	25%
Calcium	4%
Iron	2%

Chicory
Serving Size: 1 cup/250ml (180g)

Calories	40
Total Fat	0.5g 1%
Saturated Fat	0g 0%
Trans Fat	0g
Cholesterol	0mg 0%
Sodium	80mg 3%
Potassium	760mg
Total Carbohydrate	8g 3%
Dietary Fiber	7g 28%
Sugar	1g
Protein	3g
Vitamin A	210%
Vitamin C	70%
Calcium	20%
Iron	10%

Greens

1 Chinese Cabbage

Chinese cabbage is related to broccoli and cabbage, but it isn't a true cabbage. To add to the confusion, the name is sometimes incorrectly used to describe other vegetables such as Napa cabbage or bok choy. So what is it? Chinese cabbage has celery-like stalks, with bright green leaves and a mild flavor. Tightly wrap and refrigerate. Use raw, braise, or sauté within three days.

2 Collard Greens

Collard greens have long stalks topped with a loose rosette of dark green leaves. Put them in a plastic bag and refrigerate for up to five days. In Southern kitchens, collard greens are traditionally slow-cooked with salt pork or bacon. They can also be prepared like spinach or cabbage and seasoned with garlic, chile peppers, onion, ginger, or curry.

3 Curly Endive

Curly endive is similar in appearance to chicory (a close cousin) and is often mistaken for it. Curly endive's lacy green leaves are a bit prickly and taste slightly bitter. Mix it with other greens and a balsamic vinaigrette, or try it steamed and dressed with lemon juice.

4 Escarole

Escarole is another endive variety, but its broad leaves are milder in flavor than either curly or Belgian endive. Escarole looks like lettuce, but is firmer and crunchier. Tightly wrap and refrigerate for up to three days. It can be cooked like spinach or Swiss chard, braised, added to Italian-style soups, or served wilted with a warm salad dressing.

5 Fiddlehead Fern

Fiddlehead ferns are tightly coiled fern fronds that look like the scroll on the end of a violin. These young shoots are chewy and taste something like a combination of asparagus, green beans, and okra. Tightly wrap and refrigerate for no more than two days. Trim fiddlehead ferns, and then rub them between your palms to remove the fuzzy brown scales. They can then be prepared like asparagus or artichoke hearts.

6 Frisée

Frisée belongs to the chicory family. Its delicate, feathery leaves are curly and yellow-white to yellow-green. Store it unwashed in the refrigerator for up to five days. Frisée's pleasantly bitter taste makes it a welcome addition to mesclun and other green salad mixes.

7 Kale

Kale is related to cabbage and has a similar flavor. The most common variety has dark green leaves with ruffled edges, and it grows in a loose bouquet. Store in a perforated plastic bag in the refrigerator for several days; it will grow bitter if stored too long. Kale can be cooked like spinach (remove the tough center rib first). Try sautéing kale in olive oil with garlic and sun-dried tomatoes, or add finely chopped kale to lamb stew.

8 Kale, Flowering

Flowering kale's cream, violet, or pink ruffles are tipped in green, and it makes an attractive garnish. It can also be cooked and tastes similar to mild cabbage. Refrigerate for up to five days. To prepare: steam or blanch flowering kale, and then sauté until crisp-tender.

9 Kohlrabi

Kohlrabi is related to turnips and is sometimes called cabbage turnip. Its bulb-like stem can be white, purple, or green; select those that are heavy for their size and firm. The edible leaves should be deep green, with no yellowing. Tightly wrap and refrigerate for up to four days. The bulb tastes like a mild, sweet turnip, and it can be cooked like a turnip—try sautéing shredded kohlrabi in olive oil and topping with Parmesan cheese. The greens can be prepared like spinach.

10 Mustard Greens

Mustard greens are dark green, with oval leaves and scalloped edges. Wrap in plastic and refrigerate for up to a week. The peppery, pungent mustard flavor mellows with slow cooking (try flavoring with ham, onions, or bacon). Young, tender mustard greens add a pleasant bite to salads.

Nutrition Facts

SOURCE: USDA

Greens

Chinese Cabbage
Serving Size: 1/2 cup/125ml (35g)

Calories		5
Total Fat	0g	0%
Saturated Fat	0g	0%
Trans Fat	0g	
Cholesterol	0mg	0%
Sodium	25mg	1%
Potassium	90mg	
Total Carbohydrate	1g	0%
Dietary Fiber	0g	0%
Sugar	0g	
Protein	1g	
Vitamin A		30%
Vitamin C		25%
Calcium		4%
Iron		2%

Collard Greens
Serving Size: 1 cup/250ml (36g)

Calories		10
Total Fat	0g	0%
Saturated Fat	0g	0%
Trans Fat	0g	
Cholesterol	0mg	0%
Sodium	5mg	0%
Potassium	60mg	
Total Carbohydrate	2g	1%
Dietary Fiber	1g	4%
Sugar	0g	
Protein	1g	
Vitamin A		50%
Vitamin C		20%
Calcium		6%
Iron		0%

Curly Endive
Serving Size: 1 cup/250ml (50g)

Calories		10
Total Fat	0g	0%
Saturated Fat	0g	0%
Trans Fat	0g	
Cholesterol	0mg	0%
Sodium	10mg	0%
Potassium	160mg	
Total Carbohydrate	2g	1%
Dietary Fiber	2g	8%
Sugar	0g	
Protein	1g	
Vitamin A		20%
Vitamin C		6%
Calcium		2%
Iron		2%

Escarole
Serving Size: 1 cup/250ml (50g)

Calories		10
Total Fat	0g	0%
Saturated Fat	0g	0%
Trans Fat	0g	
Cholesterol	0mg	0%
Sodium	10mg	0%
Potassium	160mg	
Total Carbohydrate	2g	1%
Dietary Fiber	2g	8%
Sugar	0g	
Protein	1g	
Vitamin A		20%
Vitamin C		6%
Calcium		2%
Iron		2%

Fiddlehead Fern
Serving Size: 1 cup/250ml (50g)

Calories		15
Total Fat	0g	0%
Saturated Fat	0g	0%
Trans Fat	0g	
Cholesterol	0mg	0%
Sodium	0mg	0%
Potassium	185mg	
Total Carbohydrate	3g	1%
Dietary Fiber	1g	4%
Sugar	1g	
Protein	2g	
Vitamin A		35%
Vitamin C		20%
Calcium		2%
Iron		4%

Frisée
Serving Size: 1 cup/250ml (90g)

Calories		15
Total Fat	0g	0%
Saturated Fat	0g	0%
Trans Fat	0g	
Cholesterol	0mg	0%
Sodium	20mg	1%
Potassium	280mg	
Total Carbohydrate	3g	1%
Dietary Fiber	1g	4%
Sugar	1g	
Protein	1g	
Vitamin A		35%
Vitamin C		10%
Calcium		4%
Iron		4%

Kale
Serving Size: 1 cup/250ml (67g)

Calories		35
Total Fat	0g	0%
Saturated Fat	0g	0%
Trans Fat	0g	
Cholesterol	0mg	0%
Sodium	30mg	1%
Potassium	300mg	
Total Carbohydrate	7g	2%
Dietary Fiber	1g	4%
Sugar	2g	
Protein	2g	
Vitamin A		210%
Vitamin C		130%
Calcium		10%
Iron		6%

Kale, Flowering
Serving Size: 1 cup/250ml (67g)

Calories		30
Total Fat	0g	0%
Saturated Fat	0g	0%
Trans Fat	0g	
Cholesterol	0mg	0%
Sodium	45mg	1%
Potassium	300mg	
Total Carbohydrate	6g	2%
Dietary Fiber	1g	4%
Sugar	1g	
Protein	2g	
Vitamin A		40%
Vitamin C		150%
Calcium		15%
Iron		10%

Kohlrabi
Serving Size: 1/2 cup/125ml (68g)

Calories		20
Total Fat	0g	0%
Saturated Fat	0g	0%
Trans Fat	0g	
Cholesterol	0mg	0%
Sodium	15mg	1%
Potassium	235mg	
Total Carbohydrate	4g	1%
Dietary Fiber	2g	8%
Sugar	2g	
Protein	1g	
Vitamin A		0%
Vitamin C		70%
Calcium		2%
Iron		2%

Mustard Greens
Serving Size: 1 cup/250ml (56g)

Calories		15
Total Fat	0g	0%
Saturated Fat	0g	0%
Trans Fat	0g	
Cholesterol	0mg	0%
Sodium	15mg	1%
Potassium	200mg	
Total Carbohydrate	3g	1%
Dietary Fiber	2g	8%
Sugar	1g	
Protein	2g	
Vitamin A		120%
Vitamin C		70%
Calcium		6%
Iron		4%

Greens

Rapini/Broccoli Raab

Rapini, also called broccoli raab, grows on stalks with small, broccoli-like clusters at the end. This bitter green is favored in Italian cooking, and a classic dish calls for blanching rapini for two minutes, and then sautéing it in olive oil with garlic and red pepper flakes. Add sun-dried tomatoes and toasted pine nuts, if desired.

Spinach

Spinach is delicious raw or cooked. Look for crisp, dark green leaves and wash carefully to remove any grit. Store in a plastic bag in the refrigerator for up to three days. Use in salads, steam until wilted (use just the water that clings to the leaves after rinsing), or add to lasagna, scrambled eggs, or soups.

Swiss Chard

Swiss chard's broad green leaves grow on celery-like stalks that vary in color, depending on the type. Green Swiss chard has a pale stalk; red has a red stalk, darker leaves, and a stronger flavor. Rainbow Swiss chard is the mildest of the three, and its stalks are a collection of reds, pinks, oranges, and yellows. Store Swiss chard in a plastic bag in the refrigerator for up to three days. To prepare, trim the leaves off the stalk and cook like spinach. Cook the stalks like celery or asparagus. If you plan to use both in the same dish, cook the stalks for a few minutes before adding the leaves.

Turnip Greens

Turnip greens have flat, fuzzy leaves on long stems. Tender and sweet when young, they grow tough and strong tasting with age. Refrigerate in a plastic bag for up to three days. To prepare, trim leaves from the thick rib, and then boil, sauté, steam, or stir-fry. Southern cooks traditionally braise turnip greens in a broth with salt pork or a ham hock.

Watercress

Watercress belongs to the mustard family and shares its relatives' pungent, mustardy, peppery bite. The dark green, heart-shaped leaves make a pretty garnish, but watercress also adds a bold flavor to salads, sandwiches, soups, and other dishes. Wrap in plastic, refrigerate, and use within a few days.

Lettuces

A big salad is just the thing if you're trying to lose weight. Lettuce is low in calories and can take the edge off your appetite while providing vitamins A and C, calcium, and iron. For maximum nutrition and flavor, choose dark-colored lettuces and mix them with grated red cabbage, carrots, radicchio, or other fruits and vegetables.

But beware of that common salad pitfall: dressing. Salad dressing is the number one source of fat in women's diets. Choose a fat-free or reduced-fat dressing, or use flavored vinegar instead. Another tip is to serve salad dressing on the side, and then dip your fork into it before spearing a bite of lettuce to get the flavor with fewer calories.

Of course, lettuce isn't just for salads. Create a bed of your favorite leaves for grilled fish or make Asian-style lettuce wraps.

Look for crisp lettuce with no blemishes or browning. Wash lettuce thoroughly, and then dry it by using a salad spinner or blotting with paper towels. Store washed and dried lettuce in a plastic bag in the refrigerator for three to five days, depending on the variety. The wide selection of prewashed, bagged lettuce makes adding it to your meal even easier.

Bibb

Bibb lettuce is one of the best-known butterhead varieties (the other is Boston lettuce). The tender, dark green leaves form a loosely folded head, and they have a flavorful, almost buttery, taste.

Nutrition Facts

SOURCE: USDA

Greens

Rapini/Broccoli Raab
Serving Size: 1/2 cup/125ml (29g)

Calories		10
Total Fat	0g	0%
Saturated Fat	0g	0%
Trans Fat	0g	
Cholesterol	0mg	0%
Sodium	10mg	0%
Potassium	56mg	
Total Carbohydrate	1g	0%
Dietary Fiber	0g	0%
Sugar	0g	
Protein	1g	
Vitamin A		35%
Vitamin C		45%
Calcium		2%
Iron		2%

Turnip Greens
Serving Size: 1 cup/250ml (55g)

Calories		20
Total Fat	0g	0%
Saturated Fat	0g	0%
Trans Fat	0g	
Cholesterol	0mg	0%
Sodium	20mg	1%
Potassium	165mg	
Total Carbohydrate	4g	1%
Dietary Fiber	2g	8%
Sugar	0g	
Protein	1g	
Vitamin A		0%
Vitamin C		60%
Calcium		10%
Iron		4%

Spinach
Serving Size: 1 cup/250ml (24g)

Calories		10
Total Fat	0g	0%
Saturated Fat	0g	0%
Trans Fat	0g	
Cholesterol	0mg	0%
Sodium	40mg	2%
Potassium	135mg	
Total Carbohydrate	3g	1%
Dietary Fiber	1g	4%
Sugar	0g	
Protein	1g	
Vitamin A		15%
Vitamin C		6%
Calcium		2%
Iron		4%

Watercress
Serving Size: 1 cup/250ml (34g)

Calories		5
Total Fat	0g	0%
Saturated Fat	0g	0%
Trans Fat	0g	
Cholesterol	0mg	0%
Sodium	15mg	1%
Potassium	115mg	
Total Carbohydrate	0g	0%
Dietary Fiber	0g	0%
Sugar	0g	
Protein	1g	
Vitamin A		30%
Vitamin C		25%
Calcium		4%
Iron		0%

Swiss Chard
Serving Size: 1 cup/250ml (36g)

Calories		5
Total Fat	0g	0%
Saturated Fat	0g	0%
Trans Fat	0g	
Cholesterol	0mg	0%
Sodium	75mg	3%
Potassium	140mg	
Total Carbohydrate	1g	0%
Dietary Fiber	1g	4%
Sugar	0g	
Protein	1g	
Vitamin A		45%
Vitamin C		20%
Calcium		2%
Iron		4%

Lettuces

Bibb
Serving Size: 1 cup/250ml (55g)

Calories		5
Total Fat	0g	0%
Saturated Fat	0g	0%
Trans Fat	0g	
Cholesterol	0mg	0%
Sodium	0mg	0%
Potassium	130mg	
Total Carbohydrate	1g	0%
Dietary Fiber	1g	4%
Sugar	1g	
Protein	1g	
Vitamin A		35%
Vitamin C		4%
Calcium		2%
Iron		4%

Lettuces

Boston/Butterhead

Boston lettuce is another butterhead variety and is similar to Bibb lettuce. Its meaty, medium-size leaves are smooth, succulent, and slightly sweet.

Green Leaf

Green leaf lettuce has ruffled green leaves that may be medium to dark green, with a mild flavor and delicate crunch. The leaves form a loose bunch, rather than a tight head, and are more perishable than head lettuces such as iceberg.

Iceberg

Iceberg lettuce is a type of crisphead lettuce that has pale green leaves tightly packed into a round head. To prepare, loosen the core by smacking the head on a hard surface. Twist the core and pull it out, and then rinse the remaining cavity with cold water. Iceberg's rather plain flavor and crunchy texture are well matched by most salad dressings; it's also often added to tacos or used for Asian-style lettuce wraps. Iceberg is less nutritious than other varieties.

Red Leaf

Red leaf lettuce has red-tinged leaves, but is otherwise similar to green leaf lettuce. Use it to add color to salads, or mix it with chopped apples, toasted almonds, and a citrus vinaigrette.

Romaine

Romaine lettuce has dark green outer leaves and greenish-yellow inner leaves that together form an elongated head. This crispy lettuce adds crunch to sandwiches and is the classic choice for Caesar salads. Try tossing Romaine lettuce with toasted nuts, oranges, and poppy seed dressing.

Mushrooms

Mushrooms deliver a lot of flavor for just a few calories. These fungi contain no cholesterol and almost no fat, but do deliver plenty of B-complex vitamins and essential minerals like selenium, potassium, and copper. Research suggests that the nutrients in some mushrooms may help prevent heart disease and some forms of cancer and may even stimulate the immune system.

Chanterelle

Chanterelles are wild, trumpet-shaped mushrooms that range from bright yellow to orange. They are sold fresh or dried and have a delicate nutty, almost fruity, flavor. Use them to add a gourmet touch to cream sauces (add near the end of cooking to keep them from getting tough), or sauté them with butter, onions, and chopped apricots and serve with poultry or game.

Cultivated White

Cultivated white mushrooms are creamy white to light brown. They're called button mushrooms when small, but they can grow to a jumbo size suitable for stuffing. Serve raw on a crudités platter or in salads. Cooking intensifies their mild, woodsy flavor. Try adding them to sauces or casseroles, or sautéing them with garlic in olive oil or butter.

Cremini/Baby Portobello

Cremini mushrooms are also called Italian browns or baby portobellos. They are similar to white mushrooms, but have a heartier, earthier flavor that complements meat and game. They can be substituted for white mushrooms in most recipes.

Enoki

Enoki mushrooms are creamy white, with long, slender stems and a tiny cap. Their light, fruity flavor and crunchy texture make a pleasing addition to salads, sandwiches, and stir-fries (add them at the end to prevent overcooking). They also make a pretty garnish for soups.

Maitake

Hen-of-the-woods, called maitake in Japanese, is a dark, brownish gray cluster of fronds on a single stem. They are firm and supple at the base, with brittle, ruffled edges. Substitute for white mushrooms to give any recipe more richness.

Selecting Mushrooms

Select fresh, firm, well-shaped mushrooms that are free of spots, mold, and slime. Refrigerate unwashed mushrooms in their original packaging or in a paper bag (don't use plastic). Most varieties will keep for up to a week, but it's better to use them within a few days of purchase. To clean, wipe mushrooms with a damp cloth or soft brush, or quickly rinse in cold water and pat dry. They do not need to be peeled. Many varieties are also available dried.

Nutrition Facts

SOURCE: USDA

Lettuces

Boston/Butterhead
Serving Size: 1 cup/250ml (55g)

Calories	5
Total Fat	0g 0%
Saturated Fat	0g 0%
Trans Fat	0g
Cholesterol	0mg 0%
Sodium	0mg 0%
Potassium	130mg
Total Carbohydrate	1g 0%
Dietary Fiber	1g 4%
Sugar	1g
Protein	1g
Vitamin A	35%
Vitamin C	4%
Calcium	2%
Iron	4%

Green Leaf
Serving Size: 1 cup/250ml (36g)

Calories	5
Total Fat	0g 0%
Saturated Fat	0g 0%
Trans Fat	0g
Cholesterol	0mg 0%
Sodium	10mg 0%
Potassium	70mg
Total Carbohydrate	1g 0%
Dietary Fiber	0g 4%
Sugar	1g
Protein	0g
Vitamin A	50%
Vitamin C	10%
Calcium	2%
Iron	2%

Iceberg
Serving Size: 1 cup/250ml (55g)

Calories	10
Total Fat	0g 0%
Saturated Fat	0g 0%
Trans Fat	0g
Cholesterol	0mg 0%
Sodium	5mg 0%
Potassium	80mg
Total Carbohydrate	2g 1%
Dietary Fiber	1g 4%
Sugar	1g
Protein	0g
Vitamin A	6%
Vitamin C	2%
Calcium	0%
Iron	2%

Red Leaf
Serving Size: 1 cup/250ml (28g)

Calories	0
Total Fat	0g 0%
Saturated Fat	0g 0%
Trans Fat	0g
Cholesterol	0mg 0%
Sodium	5mg 0%
Potassium	55mg
Total Carbohydrate	1g 0%
Dietary Fiber	0g 0%
Sugar	0g
Protein	0g
Vitamin A	40%
Vitamin C	2%
Calcium	0%
Iron	2%

Romaine
Serving Size: 1 cup/250ml (56g)

Calories	10
Total Fat	0g 0%
Saturated Fat	0g 0%
Trans Fat	0g
Cholesterol	0mg 0%
Sodium	0mg 0%
Potassium	140mg
Total Carbohydrate	2g 1%
Dietary Fiber	1g 4%
Sugar	1g
Protein	1g
Vitamin A	70%
Vitamin C	20%
Calcium	2%
Iron	4%

Mushrooms

Chanterelle
Serving Size: 1/4 cup/50ml (36g)

Calories	140
Total Fat	0g 0%
Saturated Fat	0g 0%
Trans Fat	0g
Cholesterol	0mg 0%
Sodium	0mg 0%
Potassium	n/a
Total Carbohydrate	18g 6%
Dietary Fiber	9g 36%
Sugar	0g
Protein	9g
Vitamin A	0%
Vitamin C	0%
Calcium	0%
Iron	20%

Cremini/Baby Portobello
Serving Size: 1 medium (14g)

Calories	5
Total Fat	0g 0%
Saturated Fat	0g 0%
Trans Fat	0g
Cholesterol	0mg 0%
Sodium	0mg 0%
Potassium	65mg
Total Carbohydrate	1g 0%
Dietary Fiber	0g 0%
Sugar	0g
Protein	0g
Vitamin A	0%
Vitamin C	0%
Calcium	0%
Iron	0%

Cultivated White
Serving Size: 1/2 cup/125ml (35g)

Calories	10
Total Fat	0g 0%
Saturated Fat	0g 0%
Trans Fat	0g
Cholesterol	0mg 0%
Sodium	0mg 0%
Potassium	130mg
Total Carbohydrate	1g 0%
Dietary Fiber	0g 0%
Sugar	0g
Protein	1g
Vitamin A	0%
Vitamin C	2%
Calcium	0%
Iron	2%

Enoki
Serving Size: 1/2 cup/125ml (35g)

Calories	10
Total Fat	0g 0%
Saturated Fat	0g 0%
Trans Fat	0g
Cholesterol	0mg 0%
Sodium	0mg 0%
Potassium	135mg
Total Carbohydrate	2g 1%
Dietary Fiber	1g 4%
Sugar	0g
Protein	1g
Vitamin A	0%
Vitamin C	6%
Calcium	0%
Iron	2%

Maitake
Serving Size: 1/2 cup/125ml (35g)

Calories	10
Total Fat	0g 0%
Saturated Fat	0g 0%
Trans Fat	0g
Cholesterol	0mg 0%
Sodium	0mg 0%
Potassium	160mg
Total Carbohydrate	1g 0%
Dietary Fiber	0g 0%
Sugar	1g
Protein	1g
Vitamin A	0%
Vitamin C	0%
Calcium	0%
Iron	0%

Mushrooms

Morel

Morels have a spongy, honeycomb-like cap that ranges from tan to dark brown. These wild mushrooms belong to the same fungus species as truffles, and their smoky, earthy flavor turns wonderfully nutty when sautéed in butter or added to cream sauces or risotto. Wash thoroughly before use.

Oyster

Oyster mushrooms range from soft brown to gray, and their fanned shape resembles that of an oyster shell. They are velvety, with a robust flavor that turns subtly sweet when cooked. Add oyster mushrooms to pasta, polenta, rice, grains, or eggs. Cream them and serve with roast pork, or sauté and serve with seafood or poultry dishes.

Porcini

Porcini mushrooms, also called *cèpes*, have a smooth, meaty texture and a pungent, woodsy flavor. These brown mushrooms measure up to ten inches in diameter. Dried porcini are easier to find than fresh, but either adds rich character to soup, stuffing, pasta sauce, and risotto. Try fresh porcini stuffed with ham, shallots, herbs, onion, and garlic.

Portobello

The dark brown portobello is actually a fully mature cremini, and it may be as large as six inches in diameter. Portobellos have a chewy, meaty texture and a hearty flavor that's intensified by roasting or grilling. Cut them into thick slices for salads, or substitute them for meat in sandwiches. Or, try baking a whole portobello stuffed with sautéed broccoli, onion, and garlic and topped with grated Gruyère cheese.

Shiitake

Shiitake mushrooms are also called Chinese black or forest mushrooms. They have an umbrella-shaped cap and may be tan to dark brown. Remove the tough stems before cooking. Shiitakes add a woodsy, beefy flavor to Asian stir-fries, soups, and roasted vegetables.

Wood Ear

Wood Ears (also called cloud ears or tree ears) are aptly named—they are indeed ear shaped. They are also semitransparent, with a purplish-gray cap and slightly crunchy texture. These subtle mushrooms soak up flavor from other ingredients. Add them to mu shu pork and other stir-fries or scrambled eggs.

Onions

Onions are one of the world's most important ingredients.

Raw onions add a pungent bite, and cooked ones a mellow sweetness, to the foods of countless countries and cultures. Even better, onions are good for you. They're a fine source of vitamin C, potassium, and folic acid and are high in antioxidants such as quercetin that have anticancer and antimicrobial properties. Some varieties even contain substances that researchers say may reduce the risk of atherosclerosis, cardiovascular disease, heart attack, and stroke.

Onions belong to the lily family, and there are two types: dry (storage) and green (fresh). Dry onions are mature and have a thin, papery skin that can be yellow, red, or white. Their flesh is juicy, and their flavor is intense. Select dry onions that are firm and heavy for their size and that have dry, unblemished skins. Store in a cool, dry, well-ventilated place for up to two months. Wrap cut onions in plastic and refrigerate for up to four days.

Boiling

Boiling onions measure about an inch across and can be white, yellow, or red. They are typically boiled (as the name implies) and are easy to peel after cooking. They are best served whole; try pickling boiling onions or adding them to cream sauces, vegetable dishes, or casseroles.

Nutrition Facts

SOURCE: USDA

Mushrooms

Morel
Serving Size: 1/4 cup/50ml (36g)

Calories		140
Total Fat	0g	0%
Saturated Fat	0g	0%
Trans Fat		0g
Cholesterol	0mg	0%
Sodium	0mg	0%
Potassium		100mg
Total Carbohydrate	18g	6%
Dietary Fiber	0g	0%
Sugar		0g
Protein		9g
Vitamin A		0%
Vitamin C		0%
Calcium		0%
Iron		35%

Oyster
Serving Size: 1 medium (15g)

Calories		5
Total Fat	0g	0%
Saturated Fat	0g	0%
Trans Fat		0g
Cholesterol	0mg	0%
Sodium	0mg	0%
Potassium		80mg
Total Carbohydrate	1g	0%
Dietary Fiber	0g	0%
Sugar		0g
Protein		1g
Vitamin A		0%
Vitamin C		0%
Calcium		0%
Iron		2%

Porcini
Serving Size: 1/4 cup/50ml (36g)

Calories		130
Total Fat	1.5g	2%
Saturated Fat	0g	0%
Trans Fat		0g
Cholesterol	0mg	0%
Sodium	15mg	1%
Potassium		140mg
Total Carbohydrate	18g	6%
Dietary Fiber	6g	24%
Sugar		1g
Protein		11g
Vitamin A		0%
Vitamin C		0%
Calcium		0%
Iron		40%

Portobello
Serving Size: 1 medium (84g)

Calories		25
Total Fat	0g	0%
Saturated Fat	0g	0%
Trans Fat		0g
Cholesterol	0mg	0%
Sodium	5mg	0%
Potassium		410mg
Total Carbohydrate	4g	1%
Dietary Fiber	1g	4%
Sugar		2g
Protein		2g
Vitamin A		0%
Vitamin C		2%
Calcium		0%
Iron		2%

Shiitake
Serving Size: 1/2 cup/125ml (72g)

Calories		30
Total Fat	0g	0%
Saturated Fat	0g	0%
Trans Fat		0g
Cholesterol	0mg	0%
Sodium	15mg	1%
Potassium		60mg
Total Carbohydrate	4g	1%
Dietary Fiber	1g	4%
Sugar		1g
Protein		2g
Vitamin A		0%
Vitamin C		4%
Calcium		0%
Iron		6%

Wood Ear
Serving Size: 1/2 cup/125ml (50g)

Calories		10
Total Fat	0g	0%
Saturated Fat	0g	0%
Trans Fat		0g
Cholesterol	0mg	0%
Sodium	0mg	0%
Potassium		20mg
Total Carbohydrate	3g	1%
Dietary Fiber	0g	0%
Sugar		0g
Protein		0g
Vitamin A		0%
Vitamin C		0%
Calcium		0%
Iron		2%

Onions

Boiling
Serving Size: 1 medium (28g)

Calories		10
Total Fat	0g	0%
Saturated Fat	0g	0%
Trans Fat		0g
Cholesterol	0mg	0%
Sodium	0mg	0%
Potassium		40mg
Total Carbohydrate	2g	1%
Dietary Fiber	1g	4%
Sugar		2g
Protein		0g
Vitamin A		0%
Vitamin C		4%
Calcium		0%
Iron		0%

Onions

Green onions have an immature bulb and long, green leaves. When buying green onions such as scallions or leeks, look for those with crisp, bright tops and a firm, white base. Store in a plastic bag and refrigerate for up to five days.

Refrigerating an onion for at least thirty minutes before chopping will help prevent the irritating juices from making your eyes water, as will using a freshly sharpened knife. To cleanse your hands of the onion smell, rub them with lemon juice, and then wash with soap and water.

Cipollini

Cipollini, also called wild or borettana onions, are actually the bulb of another lily relative—grape hyacinths. They taste just like a juicy onion and are traditionally used in Italian cooking. Cipollini are shaped like a flat saucer and measure between one and two inches in diameter. Slow cooking brings out their savory sweetness, but they are also tasty when pickled.

Globe

Globe onions are between one and four inches across and have yellow, red, or white skins. Their flavor also varies, and they can taste mildly pungent to downright sharp.

Green Onion/Scallion

Green onions have a small, white base that has not yet developed into a bulb; scallions have a flatter base and milder flavor. Both have long, straight, green leaves, and they can be used interchangeably in recipes. Sprinkle chopped green onions or scallions on salads, soups, and other dishes.

Knob

Knob onions have thick green tops (similar to a leek) and a white, bulbous base. Sauté them in butter, add to a white sauce, or use in stir-fries.

Leek

Leeks look something like giant scallions, with flat, green leaves and a thick, white base. Cut them in half and wash carefully to remove any sand or dirt between the layers. The leaves are usually discarded or used to make stock. Add leeks to potato soup or drizzle with olive oil and gently roast until sweet.

Pearl

Pearl onions are marble-size, mild-tasting, white boiling onions. They can be creamed, pickled, marinated, or substituted for boiling onions in any recipe. Or, serve them with their classic partner: tender, young peas.

Red/Italian

Red, or Italian, onions are mildly sweet, with a reddish-purple skin and white flesh with a red tinge that adds color to salads, pizza, and pasta dishes. Or, grill thick slices until they're smoky, sweet, and soft, and then serve with hamburgers or steak.

Shallot

Shallots form in cloves, much like a head of garlic. Their whitish flesh is tinged with green or purple; the thin, papery skin might be tan, pale gray, or rose. Dry shallots will keep for a month in a cool and dry location. Fresh shallots can be refrigerated for up to a week. Avoid those that are wrinkled, soft, or sprouting. Shallots have a sweet and delicate flavor and can be used like other onions.

Spanish

Spanish onions are large, round, and mild. They typically have a yellow skin, although they may also be white.

Sweet/Spring

Sweet onions are succulent and mild, due to lower levels of the sulfuric compounds that make your eyes water. Varieties known for their high sugar content include Vidalia Sweets®, Maui Sweets, OSO Sweet, Walla Walla Sweets®, and Texas 1015 SuperSweet®. Sweet onions are tasty raw or cooked; try them in tarts, soups, or salsas.

Nutrition Facts

SOURCE: USDA

Onions

Cipollini
Serving Size: 1 medium (28g)

Calories		10
Total Fat	0g	0%
Saturated Fat	0g	0%
Trans Fat	0g	
Cholesterol	0mg	0%
Sodium	0mg	0%
Potassium	30mg	
Total Carbohydrate	2g	1%
Dietary Fiber	1g	4%
Sugar	2g	
Protein	0g	
Vitamin A		0%
Vitamin C		4%
Calcium		0%
Iron		0%

Pearl
Serving Size: 1/2 cup/125ml (80g)

Calories		35
Total Fat	0g	0%
Saturated Fat	0g	0%
Trans Fat	0g	
Cholesterol	0mg	0%
Sodium	0mg	0%
Potassium	120mg	
Total Carbohydrate	8g	3%
Dietary Fiber	1g	4%
Sugar	3g	
Protein	1g	
Vitamin A		0%
Vitamin C		8%
Calcium		2%
Iron		0%

Globe
Serving Size: 1/2 cup/125ml (80g)

Calories		35
Total Fat	0g	0%
Saturated Fat	0g	0%
Trans Fat	0g	
Cholesterol	0mg	0%
Sodium	0mg	0%
Potassium	115mg	
Total Carbohydrate	8g	3%
Dietary Fiber	1g	4%
Sugar	3g	
Protein	1g	
Vitamin A		0%
Vitamin C		8%
Calcium		2%
Iron		0%

Red/Italian
Serving Size: 1 medium (110g)

Calories		45
Total Fat	0g	0%
Saturated Fat	0g	0%
Trans Fat	0g	
Cholesterol	0mg	0%
Sodium	0mg	0%
Potassium	160mg	
Total Carbohydrate	11g	4%
Dietary Fiber	2g	8%
Sugar	5g	
Protein	1g	
Vitamin A		0%
Vitamin C		10%
Calcium		2%
Iron		2%

Green Onion/Scallion
Serving Size: 1 medium (15g)

Calories		5
Total Fat	0g	0%
Saturated Fat	0g	0%
Trans Fat	0g	
Cholesterol	0mg	0%
Sodium	0mg	0%
Potassium	45mg	
Total Carbohydrate	1g	0%
Dietary Fiber	0g	0%
Sugar	0g	
Protein	0g	
Vitamin A		2%
Vitamin C		4%
Calcium		2%
Iron		2%

Shallot
Serving Size: 3 tablespoons (30g)

Calories		20
Total Fat	0g	0%
Saturated Fat	0g	0%
Trans Fat	0g	
Cholesterol	0mg	0%
Sodium	0mg	0%
Potassium	100mg	
Total Carbohydrate	5g	2%
Dietary Fiber	0g	0%
Sugar	1g	
Protein	1g	
Vitamin A		8%
Vitamin C		4%
Calcium		12%
Iron		2%

Knob
Serving Size: 1/2 cup/125ml (80g)

Calories		25
Total Fat	0g	0%
Saturated Fat	0g	0%
Trans Fat	0g	
Cholesterol	0mg	0%
Sodium	15mg	1%
Potassium	170mg	
Total Carbohydrate	5g	2%
Dietary Fiber	1g	4%
Sugar	4g	
Protein	2g	
Vitamin A		20%
Vitamin C		35%
Calcium		2%
Iron		6%

Spanish
Serving Size: 1/2 cup/125ml (80g)

Calories		35
Total Fat	0g	0%
Saturated Fat	0g	0%
Trans Fat	0g	
Cholesterol	0mg	0%
Sodium	0mg	0%
Potassium	115mg	
Total Carbohydrate	8g	3%
Dietary Fiber	1g	4%
Sugar	3g	
Protein	1g	
Vitamin A		0%
Vitamin C		8%
Calcium		2%
Iron		0%

Leek
Serving Size: 1 medium (89g)

Calories		50
Total Fat	0g	0%
Saturated Fat	0g	0%
Trans Fat	0g	
Cholesterol	0mg	0%
Sodium	20mg	1%
Potassium	160mg	
Total Carbohydrate	13g	4%
Dietary Fiber	2g	8%
Sugar	3g	
Protein	1g	
Vitamin A		30%
Vitamin C		20%
Calcium		6%
Iron		10%

Sweet/Spring
Serving Size: 1/2 cup/125ml (50g)

Calories		15
Total Fat	0g	0%
Saturated Fat	0g	0%
Trans Fat	0g	
Cholesterol	0mg	0%
Sodium	10mg	0%
Potassium	140mg	
Total Carbohydrate	4g	2%
Dietary Fiber	1g	4%
Sugar	2g	
Protein	1g	
Vitamin A		4%
Vitamin C		15%
Calcium		4%
Iron		4%

Peppers (Chile)

There are more than 200 varieties of chile peppers worldwide, and their heat ranges from mild to "grab the fire extinguisher." They also bring floral, fruity, or smoky notes to a dish, as well as a dose of vitamins A, C, and E; potassium; and folic acid — all without adding calories, fat, or cholesterol.

Chile peppers may be large or small (general rule: the smaller, the hotter); plump or skinny; and yellow, green, red, or black. The fire in each comes from the capsaicin found in its veins and seeds. Remove those parts, and you automatically get a milder pepper. To do that, slice off the stem, cut the pepper in half lengthwise, and use a spoon to scrape out the veins and seeds.

> **Warning:** Be careful, though. The burning sensation caused by capsaicin can last for hours. Wear disposable gloves, avoid touching your face or eyes, and wash your hands thoroughly after preparation. If you eat a too-hot chile, try cooling the fire with milk, yogurt, or another dairy product, or starchy foods such as bread.

1 Anaheim

Anaheim chiles are green or red and a slender six to eight inches long. Their sweet flavor and small bite makes Anaheims a zesty addition to salsas and stuffed dishes such as chiles rellenos.

2 Cherry

Cherry peppers, also called Hungarian cherry peppers, are small, round, and deep orange to bright red. They are mild to medium-hot and slightly sweet. Pickled cherry peppers often appear on antipasto platters, while fresh ones are useful in meat and poultry dishes.

3 Fresno

Fresno chiles start out a light green and mature to bright red. They are short and cone shaped, with a jalapeño-like kick. Use them sparingly to season casseroles and savory dishes.

4 Habañero

Habañero peppers top the Scoville Heat Unit scale that measures pepper pungency and should be handled cautiously. They are lantern shaped and come in shades of green, red, orange, and yellow. Their intensity is accompanied by a fruity, tropical flavor and apricot aroma, which makes them perfect for Jamaican jerk chicken and other Caribbean-style recipes.

5 Hungarian Wax

Hungarian wax peppers are three to five inches long and not quite two inches across. This yellow chile may seem tame early in the season, but it will be fiery hot when fully mature. They are sometimes confused with banana peppers, which look much the same but are sweet and mild. Be sure you know which you're buying.

6 Jalapeño/Chipotle

Jalapeño chiles may be green or red, hot or very hot. They are about two inches long, rounded at the tip, and smooth skinned. They are a mainstay in American kitchens, mostly because they're flavorful, widely available, and easy to prepare. Use fresh jalapeños in salsas, nachos, sauces, or vegetable dishes. Dried jalapeños, called chipotles, are a standard ingredient in Southwestern and Mexican recipes.

7 Korean

Korean chiles are long, thin, and curved and can be green or red. They are used in Korean dishes such as kimchee, a pungent condiment made from pickled vegetables.

8 Pasilla/Chilaca

Fresh chilaca peppers are long and thin. They ripen from green to a deep chocolate brown, but they are rarely used fresh. Dried chilacas, called pasilla peppers, are more common. They may be medium to very hot and add a rich and fruity complexity to sauces.

Nutrition Facts

SOURCE: USDA

Peppers (Chile)

Anaheim
Serving Size: 1/4 cup/50ml (8g)

Calories	30
Total Fat	0g 0%
Saturated Fat	0g 0%
Trans Fat	0g
Cholesterol	0mg 0%
Sodium	0mg 0%
Potassium	260mg
Total Carbohydrate	4g 1%
Dietary Fiber	1g 4%
Sugar	2g
Protein	2g
Vitamin A	120%
Vitamin C	4%
Calcium	2%
Iron	0%

Hungarian Wax
Serving Size: 1 medium (27g)

Calories	10
Total Fat	0g 0%
Saturated Fat	0g 0%
Trans Fat	0g
Cholesterol	0mg 0%
Sodium	0mg 0%
Potassium	55mg
Total Carbohydrate	2g 1%
Dietary Fiber	0g 0%
Sugar	0g
Protein	0g
Vitamin A	0%
Vitamin C	40%
Calcium	0%
Iron	0%

Cherry
Serving Size: 1 medium (45g)

Calories	25
Total Fat	1g 2%
Saturated Fat	0g 0%
Trans Fat	0g
Cholesterol	0mg 0%
Sodium	0mg 0%
Potassium	260mg
Total Carbohydrate	4g 1%
Dietary Fiber	1g 4%
Sugar	2g
Protein	1g
Vitamin A	15%
Vitamin C	30%
Calcium	0%
Iron	4%

Jalapeño/Chipotle
Serving Size: 1 medium (14g)

Calories	5
Total Fat	0g 0%
Saturated Fat	0g 0%
Trans Fat	0g
Cholesterol	0mg 0%
Sodium	0mg 0%
Potassium	30mg
Total Carbohydrate	1g 0%
Dietary Fiber	0g 0%
Sugar	0g
Protein	0g
Vitamin A	2%
Vitamin C	10%
Calcium	0%
Iron	0%

Fresno
Serving Size: 1/2 cup/125ml (45g)

Calories	15
Total Fat	0g 0%
Saturated Fat	0g 0%
Trans Fat	0g
Cholesterol	0mg 0%
Sodium	0mg 0%
Potassium	100mg
Total Carbohydrate	3g 1%
Dietary Fiber	1g 4%
Sugar	1g
Protein	1g
Vitamin A	8%
Vitamin C	35%
Calcium	0%
Iron	2%

Korean
Serving Size: n/a

Calories	n/a
Total Fat	n/a .... n/a
Saturated Fat	n/a .... n/a
Trans Fat	n/a
Cholesterol	n/a .... n/a
Sodium	n/a .... n/a
Potassium	n/a
Total Carbohydrate	n/a .... n/a
Dietary Fiber	n/a .... n/a
Sugar	n/a
Protein	n/a
Vitamin A	n/a
Vitamin C	n/a
Calcium	n/a
Iron	n/a

Habañero
Serving Size: 1/2 cup/125ml (75g)

Calories	30
Total Fat	0g 0%
Saturated Fat	0g 0%
Trans Fat	0g
Cholesterol	0mg 0%
Sodium	5mg 0%
Potassium	255mg
Total Carbohydrate	7g 2%
Dietary Fiber	1g 4%
Sugar	4g
Protein	1g
Vitamin A	20%
Vitamin C	300%
Calcium	2%
Iron	6%

Pasilla/Chilaca
Serving Size: 1 medium (7g)

Calories	15
Total Fat	0g 0%
Saturated Fat	0g 0%
Trans Fat	0g
Cholesterol	0mg 0%
Sodium	0mg 0%
Potassium	160mg
Total Carbohydrate	3g 1%
Dietary Fiber	1g 4%
Sugar	1g
Protein	1g
Vitamin A	8%
Vitamin C	35%
Calcium	0%
Iron	2%

Peppers (Chile)

Poblano

Poblano chiles are a dark (almost black) green. They warm to a reddish-brown and sweeten when ripe. They grow up to five inches long and are triangular in shape. Their rich flavor is spiked with varying amounts of heat. When dried, they are called ancho chiles and are the sweetest of the dried varieties. Mulato chiles are a smoked dried poblano. All three are essential to Mexican cookery.

Scotch Bonnet

Scotch bonnet chiles come in shades of yellow, orange, and red. They are a small, wrinkled, and extremely potent relative of the habañero. Scotch bonnets are fruity and smoky, and they are frequently used in African and Caribbean recipes. Add a little—and just a little—to sauces, relishes, and meat and poultry dishes.

Serrano

Serrano chiles are at first green, then scarlet, and finally yellow and very spicy when fully ripe. They are about an inch and a half long, with a slightly pointed tip. Use them to ratchet up the heat in guacamole, salsa, and other Mexican dishes.

Thai

Thai chiles may be tiny (a little more than an inch long and quarter-inch around), but they are startlingly potent. They may be green or red and are often called bird or birds-eye chiles when dried. Use them in Thai and other Southeast Asian dishes.

How Hot Is It?

In 1912, pharmacist William Scoville invented the Scoville Heat Unit (SHU) scale to assess the heat level of chile peppers. In this somewhat subjective test, chile "tasters" sampled a chile and recorded its heat level. The chile was then diluted in the laboratory until the taster couldn't taste any more capsaicin, the compound that gives chiles their heat. The Scoville unit is a measure based on the amount of dilution—the higher the Scoville unit, the hotter the chile. Today, more sophisticated chemical tests are often used to test heat, but the results are still called Scoville units. The Chile Pepper Institute at the University of New Mexico rates orange habañero chiles a fiery 210,000 Scoville units and a bell pepper 0 Scoville units. Other chiles fall between those extremes.

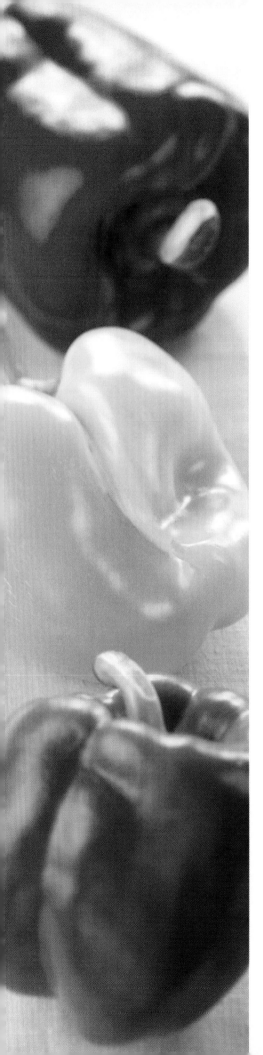

Peppers
(Sweet)

Sweet peppers belong to the same capsicum family as chile peppers, but their flesh is mild and sweet, rather than spicy hot. They add crunch, flavor, and a rainbow of colors to salads, crudités platters, stir-fries, sandwiches, soups, and casseroles. They can be grilled, roasted, steamed, sautéed, braised, or stuffed with savory fillings.

Sweet peppers are high in vitamin C (some bell peppers have more vitamin C than most citrus fruits) and are a good source of B-complex and A vitamins, calcium, and iron.

Select firm peppers that are heavy for their size, with bright, shiny skins. Avoid flabby, wrinkled, or soft peppers. Store in a plastic bag, and refrigerate for up to a week.

Nutrition Facts

SOURCE: USDA

Peppers (Chile)

Poblano
Serving Size: 1 medium (17g)

Calories	50
Total Fat	1.5g 2%
Saturated Fat	0g 0%
Trans Fat	0g
Cholesterol	0mg 0%
Sodium	5mg 0%
Potassium	410mg
Total Carbohydrate	9g 3%
Dietary Fiber	4g 16%
Sugar	0g
Protein	2g
Vitamin A	70%
Vitamin C	0%
Calcium	2%
Iron	10%

Serrano
Serving Size: 1 medium (6g)

Calories	0
Total Fat	0g 0%
Saturated Fat	0g 0%
Trans Fat	0g
Cholesterol	0mg 0%
Sodium	0mg 0%
Potassium	20mg
Total Carbohydrate	0g 0%
Dietary Fiber	0g 0%
Sugar	0g
Protein	0g
Vitamin A	2%
Vitamin C	4%
Calcium	0%
Iron	0%

Scotch Bonnet
Serving Size: 1 medium (45g)

Calories	15
Total Fat	0g 0%
Saturated Fat	0g 0%
Trans Fat	0g
Cholesterol	0mg 0%
Sodium	0mg 0%
Potassium	100mg
Total Carbohydrate	3g 1%
Dietary Fiber	1g 4%
Sugar	1g
Protein	1g
Vitamin A	8%
Vitamin C	35%
Calcium	0%
Iron	2%

Thai
Serving Size: 1 medium (45g)

Calories	20
Total Fat	0g 0%
Saturated Fat	0g 0%
Trans Fat	0g
Cholesterol	0mg 0%
Sodium	0mg 0%
Potassium	150mg
Total Carbohydrate	4g 1%
Dietary Fiber	1g 4%
Sugar	2g
Protein	1g
Vitamin A	8%
Vitamin C	110%
Calcium	0%
Iron	2%

Peppers (Sweet)

Bell (Green, Red, Yellow, Orange)

Bell peppers may be green, red, yellow, orange, or even purple. Immature red peppers are green, and then turn color as they ripen. Bell peppers are, not surprisingly, bell shaped, with a thick, crunchy flesh. Try serving raw slices with a vegetable dip or adding roasted bell peppers to pizza or pasta dishes.

Cubanelle

Cubanelle peppers are long and tapered, with a pale greenish-yellow color that ripens to vivid red. They can have a bit more bite than other sweet peppers, but are still quite mild and tasty on sandwiches or in egg dishes.

Sweet Banana

Sweet banana peppers are aptly named as they look like a long, yellow banana. Be careful, though—they also resemble the hotter Hungarian wax chiles that are sometimes sold as banana chiles or banana peppers. Be sure you get the variety you want! Use sweet banana peppers like other sweet peppers.

Potatoes

Potatoes are a good source of the complex carbohydrates that fuel the body and brain. Potatoes (eaten with the skin on) are high in vitamin C and potassium and also supply fiber, vitamin B-6, and minerals.

A medium-size baked potato has no fat, cholesterol, or sodium and just 100 calories—at least until you add butter, sour cream, or cheese. So, skip the high-fat toppings and create a filling, flavorful, and low-calorie snack or side dish by adding fresh salsa or fat-free plain yogurt instead.

Potatoes fall into two general categories: floury (or baking) and waxy. Floury potatoes are low in moisture and high in starch, which makes them the best choice for baking and mashing. Waxy potatoes contain more moisture and have a firmer texture that's ideal for boiling and roasting. New potatoes are immature potatoes of any variety; they are creamy, thin skinned, and small enough to serve whole.

Select potatoes with smooth, unblemished skins. Avoid those with soft spots, sprouting "eyes," or with a greenish tinge. Store potatoes in a cool, dark, well-ventilated place for up to two weeks. Do not refrigerate. Use new potatoes within three days of purchase.

Sweet potatoes and yams aren't really potatoes, but they can be used in the same way. They should have smooth, unblemished skins. Store both in a cool, dark, and dry place (but not the refrigerator). Use sweet potatoes within a week of purchase and yams within two weeks.

Red

Red potatoes, sometimes called boilers, are a waxy potato with a rosy skin, white flesh, and smooth, firm texture. They hold their shape when steamed, roasted, or boiled, and so are ideal for making potato salads and scalloped potatoes.

Sweet

Sweet potatoes are especially high in vitamin A. Their skins and flesh may be light yellow to bright orange to dusty red. Lighter-skinned varieties tend to be drier and less sweet than dark ones, and can be substituted for potatoes in many recipes. Try topping baked sweet potatoes with cinnamon sugar, hummus, or sautéed vegetables.

Russet

Russet, or Idaho, potatoes are long and oval shaped, with a rough, brown skin and white flesh. This floury potato makes fluffy, light mashed potatoes. It also bakes well and is tasty when topped with zesty salsa or low-fat sour cream and a sprinkling of fresh herbs.

White

White potatoes may be short and round or long and oval. Both varieties are the waxy type, with smooth and thin tan skins and white, creamy flesh. These all-purpose potatoes hold their shape well and can be used in most recipes. Tiny "baby" whites are called fingerling potatoes.

Nutrition Facts

SOURCE: USDA

Peppers (Sweet)

Bell (Green, Red, Yellow, Orange)
Serving Size: 1 medium (119g)

Calories	25
Total Fat	0g 0%
Saturated Fat	0g 0%
Trans Fat	0g
Cholesterol	0mg 0%
Sodium	0mg 0%
Potassium	210mg
Total Carbohydrate	6g 2%
Dietary Fiber	2g 8%
Sugar	3g
Protein	1g
Vitamin A	8%
Vitamin C	160%
Calcium	2%
Iron	2%

Cubanelle
Serving Size: 1 medium (148g)

Calories	30
Total Fat	0g 0%
Saturated Fat	0g 0%
Trans Fat	0g
Cholesterol	0mg 0%
Sodium	0mg 0%
Potassium	270mg
Total Carbohydrate	7g 2%
Dietary Fiber	2g 8%
Sugar	4g
Protein	1g
Vitamin A	8%
Vitamin C	190%
Calcium	2%
Iron	2%

Sweet Banana
Serving Size: 1 medium (46g)

Calories	10
Total Fat	0g 0%
Saturated Fat	0g 0%
Trans Fat	0g
Cholesterol	0mg 0%
Sodium	5mg 0%
Potassium	120mg
Total Carbohydrate	2g 1%
Dietary Fiber	2g 8%
Sugar	0g
Protein	1g
Vitamin A	4%
Vitamin C	60%
Calcium	0%
Iron	2%

Potatoes

Red
Serving Size: 1/2 cup/125ml (74g)

Calories	50
Total Fat	0g 0%
Saturated Fat	0g 0%
Trans Fat	0g
Cholesterol	0mg 0%
Sodium	0mg 0%
Potassium	335mg
Total Carbohydrate	12g 4%
Dietary Fiber	1g 4%
Sugar	1g
Protein	1g
Vitamin A	0%
Vitamin C	25%
Calcium	0%
Iron	2%

Russet
Serving Size: 1/2 cup/125ml (74g)

Calories	60
Total Fat	0g 0%
Saturated Fat	0g 0%
Trans Fat	0g
Cholesterol	0mg 0%
Sodium	0mg 0%
Potassium	310mg
Total Carbohydrate	13g 4%
Dietary Fiber	1g 4%
Sugar	0g
Protein	2g
Vitamin A	0%
Vitamin C	25%
Calcium	0%
Iron	4%

Sweet
Serving Size: 1/2 cup/125ml (67g)

Calories	50
Total Fat	0g 0%
Saturated Fat	0g 0%
Trans Fat	0g
Cholesterol	0mg 0%
Sodium	10mg 0%
Potassium	225mg
Total Carbohydrate	12g 4%
Dietary Fiber	2g 8%
Sugar	3g
Protein	1g
Vitamin A	190%
Vitamin C	25%
Calcium	2%
Iron	2%

White
Serving Size: 1/2 cup/125ml (74g)

Calories	50
Total Fat	0g 0%
Saturated Fat	0g 0%
Trans Fat	0g
Cholesterol	0mg 0%
Sodium	0mg 0%
Potassium	300mg
Total Carbohydrate	12g 4%
Dietary Fiber	2g 8%
Sugar	1g
Protein	1g
Vitamin A	0%
Vitamin C	25%
Calcium	0%
Iron	2%

Potatoes

Yam

Yams are a tropical tuber similar to and often confused with the sweet potato. There are more than 150 yam species that can vary from off-white to dark brown, with a white, yellow, purple, or pink flesh. They are higher in moisture and sugar than sweet potatoes, but can still be substituted for them in many recipes. Look for yams in Latin or specialty markets.

Yukon Gold

Yukon Gold is one of the most popular waxy, yellow-fleshed potato varieties in the U.S. They are buttery yellow to gold, both inside and out, with a creamy texture that yields excellent mashed potatoes.

Radishes

Radishes are a root vegetable from the mustard family. They have a peppery flavor and come in a variety of colors, sizes, and shapes. Radishes are a salad classic, and they also add bite to sandwiches, soups, and vegetable dishes. Roasting mellows and tames their heat, or you can highlight their zest by adding radishes to a salad of Kalamata olives, feta cheese, garlic, and yogurt.

Radishes should feel firm; those that yield to gentle pressure won't be as crisp. If the leaves are still attached, they should be green and fresh-looking. Refrigerate radishes in a plastic bag for up to five days, depending on the variety.

Radishes contain no cholesterol, little fat, and few calories. They provide vitamin C, folate, calcium, potassium, and fiber.

Black

Black radishes are round, with a rough, black skin and crunchy, white flesh. Although they can be horseradish hot, they do add a pleasing tang to salads and stir-fries and make an interesting side dish when braised or sautéed.

Daikon

Daikon (literally "large root" in Japanese) radishes can grow as big as a football. They may be creamy white or black on the outside and crisp, juicy, and white on the inside. This Asian variety is often pickled, or it can be shredded and used as a garnish or added to cooked dishes.

Red

Red radishes are the most common and may be as small as a cherry or as large as an orange. They have a bright red skin, with crisp, white flesh that has a mild bite. Try serving them raw with sea salt or thinly slice them as a topping for buttered, dark bread.

White

White radishes are also called icicle radishes because of their long (up to six inches), tapering, snowy white appearance. They are milder tasting than red radishes and are tasty raw. Or, try them steamed and served with butter.

Tasty Idea

Radishes are a superb sandwich or salad ingredient, but you can do so much more with them:

- *Make a Moroccan-style salad with chopped oranges and sliced radishes. Toss with a little honey and olive oil.*

- *Steam radishes and serve with a sprinkling of herb vinegar or a little sugar.*

- *Shred a daikon radish. Sauté it in sesame oil with a pinch of sugar and a little soy sauce.*

- *Make Asian-style "pickled" radishes. Combine ⅔ cup rice vinegar, 2 tablespoons sugar, and 1 teaspoon soy sauce. Marinate sliced radishes in vinegar mixture overnight. Drain; sprinkle with toasted sesame seeds. (You can also use this technique with cucumbers.)*

Nutrition Facts

SOURCE: USDA

Potatoes

Yam

Serving Size: 1/2 cup/125ml (75g)

Calories		90
Total Fat	0g	0%
Saturated Fat	0g	0%
Trans Fat	0g	
Cholesterol	0mg	0%
Sodium	5mg	0%
Potassium	615mg	
Total Carbohydrate	21g	7%
Dietary Fiber	3g	12%
Sugar	0g	
Protein	1g	
Vitamin A		0%
Vitamin C		20%
Calcium		2%
Iron		2%

Yukon Gold

Serving Size: 1/2 cup/125ml (74g)

Calories		60
Total Fat	0g	0%
Saturated Fat	0g	0%
Trans Fat	0g	
Cholesterol	0mg	0%
Sodium	0mg	0%
Potassium	420mg	
Total Carbohydrate	13g	4%
Dietary Fiber	1g	4%
Sugar	0g	
Protein	2g	
Vitamin A		0%
Vitamin C		25%
Calcium		0%
Iron		4%

Radishes

Black

Serving Size: 1/2 cup/125ml (57g)

Calories		10
Total Fat	0g	0%
Saturated Fat	0g	0%
Trans Fat	0g	
Cholesterol	0mg	0%
Sodium	15mg	1%
Potassium	135mg	
Total Carbohydrate	2g	1%
Dietary Fiber	1g	4%
Sugar	1g	
Protein	1g	
Vitamin A		0%
Vitamin C		20%
Calcium		0%
Iron		0%

Radishes

Daikon

Serving Size: 1/2 cup/125ml (30g)

Calories		15
Total Fat	1g	2%
Saturated Fat	0g	0%
Trans Fat	0g	
Cholesterol	0mg	0%
Sodium	0mg	0%
Potassium	135mg	
Total Carbohydrate	1g	0%
Dietary Fiber	0g	0%
Sugar	0g	
Protein	1g	
Vitamin A		2%
Vitamin C		15%
Calcium		0%
Iron		0%

Red

Serving Size: 1/2 cup/125ml (30g)

Calories		5
Total Fat	0g	0%
Saturated Fat	0g	0%
Trans Fat	0g	
Cholesterol	0mg	0%
Sodium	10mg	0%
Potassium	135mg	
Total Carbohydrate	1g	0%
Dietary Fiber	0g	0%
Sugar	1g	
Protein	0g	
Vitamin A		0%
Vitamin C		10%
Calcium		0%
Iron		0%

White

Serving Size: 1/2 cup/125ml (50g)

Calories		5
Total Fat	0g	0%
Saturated Fat	0g	0%
Trans Fat	0g	
Cholesterol	0mg	0%
Sodium	10mg	0%
Potassium	140mg	
Total Carbohydrate	1g	0%
Dietary Fiber	1g	4%
Sugar	0g	
Protein	1g	
Vitamin A		0%
Vitamin C		25%
Calcium		2%
Iron		2%

Squash

Winter squash

Winter squash, sometimes called hard squash, are harvested in the autumn. They have hard rinds in a range of whites, yellows, oranges, greens, and even blues; yellow or orange flesh; and tough seeds that should be scooped out before cooking. Select firm squash that are heavy for their size, with dull but deeply colored rinds. Avoid blemished or spotted squash. Most varieties can be stored for at least a month in a cool, dark place. Do not refrigerate.

Winter squash can be baked, roasted, stuffed, steamed, puréed, or added to stews and casseroles. Cardamom, nutmeg, cinnamon, thyme, ginger, and allspice complement the natural sweetness of most varieties.

These versatile vegetables contain no fat or cholesterol and are low in sodium. Most are a good source of vitamins A and C, beta-carotene (deep-colored squash contain the most), and fiber. They also provide riboflavin and iron.

Buttercup (Winter)

Buttercup squash are a type of turban squash. They grow to about the size of a salad plate and have a sweet, orange flesh that tastes a bit like a sweet potato. Their dark green shells are flecked with gray; there is also an orange variety. Try using this squash instead of pumpkin in pies.

Butternut (Winter)

Butternut squash are large (up to a foot long), with pear-shaped, smooth, tan shells. The sweet, orange flesh is versatile, and it makes a tasty ravioli filling, soup, or risotto.

Acorn (Winter)

Acorn squash are oval, with deeply ribbed, dark green shells and bright orange flesh. There are also white and gold varieties. Acorn squash is at its best when cut in half and baked with butter and cinnamon or brown sugar.

Chayote (Summer)

Chayote looks something like a furrowed, pale green pear. The white flesh surrounds a single seed and has a zucchini-cucumber-apple flavor. They can be split and baked like acorn squash, sautéed in butter, or used raw in salads.

Delicata (Winter)

Delicatas, also called sweet potato squash, are oblong, with green stripes along their pale, yellow skins. The flesh is yellow and creamy and tastes like a cross between butternut squash and sweet potato. Bake or steam, and then serve with a bit of butter and a squeeze of lemon juice.

Golden Nugget (Winter)

Golden nugget squash resemble small pumpkins, with a finely ridged, orange or salmon-colored rind. They have a pleasantly sweet and nutty flavor when fully mature; look for those with a dull skin, which is a sign of maturity.

Hubbard (Winter)

Hubbards are large, with bumpy shells that range in color from dark or light green to bright orange. The yellow-orange flesh is slightly dry and grainy, so it's often mashed or puréed with butter and other seasonings.

Kabocha (Winter)

Kabochas are dark green with celadon streaks, and have pale orange flesh. They're sweet and tender, and they taste like a pumpkin-sweet potato cross. These large squash can weigh up to eight pounds.

Pattypan (Summer)

Pattypans, or scalloped squash, are squat and round, with a scalloped edge. Their pale green skin turns white as the squash matures. Use them as you would other summer squashes.

Pumpkin (Winter)

Pumpkins belong to the gourd family, which also includes squash. Most pumpkins come in shades of orange, but there are also white varieties. They may weigh up to 100 pounds, but most are small, with tender and succulent orange flesh. Store pumpkins at room temperature for up to a month or in the refrigerator for three months. Pumpkins are most famously used for pie, but try substituting them for other winter squashes in recipes.

Nutrition Facts
SOURCE: USDA

Squash

Acorn
Serving Size: 1/2 cup/125ml (70g)

Calories		30
Total Fat	0g	0%
Saturated Fat	0g	0%
Trans Fat	0g	
Cholesterol	0mg	0%
Sodium	0mg	0%
Potassium	240mg	
Total Carbohydrate	7g	2%
Dietary Fiber	1g	4%
Sugar	2g	
Protein	1g	
Vitamin A		6%
Vitamin C		15%
Calcium		2%
Iron		2%

Buttercup
Serving Size: 1/2 cup/125ml (57g)

Calories		30
Total Fat	0g	0%
Saturated Fat	0g	0%
Trans Fat	0g	
Cholesterol	0mg	0%
Sodium	140mg	6%
Potassium	n/a	
Total Carbohydrate	3g	1%
Dietary Fiber	1g	4%
Sugar	3g	
Protein	3g	
Vitamin A		70%
Vitamin C		15%
Calcium		2%
Iron		2%

Butternut
Serving Size: 1/2 cup/125ml (120g)

Calories		50
Total Fat	0g	0%
Saturated Fat	0g	0%
Trans Fat	0g	
Cholesterol	0mg	0%
Sodium	0mg	0%
Potassium	420mg	
Total Carbohydrate	14g	5%
Dietary Fiber	2g	8%
Sugar	3g	
Protein	1g	
Vitamin A		260%
Vitamin C		40%
Calcium		6%
Iron		4%

Chayote
Serving Size: 1/2 cup/125ml (186g)

Calories		70
Total Fat	0g	0%
Saturated Fat	0g	0%
Trans Fat	0g	
Cholesterol	0mg	0%
Sodium	5mg	0%
Potassium	510mg	
Total Carbohydrate	17g	6%
Dietary Fiber	4g	16%
Sugar	4g	
Protein	2g	
Vitamin A		260%
Vitamin C		50%
Calcium		6%
Iron		6%

Delicata
Serving Size: 1/2 cup/125ml (57g)

Calories		30
Total Fat	0g	0%
Saturated Fat	0g	0%
Trans Fat	0g	
Cholesterol	0mg	0%
Sodium	0mg	0%
Potassium	200mg	
Total Carbohydrate	7g	2%
Dietary Fiber	1g	4%
Sugar	3g	
Protein	1g	
Vitamin A		70%
Vitamin C		15%
Calcium		2%
Iron		2%

Golden Nugget
Serving Size: 1/2 cup/125ml (58g)

Calories		20
Total Fat	0g	0%
Saturated Fat	0g	0%
Trans Fat	0g	
Cholesterol	0mg	0%
Sodium	0mg	0%
Potassium	200mg	
Total Carbohydrate	5g	2%
Dietary Fiber	1g	4%
Sugar	1g	
Protein	1g	
Vitamin A		15%
Vitamin C		10%
Calcium		2%
Iron		2%

Hubbard
Serving Size: 1/2 cup/125ml (58g)

Calories		25
Total Fat	0g	0%
Saturated Fat	0g	0%
Trans Fat	0g	
Cholesterol	0mg	0%
Sodium	0mg	0%
Potassium	190mg	
Total Carbohydrate	5g	2%
Dietary Fiber	2g	8%
Sugar	1g	
Protein	1g	
Vitamin A		15%
Vitamin C		10%
Calcium		0%
Iron		2%

Kabocha
Serving Size: 1/2 cup/125ml (57g)

Calories		30
Total Fat	0g	0%
Saturated Fat	0g	0%
Trans Fat	0g	
Cholesterol	0mg	0%
Sodium	0mg	0%
Potassium	200mg	
Total Carbohydrate	7g	2%
Dietary Fiber	1g	4%
Sugar	3g	
Protein	1g	
Vitamin A		70%
Vitamin C		15%
Calcium		2%
Iron		2%

Pattypan
Serving Size: 1/2 cup/125ml (65g)

Calories		10
Total Fat	0g	0%
Saturated Fat	0g	0%
Trans Fat	0g	
Cholesterol	0mg	0%
Sodium	0mg	0%
Potassium	120mg	
Total Carbohydrate	2g	1%
Dietary Fiber	1g	4%
Sugar	1g	
Protein	1g	
Vitamin A		2%
Vitamin C		20%
Calcium		2%
Iron		2%

Pumpkin
Serving Size: 1/2 cup/125ml (58g)

Calories		15
Total Fat	0g	0%
Saturated Fat	0g	0%
Trans Fat	0g	
Cholesterol	0mg	0%
Sodium	0mg	0%
Potassium	200mg	
Total Carbohydrate	4g	1%
Dietary Fiber	0g	0%
Sugar	1g	
Protein	1g	
Vitamin A		90%
Vitamin C		8%
Calcium		2%
Iron		2%

Squash

Summer squash

Summer squash such as zucchini and pattypan have tender, edible rinds and soft seeds. Select firm squash with shiny, smooth skins. Avoid any with blemishes or that are withered at either end. Store in a plastic bag and refrigerate for up to five days.

Summer squash contain few calories and no sodium or fat. They are a source of vitamins A and C. They can be lightly cooked — try sautéing, baking, grilling, steaming, or stir-frying them. Summer squash can be stuffed, added to soup or salad, or served as crudités. Varieties are interchangeable in most recipes.

Spaghetti (Winter)

Spaghetti squash are watermelon shaped, with a smooth, creamy yellow skin. After cooking, the yellow-gold flesh separates into spaghetti-like strands that can be served with pasta sauce or topped with butter and seasonings.

Yellow (Summer)

Yellow, or crookneck squash have long, curved, tapering necks. Their yellow skin is somewhat bumpy. The flesh is creamy yellow. Use as you would zucchini or other summer squash.

Turban (Winter)

Turban squash have a hard, bumpy shell that's bright orange with touches of green. There is a turban-shaped cap on the blossom end, hence the name. The finely textured, orange flesh may taste mild to sweet.

Zucchini (Summer)

Zucchini is the quintessential summer squash. It is cucumber shaped, long (four to eight inches), and can be light to dark green. The pale green, mild-flavored flesh is tasty when sautéed in olive oil with tomatoes and onions.

Tomatoes

Tomatoes are versatile, and they star in cuisines around the world. They come in many sizes and shapes, and while red and yellow are the most common colors, there are also green, orange, and purple varieties, as well as heirloom varieties. Botanically a fruit, the tomato is used like a vegetable and can be served raw, sautéed, fried, grilled, broiled, baked, or stewed.

A medium-size tomato is a nutritional bargain with about 30 calories. It's a good source of vitamins C and A. Tomatoes also contain fiber, potassium, calcium, and iron, and they are loaded with lycopene, a phytochemical that makes them red and may help prevent heart disease and some forms of cancer.

Select fragrant, blemish-free tomatoes that are heavy for their size and have a bright, even color. Ripe tomatoes will yield slightly to pressure. Beefsteak and other round tomatoes are good raw, while plum or Roma tomatoes are better for cooking, sauces, and pizzas. Cherry and grape tomatoes are great raw or cooked.

Beefsteak

Beefsteak tomatoes are big, bright red ovals. They are tasty raw or cooked. Try them in a summer salad, drizzled with olive oil and balsamic vinegar and sprinkled with chopped, fresh basil.

Cherry

A cherry tomato is about the size of a large gumball and can be a glossy red or yellow. They make a great snack, or try roasting them whole with olive oil and fresh herbs.

Nutrition Facts
SOURCE: USDA

Squash

Spaghetti
Serving Size: 1/2 cup/125ml (51g)

Calories		15
Total Fat	0g	0%
Saturated Fat	0g	0%
Trans Fat	0g	
Cholesterol	0mg	0%
Sodium	10mg	0%
Potassium	55mg	
Total Carbohydrate	3g	1%
Dietary Fiber	1g	4%
Sugar	2g	
Protein	0g	
Vitamin A		0%
Vitamin C		2%
Calcium		2%
Iron		0%

Turban
Serving Size: 1/2 cup/125ml (57g)

Calories		20
Total Fat	0g	0%
Saturated Fat	0g	0%
Trans Fat	0g	
Cholesterol	0mg	0%
Sodium	0mg	0%
Potassium	240mg	
Total Carbohydrate	5g	2%
Dietary Fiber	1g	4%
Sugar	2g	
Protein	1g	
Vitamin A		45%
Vitamin C		10%
Calcium		2%
Iron		2%

Yellow
Serving Size: 1/2 cup/125ml (65g)

Calories		10
Total Fat	0g	0%
Saturated Fat	0g	0%
Trans Fat	0g	
Cholesterol	0mg	0%
Sodium	0mg	0%
Potassium	140mg	
Total Carbohydrate	3g	1%
Dietary Fiber	1g	4%
Sugar	1g	
Protein	1g	
Vitamin A		2%
Vitamin C		10%
Calcium		2%
Iron		2%

Squash

Zucchini
Serving Size: 1/2 cup/125ml (62g)

Calories		10
Total Fat	0g	0%
Saturated Fat	0g	0%
Trans Fat	0g	
Cholesterol	0mg	0%
Sodium	5mg	0%
Potassium	160mg	
Total Carbohydrate	2g	1%
Dietary Fiber	1g	4%
Sugar	1g	
Protein	1g	
Vitamin A		2%
Vitamin C		20%
Calcium		0%
Iron		2%

Tomatoes

Beefsteak
Serving Size: 1 medium (149g)

Calories		25
Total Fat	0g	0%
Saturated Fat	0g	0%
Trans Fat	0g	
Cholesterol	0mg	0%
Sodium	5mg	0%
Potassium	350mg	
Total Carbohydrate	6g	2%
Dietary Fiber	2g	8%
Sugar	4g	
Protein	1g	
Vitamin A		25%
Vitamin C		30%
Calcium		2%
Iron		2%

Cherry
Serving Size: 1/2 cup/125ml (75g)

Calories		15
Total Fat	0g	0%
Saturated Fat	0g	0%
Trans Fat	0g	
Cholesterol	0mg	0%
Sodium	0mg	0%
Potassium	180mg	
Total Carbohydrate	3g	1%
Dietary Fiber	1g	4%
Sugar	2g	
Protein	1g	
Vitamin A		10%
Vitamin C		15%
Calcium		0%
Iron		2%

Tomatoes

Grape

Grape tomatoes are actually baby red Romas. These small ovals are intensely sweet. Eat them out of hand, substitute for cherry tomatoes in recipes, or serve them with cottage cheese.

Sun-Dried

Sun-dried tomatoes are slightly salty, with the chewy texture of raisins. Their intense tomato taste enlivens pasta sauces, bread, meatloaf, vegetable sautés, and salads. They may be either dry or packed in oil. To soften the dry-packed version, cover with boiling water, and then let stand for five minutes. Drain and use.

Plum/Roma

Plum tomatoes, also called Italian plum or Roma tomatoes, are egg shaped and either red or yellow. Thick-fleshed and meaty, plum tomatoes are perfect for sauces, stir-fries, stews, casseroles, or pizza.

Teardrop

Teardrop tomatoes are shaped like a teardrop or tiny pear, and there are both red and yellow varieties. They are about the size of cherry tomatoes and can be used in the same way. Try serving them fresh with a selection of Italian cheeses.

In the Kitchen

To peel tomatoes, cut an "X" in the bottom with a sharp knife. Place two or three at a time into a pot of boiling water. Boil for 15 to 30 seconds. Remove with a slotted spoon. Rinse with cold water, and then slip the skins off (use a paring knife if needed).

Other Vegetables

Nothing beats the flavor of ripe produce fresh from the market. Most vegetables are low in calories, and high in fiber, vitamins, minerals, and natural substances that help protect the body from disease. Vegetables — both familiar and unusual — taste great, especially when cooked using low-fat methods like steaming, stir-frying, or sautéing. Try seasoning vegetables with herbs and spices instead of fats like butter or oil, and eat a variety for the greatest health and weight-loss benefits.

Alfalfa Sprouts

Alfalfa sprouts are germinated alfalfa seeds. Usually eaten raw, they add a crispness and peppery flavor to salads and sandwiches. Look for crisp sprouts with the buds attached. Avoid any that smell musty or look dark or slimy. Refrigerate for up to two days in a perforated plastic bag or the ventilated plastic container they came in.

Artichoke

Artichokes are the head of an edible thistle, and they come in many sizes. Look for deep green artichokes that are heavy for their size and that have tightly formed leaves that "squeak" when pressed. Avoid those with dry, brown, or split leaves. Refrigerate unwashed in a plastic bag for up to four days, and then boil, steam, or microwave. Globe artichokes (the most common type) are low in calories, have no fat, and are a source of vitamin C, potassium, folate, magnesium, and fiber.

Tasty Idea

Stuffed artichokes make a delicious and elegant first course. To prepare, trim stem end and any thorny tips. Boil for 15 minutes. Cool slightly; spread leaves and scoop out fuzzy choke in center. Stuff center and leaves with a mixture of bread crumbs, garlic, and oregano drizzled with a little olive oil. Steam until done (about 30 to 40 minutes).

Asparagus, Green

Asparagus is a low-calorie, low-sodium source of vitamins A and B6, folate, and phytochemicals that may help prevent disease. Look for bright green stalks, with compact and firm tips. Refrigerate for up to four days in a plastic bag or standing upright in water (like flowers in a vase). Before using, snap stalks off at their natural bend. Peel more mature or larger stalks. Boil, steam, or stir-fry until crisp-tender, or roast with olive oil and Parmesan cheese.

Asparagus, White

White asparagus is grown underground, which keeps it from turning green. Look for thick, smooth, pale ivory stalks with closed heads. Peel before cooking. Use like green asparagus.

Bean Sprouts

Bean sprouts are a popular Asian ingredient. The most common are mung bean sprouts. Look for crisp sprouts that smell fresh, look firm, and have buds still attached. Refrigerate in a plastic bag for up to three days. Use them to add crunch and flavor to stir-fries and other lightly cooked dishes.

Nutrition Facts

SOURCE: USDA

Tomatoes

Grape
Serving Size: 1/2 cup/125ml (75g)

Calories	15
Total Fat	0g ... 0%
Saturated Fat	0g ... 0%
Trans Fat	0g
Cholesterol	0mg ... 0%
Sodium	0mg ... 0%
Potassium	180mg
Total Carbohydrate	3g ... 1%
Dietary Fiber	1g ... 4%
Sugar	2g
Protein	1g
Vitamin A	10%
Vitamin C	15%
Calcium	0%
Iron	2%

Plum/Roma
Serving Size: 1/2 cup/125ml (75g)

Calories	15
Total Fat	0g ... 0%
Saturated Fat	0g ... 0%
Trans Fat	0g
Cholesterol	0mg ... 0%
Sodium	0mg ... 0%
Potassium	180mg
Total Carbohydrate	3g ... 1%
Dietary Fiber	1g ... 4%
Sugar	2g
Protein	1g
Vitamin A	10%
Vitamin C	15%
Calcium	0%
Iron	2%

Sun-Dried
Serving Size: 1/4 cup/50ml (14g)

Calories	35
Total Fat	0g ... 0%
Saturated Fat	0g ... 0%
Trans Fat	0g
Cholesterol	0mg ... 0%
Sodium	280mg ... 12%
Potassium	470mg
Total Carbohydrate	8g ... 3%
Dietary Fiber	2g ... 8%
Sugar	5g
Protein	2g
Vitamin A	2%
Vitamin C	8%
Calcium	2%
Iron	6%

Teardrop
Serving Size: 1/2 cup/125ml (75g)

Calories	15
Total Fat	0g ... 0%
Saturated Fat	0g ... 0%
Trans Fat	0g
Cholesterol	0mg ... 0%
Sodium	0mg ... 0%
Potassium	180mg
Total Carbohydrate	3g ... 1%
Dietary Fiber	1g ... 4%
Sugar	2g
Protein	1g
Vitamin A	10%
Vitamin C	15%
Calcium	0%
Iron	2%

Other Vegetables

Alfalfa Sprouts
Serving Size: 1/2 cup/125ml (17g)

Calories	5
Total Fat	0g ... 0%
Saturated Fat	0g ... 0%
Trans Fat	0g
Cholesterol	0mg ... 0%
Sodium	0mg ... 0%
Potassium	15mg
Total Carbohydrate	1g ... 0%
Dietary Fiber	0g ... 0%
Sugar	0g
Protein	1g
Vitamin A	0%
Vitamin C	2%
Calcium	0%
Iron	0%

Artichoke
Serving Size: 1 medium (128g)

Calories	60
Total Fat	0g ... 0%
Saturated Fat	0g ... 0%
Trans Fat	0g
Cholesterol	0mg ... 0%
Sodium	120mg ... 5%
Potassium	480mg
Total Carbohydrate	13g ... 4%
Dietary Fiber	6g ... 24%
Sugar	3g
Protein	4g
Vitamin A	4%
Vitamin C	25%
Calcium	6%
Iron	10%

Asparagus, Green
Serving Size: 1/2 cup/125ml (67g)

Calories	35
Total Fat	0g ... 0%
Saturated Fat	0g ... 0%
Trans Fat	0g
Cholesterol	0mg ... 0%
Sodium	0mg ... 0%
Potassium	135mg
Total Carbohydrate	3g ... 1%
Dietary Fiber	1g ... 4%
Sugar	1g
Protein	1g
Vitamin A	10%
Vitamin C	6%
Calcium	2%
Iron	8%

Asparagus, White
Serving Size: 1/2 cup/125ml (58g)

Calories	15
Total Fat	0g ... 0%
Saturated Fat	0g ... 0%
Trans Fat	0g
Cholesterol	0mg ... 0%
Sodium	0mg ... 0%
Potassium	160mg
Total Carbohydrate	3g ... 1%
Dietary Fiber	1g ... 4%
Sugar	1g
Protein	1g
Vitamin A	6%
Vitamin C	15%
Calcium	0%
Iron	2%

Bean Sprouts
Serving Size: 1/2 cup/125ml (52g)

Calories	15
Total Fat	0g ... 0%
Saturated Fat	0g ... 0%
Trans Fat	0g
Cholesterol	0mg ... 0%
Sodium	0mg ... 0%
Potassium	80mg
Total Carbohydrate	3g ... 1%
Dietary Fiber	1g ... 4%
Sugar	2g
Protein	2g
Vitamin A	0%
Vitamin C	10%
Calcium	0%
Iron	2%

Other Vegetables

Beet

Beets may be garnet to white, with firm, smooth skins. They provide some vitamin C and iron. Small beets are usually more tender than large ones. If the greens (a nutritious vegetable in themselves) are attached, they should be crisp and bright. Remove greens, leaving about an inch of the stem, cook, and then peel. Refrigerate beets in a plastic bag for up to three weeks. Add raw, grated beets to a salad, or roast and serve as a salad with arugula and fresh goat cheese.

Broccoli

Broccoli is an excellent source of vitamin C and also contains vitamin A, riboflavin, calcium, iron, and a natural compound that may help prevent some cancers. Look for heads with tightly closed, vivid green buds; avoid those that are yellowing or brown. Refrigerate unwashed for up to four days. Trim and peel stalks before using. Serve raw broccoli with a dip or grate and substitute for cabbage in coleslaw. Broccoli can also be steamed, stir-fried, or boiled; or, try sautéing in olive oil with garlic or shallots.

Broccoli Sprouts

Sprouted broccoli seeds are high in phytochemicals that may help prevent some forms of cancer—one ounce contains almost as much as two pounds of mature broccoli. Sprinkle broccoli sprouts on salads, or add them to sandwiches for extra crunch.

In the Kitchen

When boiling white cauliflower, add 1 cup of milk or a tablespoon of lemon juice to the cooking water to keep it from discoloring.

Brussels Sprouts

Brussels sprouts look like tiny heads of cabbage. They're high in vitamins A and C and fiber, and like other cruciferous vegetables, may help prevent certain forms of cancer. Look for compact, firm, and bright green Brussels sprouts. Refrigerate in a plastic bag for no more than three days. Microwave, steam, boil, or roast Brussels sprouts. Their nutty, sweet flavor is especially good with caramelized onions and fennel.

Carrot

Carrots are high in vitamin A, making them as healthful as they are versatile. Look for firm, smooth carrots; avoid withered or cracked ones. Wrap in plastic and refrigerate (store separately from apples, which emit ethylene gas and make carrots taste bitter). Very young or baby carrots don't need to be peeled before use. Serve raw as crudités, grate for salads, steam, boil, microwave, or add to stir-fries, casseroles, soups, or stews. Or, cut them into finger-long pieces, toss with thyme and honey, and roast until tender.

Cauliflower

Cauliflower is high in vitamin C and is a source of iron. Cauliflower is usually white, although green and purple varieties are sometimes available. Look for firm heads with compact florets and green, crisp leaves. Wrap tightly and refrigerate for up to five days. Cauliflower can be boiled, steamed, microwaved, sautéed, roasted, or served raw. Try substituting cauliflower for broccoli in recipes, or serve puréed cauliflower instead of mashed potatoes.

Celeriac

Celeriac is the knobby, brown root of a special celery variety. It's also called celery root, celery knob, or knob celery. Look for small and firm roots that are heavy for their size; avoid those with soft spots or that are excessively bumpy. Refrigerate in a plastic bag for up to ten days. Celeriac has a celery-parsley flavor and can be eaten raw or cooked (peel first). Purée and mix with mashed potatoes. Or, grate raw celeriac and apples and mix with a creamy mustard salad dressing.

Celery

Green celery is the most common celery, although there is also a gold variety. Celery is a low-calorie source of fiber and vitamin C. It brings a lively crunch to salads and an assertive, herbaceous flavor to soups, casseroles, and vegetable dishes. Choose firm, tight bunches with crisp leaves, which can be chopped and used like an herb. Refrigerate in a plastic bag for up to two weeks. Try stuffing celery with reduced fat cheese or peanut butter for a snack, or braise and serve with roasted meats or poultry.

Nutrition Facts
SOURCE: USDA

Other Vegetables

Beet
Serving Size: 1/2 cup/125ml (68g)

Calories	30
Total Fat	0g 0%
Saturated Fat	0g 0%
Trans Fat	0g
Cholesterol	0mg 0%
Sodium	55mg 2%
Potassium	221mg
Total Carbohydrate	7g 2%
Dietary Fiber	2g 8%
Sugar	5g
Protein	1g
Vitamin A	0%
Vitamin C	6%
Calcium	2%
Iron	4%

Carrot
Serving Size: 1 medium (61g)

Calories	25
Total Fat	0g 0%
Saturated Fat	0g 0%
Trans Fat	0g
Cholesterol	0mg 0%
Sodium	40mg 2%
Potassium	200mg
Total Carbohydrate	6g 2%
Dietary Fiber	2g 8%
Sugar	3g
Protein	1g
Vitamin A	150%
Vitamin C	6%
Calcium	2%
Iron	4%

Broccoli
Serving Size: 1/2 cup/125ml (36g)

Calories	10
Total Fat	0g 0%
Saturated Fat	0g 0%
Trans Fat	0g
Cholesterol	0mg 0%
Sodium	10mg 0%
Potassium	115mg
Total Carbohydrate	2g 1%
Dietary Fiber	1g 4%
Sugar	1g
Protein	1g
Vitamin A	4%
Vitamin C	50%
Calcium	2%
Iron	2%

Cauliflower
Serving Size: 1/2 cup/125ml (32g)

Calories	10
Total Fat	0g 0%
Saturated Fat	0g 0%
Trans Fat	0g
Cholesterol	0mg 0%
Sodium	5mg 0%
Potassium	100mg
Total Carbohydrate	2g 1%
Dietary Fiber	1g 4%
Sugar	1g
Protein	1g
Vitamin A	0%
Vitamin C	45%
Calcium	2%
Iron	2%

Broccoli Sprouts
Serving Size: 1/2 cup/125ml (43g)

Calories	20
Total Fat	0g 0%
Saturated Fat	0g 0%
Trans Fat	0g
Cholesterol	0mg 0%
Sodium	15mg 1%
Potassium	230mg
Total Carbohydrate	3g 1%
Dietary Fiber	2g 8%
Sugar	0g
Protein	1g
Vitamin A	6%
Vitamin C	30%
Calcium	4%
Iron	2%

Celeriac
Serving Size: 1/2 cup/125ml (78g)

Calories	35
Total Fat	0g 0%
Saturated Fat	0g 0%
Trans Fat	0g
Cholesterol	0mg 0%
Sodium	80mg 3%
Potassium	235mg
Total Carbohydrate	7g 2%
Dietary Fiber	1g 4%
Sugar	1g
Protein	1g
Vitamin A	0%
Vitamin C	10%
Calcium	4%
Iron	4%

Brussels Sprouts
Serving Size: 1/2 cup/125ml (44g)

Calories	20
Total Fat	0g 0%
Saturated Fat	0g 0%
Trans Fat	0g
Cholesterol	0mg 0%
Sodium	10mg 0%
Potassium	170mg
Total Carbohydrate	4g 1%
Dietary Fiber	2g 8%
Sugar	1g
Protein	1g
Vitamin A	6%
Vitamin C	60%
Calcium	2%
Iron	4%

Celery
Serving Size: 1/2 cup/125ml (60g)

Calories	10
Total Fat	0g 0%
Saturated Fat	0g 0%
Trans Fat	0g
Cholesterol	0mg 0%
Sodium	50mg 2%
Potassium	160mg
Total Carbohydrate	2g 1%
Dietary Fiber	1g 4%
Sugar	1g
Protein	0g
Vitamin A	6%
Vitamin C	4%
Calcium	2%
Iron	0%

1

5

2

3

4

6

7

8

9

1 Corn

Most corn is yellow or white. Yellow corn has large, full-flavored kernels. White kernels are typically smaller and sweeter. There are also many hybrid bicolor varieties that are extremely sweet. Corn is a source of fiber and vitamins A and C. Fresh corn begins losing flavor immediately after picking, so buy as soon after harvest as possible. Select ears with bright green, tight husks; golden brown silk; and plump, milky kernels in tightly spaced rows. Refrigerate in the husk for no more than a day, and then roast, grill, boil, or microwave. Or, cut corn from the cob for soup, salsa, salads, or casseroles. Baby corn is typically sold canned or frozen and used in Asian cooking.

2 Fennel

Fennel is crunchy and sweet, with a delicate and vaguely anise-like flavor. The entire plant is edible, from bulb to feathery leaves (snip and use as an herb). Fennel is marketed as fresh anise in some parts of the country. Look for crisp bulbs with fresh, green leaves. Wrap in plastic and refrigerate for up to five days. Roast with veal or other meats, or combine with blood oranges and Parmesan cheese for an Italian-style salad.

3 Jerusalem Artichoke/ Sunchoke

Jerusalem artichokes, also called sunchokes, are the roots of a particular sunflower. They are gnarled and brown and look something like a round knob of ginger. The white flesh is a nutty, sweet, and crunchy source of iron. Look for firm Jerusalem artichokes and refrigerate in a plastic bag for up to a week. Serve raw or cooked (no need to peel first). Try roasting with garlic and herbs.

4 Okra

Okra is green, with a tapered, ribbed pod that is filled with white seeds. Okra provides vitamins A and C, and it's prized for its flavor in the South. Select brightly colored, firm pods and refrigerate for up to three days. When cooked, okra releases a sticky juice that acts as a thickener. It's a key ingredient in gumbo and Creole dishes, and it can also be sautéed, battered and deep-fried, boiled, braised, pickled, or steamed. Try pairing with stewed tomatoes.

5 Parsnip

Parsnips look like white carrots and have a sweet, nutty flavor. They provide vitamin C, fiber, and iron. Look for small to medium, evenly tapered, and firm parsnips. Refrigerate in a plastic bag for up to two weeks. Boil and mash like potatoes, steam, add to soups and stews, or roast with rosemary and olive oil.

6 Radicchio

Radicchio is a slightly bitter Italian chicory, with either a loose or tight head, pink to dark red leaves, and white ribs. The leaves should be crisp and full-colored, without any browning. Refrigerate in plastic for up to a week. Radicchio can be grilled, sautéed, baked, or added to salads or dishes such as risotto. Try substituting it for Belgian endive or escarole in recipes.

7 Rhubarb

Rhubarb has celery-like stalks and may be pink to cherry red. Select crisp, bright stalks with fresh leaves (don't eat, though—rhubarb's leaves and roots are toxic). Wrap in plastic and refrigerate for up to three days. Rhubarb's sharp tartness makes it best for sauces, jams, or desserts (like rhubarb-strawberry pie) that are made with lots of sugar.

8 Rutabaga

Rutabagas, also called Swedes, look like large, yellowish turnips. They are a cruciferous vegetable that contains fiber and vitamin C. The yellow flesh is firm and slightly sweet. Look for hard, smooth, and heavy rutabagas and refrigerate for up to two weeks. Boil and mash with potatoes, substitute for turnips in recipes, or add to beef or lamb stew.

9 Turnip

Turnips are white, with a tinge of purple at the top and white flesh. They're a fair source of vitamin C and phytochemicals that may help prevent some forms of cancer. Look for small turnips that are heavy for their size. They will be sweeter than large turnips, which may have a woody texture and peppery bite. Store in a cool, well-ventilated area or refrigerate for up to two weeks. Stir-fry, roast, steam and purée, or add turnips to stews. Add raw turnips to salads.

Nutrition Facts
Other Vegetables

SOURCE: USDA

Corn
Serving Size: 1 medium (90g)

Calories	80
Total Fat	1g 2%
Saturated Fat	0g 0%
Trans Fat	0g
Cholesterol	0mg 0%
Sodium	15mg 1%
Potassium	250mg
Total Carbohydrate	17g 6%
Dietary Fiber	2g 8%
Sugar	3g
Protein	3g
Vitamin A	4%
Vitamin C	10%
Calcium	0%
Iron	2%

Fennel
Serving Size: 1/2 cup/125ml (44g)

Calories	15
Total Fat	0g 0%
Saturated Fat	0g 0%
Trans Fat	0g
Cholesterol	0mg 0%
Sodium	25mg 1%
Potassium	180mg
Total Carbohydrate	3g 1%
Dietary Fiber	1g 4%
Sugar	0g
Protein	1g
Vitamin A	2%
Vitamin C	8%
Calcium	2%
Iron	2%

Jerusalem Artichoke
Serving Size: 1/2 cup/125ml (75g)

Calories	60
Total Fat	0g 0%
Saturated Fat	0g 0%
Trans Fat	0g
Cholesterol	0mg 0%
Sodium	0mg 0%
Potassium	330mg
Total Carbohydrate	13g 4%
Dietary Fiber	1g 4%
Sugar	7g
Protein	1g
Vitamin A	0%
Vitamin C	6%
Calcium	2%
Iron	15%

Okra
Serving Size: 1/2 cup/125ml (50g)

Calories	15
Total Fat	0g 0%
Saturated Fat	0g 0%
Trans Fat	0g
Cholesterol	0mg 0%
Sodium	0mg 0%
Potassium	160mg
Total Carbohydrate	4g 1%
Dietary Fiber	2g 8%
Sugar	1g
Protein	1g
Vitamin A	4%
Vitamin C	20%
Calcium	4%
Iron	2%

Parsnip
Serving Size: 1/2 cup/125ml (67g)

Calories	50
Total Fat	0g 0%
Saturated Fat	0g 0%
Trans Fat	0g
Cholesterol	0mg 0%
Sodium	5mg 0%
Potassium	250mg
Total Carbohydrate	12g 4%
Dietary Fiber	3g 12%
Sugar	3g
Protein	1g
Vitamin A	0%
Vitamin C	20%
Calcium	2%
Iron	2%

Radicchio
Serving Size: 1/2 cup/125ml (20g)

Calories	5
Total Fat	0g 0%
Saturated Fat	0g 0%
Trans Fat	0g
Cholesterol	0mg 0%
Sodium	0mg 0%
Potassium	60mg
Total Carbohydrate	1g 0%
Dietary Fiber	0g 0%
Sugar	0g
Protein	0g
Vitamin A	0%
Vitamin C	2%
Calcium	0%
Iron	0%

Rhubarb
Serving Size: 1/2 cup/125ml (122g)

Calories	15
Total Fat	0g 0%
Saturated Fat	0g 0%
Trans Fat	0g
Cholesterol	0mg 0%
Sodium	0mg 0%
Potassium	350mg
Total Carbohydrate	3g 1%
Dietary Fiber	1g 4%
Sugar	1g
Protein	1g
Vitamin A	2%
Vitamin C	8%
Calcium	6%
Iron	0%

Rutabaga
Serving Size: 1/2 cup/125ml (70g)

Calories	25
Total Fat	0g 0%
Saturated Fat	0g 0%
Trans Fat	0g
Cholesterol	0mg 0%
Sodium	15mg 1%
Potassium	240mg
Total Carbohydrate	6g 2%
Dietary Fiber	2g 8%
Sugar	4g
Protein	1g
Vitamin A	0%
Vitamin C	30%
Calcium	4%
Iron	2%

Turnip
Serving Size: 1/2 cup/125ml (65g)

Calories	20
Total Fat	0g 0%
Saturated Fat	0g 0%
Trans Fat	0g
Cholesterol	0mg 0%
Sodium	45mg 2%
Potassium	125mg
Total Carbohydrate	4g 1%
Dietary Fiber	1g 4%
Sugar	2g
Protein	1g
Vitamin A	0%
Vitamin C	25%
Calcium	2%
Iron	2%

Ethnic Vegetables

1 Bamboo Shoot

Fresh, pale yellow bamboo shoots are tender-crisp and slightly sweet. They're commonly used in Chinese cooking and are a good source of fiber. Wrap unpeeled shoots in plastic and refrigerate for up to two weeks (they grow bitter with longer storage). To use, remove the roots and tough ends, and then peel. Boil uncovered for 20 minutes to leach any bitterness. Do not use raw. Add cooked bamboo shoots to vegetable dishes, or stir-fry with shiitake mushrooms, bok choy, and garlic.

2 Bitter Melon

Bitter melon, also called balsam pear, is a fruit that's used as a vegetable in Chinese cooking. It looks like a long, warty cucumber and is a good source of vitamin C. When picked young, bitter melon is yellowish-green and has a delicately sour flavor. Mature bitter melon is yellowish-orange and sharp tasting. Refrigerate unwashed bitter melon for up to a week. To prepare, cut in half and scoop out the seeds and fibrous core. Do not peel. Blanch for two to three minutes to reduce the bitterness, or salt, rinse, and drain as you would eggplant. Try it stir-fried, stewed, curried, or pickled, or stuff with a savory filling.

3 Boniato

The boniato, also called the Cuban sweet potato, is a tropical sweet potato popular in Latin American and Caribbean cooking. Its skin may be red to brown, and it has creamy, white flesh. Select unblemished boniatos (avoid those that have sprouted) and store in a cool, dark, well-ventilated location for up to a month. The boniato has a chestnut-like flavor and a dry, fluffy texture. Cook like potatoes or yams. Try mashing with garlic and serving with roasted pork.

4 Breadfruit

Breadfruit is an incredibly versatile native of the Pacific islands. There are many varieties—round or oblong, small or large (up to twelve pounds), with a white or yellow flesh—that can be eaten at almost any stage of maturity. Breadfruit does not store well, so use immediately after purchase. To prepare, slice off the stem, cut into quarters, and core. Remove the skin after cooking. Immature breadfruit has a bumpy, green rind and is used like squash or other vegetables; try it pickled or marinated. Mature breadfruit is yellowish and softer. The flesh is sweetly fragrant and can be eaten raw, used in pies or cakes, or substituted for potatoes or rice. It can be steamed, boiled, deep-fried, or candied. Baked breadfruit has the flavor and texture of freshly baked bread, hence the name. Try serving baked breadfruit with coconut cream, sugar, and cinnamon.

5 Cactus Leaves/Nopales

Cactus leaves, or nopales, are the leaves of the prickly pear (nopal) cactus. Widely used in Mexican cooking, cactus leaves are fleshy and taste something like green beans and asparagus. They're also a source of vitamins A and C. Look for small and firm pale green leaves. Wrap tightly and refrigerate for up to a week. To prepare, use a vegetable peeler to shave off thorns and cut away any dry or fibrous spots. Cactus leaves can be eaten raw, but they're best when sliced into small strips and steamed or boiled. Add to salads or scrambled eggs or serve with salsa.

6 Calabaza

Calabaza is a pumpkin-like squash used throughout the Caribbean and South and Central America. It varies in color (green to light orange, solid or mottled) and size (fifteen to thirty pounds) and is a good source of fiber. Calabaza is often sold already cut into chunks, and the bright orange flesh is succulent and sweet. Look for unblemished squash that are heavy for their size and store in a cool, dark place for up to six weeks. Wrap cut squash in plastic and refrigerate for a week. Calabaza can be substituted for butternut or other winter squash, or try combining it with eggplant, tomatoes, green plantains, and onions for a Caribbean-style ratatouille.

7 Cardoon

Cardoons grow in wide, flat, celery-like stalks and are popular in France, Italy, and Spain. They belong to the same thistle family as artichokes and taste like a combination of artichoke, celery, and salsify. Cardoons are a good source of potassium, but they're also high in sodium. Look for firm, silvery green stalks. Refrigerate in a plastic bag for up to two weeks. To prepare, remove tough outer ribs, cut to size, and rub with lemon juice or dip in acidulated water to prevent browning. Cardoons can be boiled, braised, or baked. Try serving parboiled cardoons with *bagna cauda*, a hot, anchovy-flavored Italian dip.

8 Choy Sum/Chinese Flowering Cabbage

Choy sum is also known as Chinese flowering cabbage or yu choy sum. Its green leaves grow on pale green stalks; there are also sometimes tiny, yellow, edible flowers. Choy sum is a good source of vitamins A and C. Look for firm, fresh bunches free of browning. Refrigerate in plastic or an airtight container and use within four days. Choy sum's sweet leaves and slightly bitter stalks can be prepared like broccoli, or try stir-frying them with garlic.

Nutrition Facts

SOURCE: USDA

Ethnic Vegetables

Bamboo Shoot
Serving Size: 1/2 cup/125ml (76g)

Calories	20	
Total Fat	0g	0%
Saturated Fat	0g	0%
Trans Fat	0g	
Cholesterol	0mg	0%
Sodium	0mg	0%
Potassium	410mg	
Total Carbohydrate	4g	1%
Dietary Fiber	2g	8%
Sugar	2g	
Protein	2g	
Vitamin A		0%
Vitamin C		6%
Calcium		0%
Iron		2%

Cactus Leaves/Nopales
Serving Size: 1/2 cup/125ml (43g)

Calories	10	
Total Fat	0g	0%
Saturated Fat	0g	0%
Trans Fat	0g	
Cholesterol	0mg	0%
Sodium	0mg	0%
Potassium	110mg	
Total Carbohydrate	2g	1%
Dietary Fiber	1g	4%
Sugar	0g	
Protein	0g	
Vitamin A		4%
Vitamin C		70%
Calcium		0%
Iron		2%

Bitter Melon
Serving Size: 1/2 cup/125ml (47g)

Calories	10	
Total Fat	0g	0%
Saturated Fat	0g	0%
Trans Fat	0g	
Cholesterol	0mg	0%
Sodium	0mg	0%
Potassium	140mg	
Total Carbohydrate	2g	1%
Dietary Fiber	1g	4%
Sugar	0g	
Protein	0g	
Vitamin A		4%
Vitamin C		70%
Calcium		0%
Iron		2%

Calabaza
Serving Size: 1/2 cup/125ml (140g)

Calories	60	
Total Fat	1g	2%
Saturated Fat	0g	0%
Trans Fat	0g	
Cholesterol	0mg	0%
Sodium	0mg	0%
Potassium	400mg	
Total Carbohydrate	15g	5%
Dietary Fiber	1g	4%
Sugar	1g	
Protein	2g	
Vitamin A		200%
Vitamin C		45%
Calcium		n/a
Iron		n/a

Boniato
Serving Size: 1/2 cup/125ml (70g)

Calories	60	
Total Fat	0g	0%
Saturated Fat	0g	0%
Trans Fat	0g	
Cholesterol	0mg	0%
Sodium	8mg	1%
Potassium	20mg	
Total Carbohydrate	20g	4%
Dietary Fiber	2g	8%
Sugar	0g	
Protein	1g	
Vitamin A		0%
Vitamin C		25%
Calcium		0%
Iron		2%

Cardoon
Serving Size: 1/2 cup/125ml (89g)

Calories	20	
Total Fat	0g	0%
Saturated Fat	0g	0%
Trans Fat	0g	
Cholesterol	0mg	0%
Sodium	150mg	6%
Potassium	360mg	
Total Carbohydrate	4g	1%
Dietary Fiber	1g	4%
Sugar	2g	
Protein	1g	
Vitamin A		2%
Vitamin C		2%
Calcium		6%
Iron		4%

Breadfruit
Serving Size: 1/2 cup/125ml (110g)

Calories	110	
Total Fat	0g	0%
Saturated Fat	0g	0%
Trans Fat	0g	
Cholesterol	0mg	0%
Sodium	0mg	0%
Potassium	540mg	
Total Carbohydrate	30g	10%
Dietary Fiber	5g	20%
Sugar	12g	
Protein	1g	
Vitamin A		0%
Vitamin C		50%
Calcium		2%
Iron		4%

Choy Sum
Serving Size: 1/2 cup/125ml (43g)

Calories	10	
Total Fat	0g	0%
Saturated Fat	0g	0%
Trans Fat	0g	
Cholesterol	0mg	0%
Sodium	10mg	0%
Potassium	90mg	
Total Carbohydrate	2g	1%
Dietary Fiber	0g	0%
Sugar	0g	
Protein	1g	
Vitamin A		90%
Vitamin C		90%
Calcium		10%
Iron		4%

Ethnic Vegetables

Americans are adopting traditional recipes and cooking styles from Asia, Latin America, the Caribbean, and the Mediterranean and making them their own. This has, in turn, spurred growing demand for specialty and ethnic produce. Food retailers have responded by providing a dazzling array of fresh vegetables from every corner of the globe. Trying just one new item a week is an easy way to expand your repertoire of healthy, low-calorie foods and introduce your family to a world of flavor.

Gai Choy/ Chinese Mustard

Gai choy is a type of cabbage with dark green leaves that form in a loose head and have a strong, mustardy flavor. It's high in vitamins A and C. Look for firm, blemish-free heads, wrap in plastic, and refrigerate for up to a week. Young, tender gai choy is milder and can be added to salads. Try using gai choy in soups, or stir-fry with beef, garlic, ginger, and other vegetables.

Gai Lan/Chinese Broccoli/Chinese Kale

Gai lan is also called Chinese broccoli or Chinese kale, and it's a good source of vitamin C. It has green leaves and stalks, sometimes with white buds or flowers, and a sweet broccoli-like flavor. Wrap loosely and store unwashed in the refrigerator for several days. Gai lan cooks quickly and can be steamed or boiled. Substitute for broccoli in Chinese recipes, add to soups, or chop and stir-fry with Chinese long beans and enoki mushrooms.

Gil Choy/ Chinese Chives

Gil choy, or Chinese chives, have flat, grass-like leaves that grow up to ten inches long. It has a strong, garlicky-chive flavor and petite, edible, white flowers. Select brightly colored gil choy, tightly wrap, and refrigerate for up to four days. Use interchangeably with chives.

Gobo Root/ Burdock

Gobo is the Japanese name for burdock, a high-fiber root vegetable popular in Japan. Burdock roots are long, slender, and brown; the flesh is tender-crisp. Young burdock has the best sweet earthy flavor; look for roots less than eighteen inches long. Wrap roots in plastic and store unwashed in the refrigerator for up to four days. Scrub, but don't peel, before using. Cook with other vegetables or grains. Or, try a traditional Japanese favorite: lightly sauté burdock and carrot, then cook with sugar and soy sauce and sprinkle with sesame seeds.

Jicama

Jicama is a large (up to four pounds), round root vegetable, with crunchy, white flesh that tastes nutty and sweet. It's a source of vitamin C and can be used either raw or cooked. Look for firm, smooth roots. Wrap in plastic and refrigerate for up to two weeks. Peel the thin brown skin before using. Grate jicama and add to salads, or substitute for water chestnuts. Or, for Latin-inspired crudités, cut jicama into sticks and sprinkle with fresh lime juice and chile powder.

Kan Choy/Chinese Celery

Kan choy, or Chinese celery, is juicy, strong flavored, and aromatic, with thin, hollow ribs and an abundance of leaves. Store in a plastic bag in the refrigerator. Kan choy ribs are usually cooked with vegetables; add them to soups, casseroles, or stir-fries, or substitute for celery in other dishes. Use the leaves as an herb.

Lo Bok

Lo bok is related to daikon and other Asian radishes. The roots can be long (between one and two feet) and weigh up to five pounds. The skin is pale green at the top and beige at the root end. The flesh is white, crisp, and juicy, with a sharp flavor. Select firm and smooth roots; wrap tightly and refrigerate for up to a week. Grate lo bok and serve raw in salads, or add to soups or stir-fries.

Malanga

Malanga is a tuber from the West Indies that's sometimes confused with the distantly related and better known taro. Malanga has a tough, shaggy brown or yellowish-brown skin. Its yellow or ivory flesh has a smooth, nutty flavor and is a source of calcium, riboflavin, and thiamine. It varies in shape and may weigh up to two pounds. Some varieties are grown for their leaves, which are used like spinach in the Caribbean. Look for firm tubers free of blemishes or soft spots. Store in a cool, dry spot for up to a week. Malanga is usually peeled and boiled. Use it to thicken soups or thin puréed malanga with hot milk and serve with sugar and nutmeg.

Opo

Opo squash, also called bottle gourd, belongs to the cucumber family. The skin ranges from yellow to chartreuse, and the flesh is white, with small, edible seeds. This long squash grows in the shape of a baseball bat and tastes like a cross between cucumber and zucchini. The flavor grows increasingly bitter as the squash matures. Wrap in plastic and refrigerate for no more than four days. Grate and add to salads, or steam, bake, boil, microwave, or sauté. Use in stir-fries, soups, stews, casseroles, or other dishes.

Nutrition Facts

SOURCE: USDA

Ethnic Vegetables

Gai Choy/Chinese Mustard
Serving Size: 1/2 cup/125ml (125g)
Calories 10
Total Fat ....0g 0%
   Saturated Fat ....0g 0%
   Trans Fat 0g
Cholesterol ....0mg 0%
Sodium ....10mg 0%
Potassium 0mg
Total Carbohydrate ......2g 1%
   Dietary Fiber ....1g 4%
   Sugar 0g
Protein 1g
Vitamin A 45%
Vitamin C 50%
Calcium 4%
Iron 2%

Gai Lan/Chinese Broccoli
Serving Size: 1/2 cup/125ml (28g)
Calories 5
Total Fat ....0g 0%
   Saturated Fat ....0g 0%
   Trans Fat 0g
Cholesterol ....0mg 0%
Sodium ....10mg 0%
Potassium 60mg
Total Carbohydrate ......1g 0%
   Dietary Fiber ....0g 0%
   Sugar 0g
Protein 0g
Vitamin A 8%
Vitamin C 30%
Calcium 2%
Iron 2%

Gil Choy/Chinese Chives
Serving Size: 1/2 cup/125ml (32g)
Calories 0
Total Fat ....0g 0%
   Saturated Fat ....0g 0%
   Trans Fat 0g
Cholesterol ....0mg 0%
Sodium ....0mg 0%
Potassium ....n/a
Total Carbohydrate ......0g 0%
   Dietary Fiber ....0g 0%
   Sugar 0g
Protein 0g
Vitamin A 30%
Vitamin C 30%
Calcium 0%
Iron 0%

Gobo Root/Burdock
Serving Size: 1/2 cup/125ml (59g)
Calories 40
Total Fat ....0g 0%
   Saturated Fat ....0g 0%
   Trans Fat 0g
Cholesterol ....0mg 0%
Sodium ....0mg 0%
Potassium 190mg
Total Carbohydrate ....10g 3%
   Dietary Fiber ....2g 8%
   Sugar 2g
Protein 1g
Vitamin A 0%
Vitamin C 2%
Calcium 2%
Iron 2%

Jicama
Serving Size: 1/2 cup/125ml (65g)
Calories 25
Total Fat ....0g 0%
   Saturated Fat ....0g 0%
   Trans Fat 0g
Cholesterol ....0mg 0%
Sodium ....0mg 0%
Potassium 100mg
Total Carbohydrate ......6g 2%
   Dietary Fiber ....3g 12%
   Sugar 1g
Protein 0g
Vitamin A 0%
Vitamin C 20%
Calcium 0%
Iron 2%

Kan Choy/Chinese Celery
Serving Size: 1 ounce (26g)
Calories 5
Total Fat ....0g 0%
   Saturated Fat ....0g 0%
   Trans Fat 0g
Cholesterol ....0mg 0%
Sodium ....45mg 2%
Potassium 90mg
Total Carbohydrate ......1g 0%
   Dietary Fiber ....1g 4%
   Sugar 0g
Protein 1g
Vitamin A 15%
Vitamin C 25%
Calcium 8%
Iron 20%

Lo Bok
Serving Size: 1/2 cup/125ml (64g)
Calories 20
Total Fat ....0g 0%
   Saturated Fat ....0g 0%
   Trans Fat 0g
Cholesterol ....0mg 0%
Sodium ....40mg 2%
Potassium 40mg
Total Carbohydrate ......4g 1%
   Dietary Fiber ....2g 8%
   Sugar 2g
Protein 1g
Vitamin A 0%
Vitamin C 25%
Calcium 2%
Iron 0%

Malanga
Serving Size: 1/2 cup/125ml (70g)
Calories 70
Total Fat ....0g 0%
   Saturated Fat ....0g 0%
   Trans Fat 0g
Cholesterol ....0mg 0%
Sodium ....0mg 0%
Potassium ....n/a
Total Carbohydrate ....17g 6%
   Dietary Fiber ....1g 4%
   Sugar 15g
Protein 2g
Vitamin A 0%
Vitamin C 6%
Calcium 6%
Iron 2%

Opo
Serving Size: 1/2 cup/125ml (64g)
Calories 10
Total Fat ....0g 0%
   Saturated Fat ....0g 0%
   Trans Fat 0g
Cholesterol ....0mg 0%
Sodium ....0mg 0%
Potassium 0mg
Total Carbohydrate ......2g 1%
   Dietary Fiber ....0g 0%
   Sugar 0g
Protein 1g
Vitamin A 0%
Vitamin C 10%
Calcium 2%
Iron 0%

Ethnic Vegetables

Salsify

Salsify is a favorite European root vegetable. There are several varieties, but the most common has grayish skin and a white flesh. Salsify is also called oyster plant because of its delicate oyster (although some say artichoke) flavor. The parsnip-shaped root may be up to a foot long; select those that are heavy for their size and not too bumpy. Wrap in plastic and refrigerate for up to two weeks. You can remove the skin after cooking. Or, if you prefer to peel before using, dip each piece in acidulated water to prevent browning and wear rubber gloves to keep the salsify from staining your hands. Salsify can be steamed or braised. Boil until tender (10 to 15 minutes), and then sauté in olive oil with fresh thyme and snipped chives for a simple side dish.

Sin Qua/Chinese Okra

Sin qua, also called Chinese okra (although it's not related to okra), is used in Chinese cooking. It has a dull green skin with deep ribs that create a star shape when sliced. Sin qua tastes like a faintly bitter cross between zucchini and cucumber. This squash can grow up to a foot long; when fully mature, some varieties are harvested to make natural loofah sponges. Look for those that are no more than eight inches long, and refrigerate for up to a week. Prepare like zucchini, and then steam, braise, sauté, or stir-fry or add raw slices to salads.

Tamarillo

The tamarillo, also called the tree tomato, is egg shaped and may be a glossy red, purple, or yellow. The succulent flesh is apricot colored and surrounds tiny, edible, black seeds. It's a good source of vitamins A and C. Look for firm, unblemished, and fragrant tamarillos that are heavy for their size and that yield slightly to pressure. Wrap in plastic and refrigerate for up to two weeks. Peel the tough skin before using. Sweeten with sugar, and then add raw to fruit compotes or cook and use in sauces, chutneys, relishes, or curries.

Tamarind

The tamarind, or the Indian date, is a brown, bean-like pod that encases small seeds and a reddish-brown pulp. The pulp has a sweet-tart, fruity flavor that turns quite sour when dried. It's used as a flavoring in East Indian and Middle Eastern cooking and is an important ingredient in Worcestershire sauce. Use tamarind instead of lemon juice or vinegar to give an authentic flavor to beverages, curries, chutneys, or other dishes.

Taro Root

Taro is a potato-like tropical tuber that's a staple in West Africa, the Caribbean, and the Polynesian islands (it's used to make poi, the famous Hawaiian dish). It can be up to a foot long. Taro root has a rough brown skin and gray-white flesh that tastes slightly nutty when cooked. Taro leaves are also edible and can be cooked like turnip or mustard greens. Select firm, smooth roots, and refrigerate for up to four days. Taro can be used like potatoes in soups or stews or baked, boiled, or fried. It's too dry to serve mashed, though. Cook taro thoroughly; some varieties are toxic if undercooked.

Tomatillo

Tomatillos look like green cherry tomatoes wrapped in papery husks. They're also called Mexican green tomatoes. Select firm tomatillos with tight-fitting husks; refrigerate in a paper bag for up to a month. Tomatillos have a lemon-apple-herb flavor that works well in a variety of Mexican and Southwestern dishes. Use cooked tomatillos in *salsa verde* or guacamole, or slice and add raw to salads.

Winter Melon

Winter melon is a green muskmelon that resembles a honeydew melon, with white flesh that tastes like zucchini. Winter melons are large (they weigh up to thirty pounds) and are often sold by the slice. Whole melons keep in a cool place for several months; sliced melon should be used within two days. This fruit is used like a vegetable in Asia. Parboil and add to stir-fries, or steam, simmer, or braise. Try making a soup with it, or stir-fry with bamboo shoots, gingerroot, soy sauce, and a pinch of sugar.

Yuca/Cassava

Yuca, also called cassava or manioc, is a root vegetable with brown, bark-like skin and white flesh. It is a staple in Africa and is also widely used in Latin America and the Caribbean. Yuca may be sweet or bitter; bitter yuca is poisonous if undercooked or eaten raw. Sweet yuca is used to make tapioca. Look for firm, unblemished roots and refrigerate for up to four days. Sauté, boil, or stew yuca, or add to stir-fries, soups, or stews.

Herbs

Fresh herbs give a burst of flavor to grilled or roasted meats, salads, vegetables, soups, sauces, and even fruit without adding calories, fat, or salt.

Herbs have also been valued through the centuries for their medicinal properties, and our ancestors may have been on the right track. Preliminary research now indicates that many herbs possess antioxidant properties. Some, such as chives and parsley, are also a good source of vitamins — just one more reason to cook with them.

Select fresh, brightly colored herbs with a clean fragrance. Avoid wilted or brown herbs. Wrap most herbs with a slightly damp paper towel, seal in an airtight container, and refrigerate for up to five days. Place bunched herbs such as mint or parsley in a glass of water (like flowers in a vase), cover loosely with a plastic bag, and refrigerate for up to ten days (change the water every two days), depending on the variety. Rinse herbs and blot dry with paper towels just before using.

Nutrition Facts

SOURCE: USDA

Ethnic Vegetables

Salsify
Serving Size: 1/2 cup/125ml (67g)

Calories		50
Total Fat	0g	0%
Saturated Fat	0g	0%
Trans Fat	0g	
Cholesterol	0mg	0%
Sodium	15mg	1%
Potassium	260mg	
Total Carbohydrate	12g	4%
Dietary Fiber	2g	8%
Sugar	2g	
Protein	2g	
Vitamin A		0%
Vitamin C		8%
Calcium		4%
Iron		2%

Taro Root
Serving Size: 1/2 cup/125ml (52g)

Calories		60
Total Fat	0g	0%
Saturated Fat	0g	0%
Trans Fat	0g	
Cholesterol	0mg	0%
Sodium	5mg	0%
Potassium	310mg	
Total Carbohydrate	14g	5%
Dietary Fiber	2g	8%
Sugar	0g	
Protein	1g	
Vitamin A		0%
Vitamin C		4%
Calcium		2%
Iron		2%

Sin Qua/Chinese Okra
Serving Size: 1/2 cup/150ml (89g)

Calories		30
Total Fat	0g	0%
Saturated Fat	0g	0%
Trans Fat	0g	
Cholesterol	0mg	0%
Sodium	0mg	0%
Potassium	290mg	
Total Carbohydrate	6g	2%
Dietary Fiber	2g	8%
Sugar	n/a	
Protein	2g	
Vitamin A		10%
Vitamin C		25%
Calcium		6%
Iron		2%

Tomatillo
Serving Size: 1 medium (34g)

Calories		10
Total Fat	0g	0%
Saturated Fat	0g	0%
Trans Fat	0g	
Cholesterol	0mg	0%
Sodium	0mg	0%
Potassium	90mg	
Total Carbohydrate	2g	1%
Dietary Fiber	1g	4%
Sugar	1g	
Protein	0g	
Vitamin A		0%
Vitamin C		6%
Calcium		0%
Iron		2%

Tamarillo
Serving Size: 1 medium (140g)

Calories		35
Total Fat	0g	0%
Saturated Fat	0g	0%
Trans Fat	0g	
Cholesterol	0mg	0%
Sodium	0mg	0%
Potassium	392mg	
Total Carbohydrate	8g	3%
Dietary Fiber	2g	8%
Sugar	5g	
Protein	7g	
Vitamin A		150%
Vitamin C		35%
Calcium		0%
Iron		2%

Winter Melon
Serving Size: 1/2 cup/125ml (66g)

Calories		10
Total Fat	0g	0%
Saturated Fat	0g	0%
Trans Fat	0g	
Cholesterol	0mg	0%
Sodium	75mg	3%
Potassium	4mg	
Total Carbohydrate	3g	1%
Dietary Fiber	1g	4%
Sugar	1g	
Protein	0g	
Vitamin A		0%
Vitamin C		15%
Calcium		2%
Iron		2%

Tamarind
Serving Size: 1 medium (2g)

Calories		5
Total Fat	0g	0%
Saturated Fat	0g	0%
Trans Fat	0g	
Cholesterol	0mg	0%
Sodium	0mg	0%
Potassium	15mg	
Total Carbohydrate	1g	0%
Dietary Fiber	0g	0%
Sugar	1g	
Protein	0g	
Vitamin A		0%
Vitamin C		0%
Calcium		0%
Iron		0%

Yuca/Cassava
Serving Size: 1/2 cup/125ml (103g)

Calories		160
Total Fat	0g	0%
Saturated Fat	0g	0%
Trans Fat	0g	
Cholesterol	0mg	0%
Sodium	15mg	1%
Potassium	280mg	
Total Carbohydrate	39g	13%
Dietary Fiber	2g	8%
Sugar	2g	
Protein	1g	
Vitamin A		0%
Vitamin C		35%
Calcium		2%
Iron		2%

1 Basil

Basil belongs to the mint family and is highly aromatic. The many varieties of basil include lemon, anise, clove, and cinnamon, whose names match their flavor or fragrance. Basil is a key ingredient in pesto, and it's delicious with pasta or pizza. Make a classic Italian summer salad with ripe tomatoes, fresh basil, fresh mozzarella, and a drizzle of olive oil.

2 Bay Leaf

Bay leaf is an aromatic and spicy native of the Mediterranean that is widely used in French, Moroccan, and Turkish cooking. Fresh bay leaves are sometimes available; dried are more common. Try using it in soups, stews, stock, or poultry or tomato dishes. Remove before serving.

3 Chervil

Chervil, like other members of the parsley family, has green, lacy leaves. Its delicate flavor offers hints of parsley and anise, and it is essential to French cuisine. Fresh chervil is stronger than dried. Use like parsley, combine with other herbs in blends like *fines herbes*, or try with asparagus, pasta, or ham.

Tasty Idea

Make iced mint tea for a refreshing twist on traditional iced tea. Simply pour hot water over tea bags and a handful of fresh mint leaves (reserve some for a garnish). Let tea steep for five minutes. Remove tea bags and stir in sugar to taste, if desired. Allow the fresh mint leaves to steep for five more minutes. Remove mint leaves. Serve tea over ice, garnished with sprigs of fresh mint.

4 Chives

Chives are related to onions, but they have a milder flavor. The slender, reed-like, and bright green stems can be snipped (use kitchen scissors) over potato salad, stir-fries, egg dishes, soups, or vegetable casseroles. The pale purple flowers are also edible.

5 Cilantro

Cilantro's green leaves and tender stems come from the coriander plant, and it sometimes goes by that name. The distinctively pungent flavor is sometimes described as "soapy." Cilantro is an important ingredient in Asian, Latin American, and Caribbean cooking, and it provides a fresh contrast to spicy foods. Use in salsa, bean dip, chutney, or salads.

6 Dill

Fresh dill's green and feathery leaves, also called dill weed, have a subtle flavor that fades when cooked. Dill seeds are also edible, and they have a strong taste that intensifies with cooking. Dill seeds are often used in pickling. Try sprinkling fresh dill weed over green beans, carrots, poultry, eggs, lamb, or potatoes. Or, make a dressing for sliced cucumbers with fresh dill, chopped garlic, and fat-free plain yogurt.

7 Galangal

Galangal has a gingery-peppery to spicy hot flavor, and the rhizome is essential to Thai cooking. Greater galangal is the most common variety sold in the U.S., and its white flesh is often substituted for gingerroot. Galangal is often used in Thai soups and curries; elsewhere in Southeast Asia, it's combined with garlic, ginger, chile, and lemon or tamarind and served with seafood.

Nutrition Facts

SOURCE: USDA

Herbs

Basil
Serving Size: 4 teaspoons (4g)

Calories		0
Total Fat	0g	0%
Saturated Fat	0g	0%
Trans Fat	0g	
Cholesterol	0mg	0%
Sodium	0mg	0%
Potassium	20mg	
Total Carbohydrate	0g	0%
Dietary Fiber	0g	0%
Sugar	0g	
Protein	0g	
Vitamin A		4%
Vitamin C		2%
Calcium		0%
Iron		0%

Bay Leaf
Serving Size: 4 teaspoons (4g)

Calories		15
Total Fat	0g	0%
Saturated Fat	0g	0%
Trans Fat	0g	
Cholesterol	0mg	0%
Sodium	0mg	0%
Potassium	24mg	
Total Carbohydrate	3g	1%
Dietary Fiber	1g	4%
Sugar	0g	
Protein	0g	
Vitamin A		4%
Vitamin C		4%
Calcium		4%
Iron		10%

Chervil
Serving Size: 1 tablespoon (4g)

Calories		0
Total Fat	0g	0%
Saturated Fat	0g	0%
Trans Fat	0g	
Cholesterol	0mg	0%
Sodium	0mg	0%
Potassium	0mg	
Total Carbohydrate	1g	0%
Dietary Fiber	0g	0%
Sugar	0g	
Protein	0g	
Vitamin A		0%
Vitamin C		0%
Calcium		0%
Iron		0%

Chives
Serving Size: 1 tablespoon (4g)

Calories		0
Total Fat	0g	0%
Saturated Fat	0g	0%
Trans Fat	0g	
Cholesterol	0mg	0%
Sodium	0mg	0%
Potassium	10mg	
Total Carbohydrate	0g	0%
Dietary Fiber	0g	0%
Sugar	0g	
Protein	0g	
Vitamin A		4%
Vitamin C		4%
Calcium		0%
Iron		0%

Cilantro
Serving Size: 4 tablespoons (4g)

Calories		0
Total Fat	0g	0%
Saturated Fat	0g	0%
Trans Fat	0g	
Cholesterol	0mg	0%
Sodium	0mg	0%
Potassium	20mg	
Total Carbohydrate	0g	0%
Dietary Fiber	0g	0%
Sugar	0g	
Protein	0g	
Vitamin A		6%
Vitamin C		2%
Calcium		0%
Iron		0%

Dill
Serving Size: 4 tablespoons (4g)

Calories		0
Total Fat	0g	0%
Saturated Fat	0g	0%
Trans Fat	0g	
Cholesterol	0mg	0%
Sodium	0mg	0%
Potassium	30mg	
Total Carbohydrate	0g	0%
Dietary Fiber	0g	0%
Sugar	0g	
Protein	0g	
Vitamin A		6%
Vitamin C		6%
Calcium		0%
Iron		2%

Galangal
Serving Size: 1 tablespoon (4g)

Calories		5
Total Fat	0g	0%
Saturated Fat	0g	0%
Trans Fat	0g	
Cholesterol	0mg	0%
Sodium	0mg	0%
Potassium	10mg	
Total Carbohydrate	1g	0%
Dietary Fiber	0g	0%
Sugar	0g	
Protein	0g	
Vitamin A		0%
Vitamin C		0%
Calcium		0%
Iron		0%

Herbs

Add fresh herbs near the end of cooking, because heat causes the essential oils and flavors to dissipate. When using herbs in recipes that don't require cooking, refrigerate the final dish for two hours to allow the flavors to mingle.

Fresh herbs can also be substituted for dried. Double the amount called for in the recipe, taste, and then add more if desired. Leftover fresh herbs can also be dried or frozen for later use.

Garlic

Garlic belongs to the lily family; its cousins include onions, shallots, and leeks. The bulb or head is made up of individual cloves with white or purple parchment-like skins. Some varieties are about the size of a marble, while others are as large as an orange. Select firm, plump heads with tight cloves and dry skin. Avoid shriveled, sprouting, or moldy bulbs. Store whole heads in a cool, dry, and dark spot (not the refrigerator) for up to two months. Individual cloves can be stored for three to ten days. Garlic is pungent, aromatic, and versatile. Peel and mince, chop, or slice as many cloves as you like, and then add them to salad dressings or soups, sauté with vegetables, or roast with chicken. Try roasting whole heads of garlic, and then pop the mellowed and nutty cloves from their skins to spread on rustic breads instead of butter.

Gingerroot

Gingerroot is a knobby, tan rhizome with pale greenish-yellow to ivory flesh. Mature ginger must be peeled; young ginger (also called spring ginger) does not. Look for smooth roots with a fresh fragrance. Tightly wrapped roots can be refrigerated for three weeks or frozen for six months. Gingerroot's assertive flavor is at once peppery, spicy, and slightly sweet. It's essential in Asian and Indian cookery, where it's used in salads, chutneys, sauces, and meat and seafood dishes. Dried, ground ginger has a completely different character and cannot be substituted for fresh.

Horseradish

Horseradish is an ancient herb and one of the five bitter herbs of the Jewish Passover festival. Its large, white, pungent, and spicy roots are typically grated and used as a condiment or in sauces. Look for firm, smooth, and unblemished roots; peel before using. Try adding horseradish to mashed potatoes, beans, or lamb stew. Mix with fat-free sour cream or plain yogurt to make a sauce for roasted meats.

Lemon Grass

Lemon grass has a bulbous base with long, thin grayish-green leaves, and it looks something like a large scallion. It contains an essential oil also found in lemon rind, which gives it a similar lemon-like tartness and aroma. Look for blemish-free stalks, with bright leaves and a white base. Refrigerate lemon grass in a plastic bag for up to two weeks. Use the bulb in Thai- or Vietnamese-style soups, curries, vegetable dishes, pickles, salads, or marinades.

Marjoram

Marjoram is related to oregano, but it has a milder, sweeter flavor. Sweet marjoram is the most familiar variety, and it has pale green, velvety, oval leaves. It is widely used in Italian, French, North African, and Middle Eastern cooking. Try using marjoram to season legumes, corn, eggplant, pasta, tomatoes, lamb, or veal. It can also be substituted for oregano.

Mint

Mint is aromatic, with a not-unexpected cool and refreshing aftertaste. Peppermint and spearmint are the most common of the more than thirty mint species. Peppermint has bright green leaves and purple stems; it's more pungent than the gray-green spearmint. Mint is used in kitchens around the world, and it enlivens fruit salads, iced tea, tabbouleh, or steamed vegetables—try it with peas, corn, carrots, or potatoes.

Oregano

Oregano's flavor is similar to, but stronger than, marjoram's. Mediterranean oregano has bright green leaves and is often sold fresh. Mexican oregano is more pungent and is usually dried. Try adding fresh oregano to Italian or Mediterranean recipes, pasta or salmon dishes, steamed summer squash or other vegetables, or anything made with tomatoes.

Parsley

Parsley is high in vitamins A and C, and so is as healthful as it is attractive. Italian (or flat-leaf) and curly-leaf parsley are the best known varieties of this universal herb. Italian parsley is more strongly flavored, but both lend a peppery freshness to all kinds of foods. Parsley is a key ingredient in Middle Eastern dishes such as tabbouleh and in gremolata, an Italian garnish made with lemon peel and garlic and served with meats. Add parsley to mashed potatoes, use the stalks in stock, or mince and sprinkle over grilled fish.

Parsley Root

Parsley root is grown especially for its creamy beige roots, which taste like a cross between carrots and celery. Select firm roots (they look like mini-parsnips) with feathery, bright green leaves. Wrap in a plastic bag and refrigerate for up to a week. Purée and mix with mashed potatoes, or add to carrots, onions, or root vegetables. Bonus: the leaves can be used like any other type of parsley.

Nutrition Facts
SOURCE: USDA

Herbs

Garlic
Serving Size: 1 medium clove (4g)

Calories		5
Total Fat	0g	0%
Saturated Fat	0g	0%
Trans Fat		0g
Cholesterol	0mg	0%
Sodium	0mg	0%
Potassium		16mg
Total Carbohydrate	1g	0%
Dietary Fiber	0g	0%
Sugar		0g
Protein		0g
Vitamin A		0%
Vitamin C		2%
Calcium		0%
Iron		0%

Gingerroot
Serving Size: 2 teaspoons (4g)

Calories		5
Total Fat	0g	0%
Saturated Fat	0g	0%
Trans Fat		0g
Cholesterol	0mg	0%
Sodium	0mg	0%
Potassium		20mg
Total Carbohydrate	1g	0%
Dietary Fiber	0g	0%
Sugar		0g
Protein		0g
Vitamin A		0%
Vitamin C		0%
Calcium		0%
Iron		0%

Horseradish
Serving Size: 1 teaspoon (4g)

Calories		5
Total Fat	0g	0%
Saturated Fat	0g	0%
Trans Fat		0g
Cholesterol	0mg	0%
Sodium	0mg	0%
Potassium		20mg
Total Carbohydrate	1g	0%
Dietary Fiber	0g	0%
Sugar		0g
Protein		0g
Vitamin A		0%
Vitamin C		0%
Calcium		0%
Iron		0%

Lemon Grass
Serving Size: 3 teaspoons (4g)

Calories		5
Total Fat	0g	0%
Saturated Fat	0g	0%
Trans Fat		0g
Cholesterol	0mg	0%
Sodium	0mg	0%
Potassium		30mg
Total Carbohydrate	1g	0%
Dietary Fiber	0g	0%
Sugar		0g
Protein		0g
Vitamin A		0%
Vitamin C		0%
Calcium		0%
Iron		2%

Marjoram
Serving Size: 1 tablespoon (4g)

Calories		0
Total Fat	0g	0%
Saturated Fat	0g	0%
Trans Fat		0g
Cholesterol	0mg	0%
Sodium	0mg	0%
Potassium		n/a
Total Carbohydrate	0g	0%
Dietary Fiber	0g	0%
Sugar		0g
Protein		1g
Vitamin A		n/a
Vitamin C		4%
Calcium		n/a
Iron		n/a

Mint
Serving Size: 2 teaspoons (4g)

Calories		0
Total Fat	0g	0%
Saturated Fat	0g	0%
Trans Fat		0g
Cholesterol	0mg	0%
Sodium	0mg	0%
Potassium		20mg
Total Carbohydrate	0g	0%
Dietary Fiber	0g	0%
Sugar		0g
Protein		0g
Vitamin A		4%
Vitamin C		0%
Calcium		0%
Iron		2%

Oregano
Serving Size: 2 teaspoons (4g)

Calories		5
Total Fat	0g	0%
Saturated Fat	0g	0%
Trans Fat		0g
Cholesterol	0mg	0%
Sodium	0mg	0%
Potassium		15mg
Total Carbohydrate	0g	0%
Dietary Fiber	0g	0%
Sugar		0g
Protein		0g
Vitamin A		2%
Vitamin C		4%
Calcium		2%
Iron		0%

Parsley
Serving Size: 1 tablespoon (4g)

Calories		0
Total Fat	0g	0%
Saturated Fat	0g	0%
Trans Fat		0g
Cholesterol	0mg	0%
Sodium	0mg	0%
Potassium		25mg
Total Carbohydrate	0g	0%
Dietary Fiber	0g	0%
Sugar		0g
Protein		0g
Vitamin A		6%
Vitamin C		8%
Calcium		0%
Iron		2%

Parsley Root
Serving Size: 1 1/2 teaspoons (4g)

Calories		0
Total Fat	0g	0%
Saturated Fat	0g	0%
Trans Fat		0g
Cholesterol	0mg	0%
Sodium	0mg	0%
Potassium		10mg
Total Carbohydrate	0g	0%
Dietary Fiber	0g	0%
Sugar		0g
Protein		0g
Vitamin A		0%
Vitamin C		0%
Calcium		0%
Iron		0%

Herbs

Rosemary

Rosemary, a Mediterranean native, has an assertive flavor with a hint of pine and lemon. The tough needles are silvery green and needle-like; strip them from their branches before using. Try chopped, fresh rosemary with roasted lamb, pork, or potatoes. Or, thread chunks of chicken, pork, or seafood on rosemary "skewers" and grill.

Sage

Sage has oval, slightly furry, gray-green leaves. They are powerful, slightly bitter, and taste a little like musty mint. Sage is a traditional ingredient in sausage or poultry stuffing, but it also works well in pork, cheese, and bean dishes. Or, try sautéing sage leaves in a small amount of butter until crisp and lightly browned, and then using both the leaves and infused butter as a light sauce for gnocchi. Pineapple sage has a delicate, tropical, and slightly sweet flavor; use it in fruit salads and cold soups.

Savory

There are two primary kinds of savory: summer and winter. Summer savory is milder, but both have an assertive taste reminiscent of mint and thyme. Use savory in soups or stews, or add to hearty meat, bean, or vegetable dishes.

Sorrel

Sorrel, a member of the buckwheat family, is a source of vitamin A. It has spinach-like leaves and a lemony tang that sharpens as it matures, although some varieties are quite acidic to begin with. Use in salads, cream soups, or omelets. Or, cook tender, young sorrel leaves like spinach (but don't use a metal or iron pan, which will impart a metallic taste).

Tarragon

Tarragon's narrow, pointed leaves are dark green and have a distinctive, anise-like flavor. It holds up well during cooking, but can overwhelm other ingredients, so use it judiciously. Tarragon is used in classic French sauces (béarnaise is the most famous) and dishes, and it combines well with tomatoes, artichokes, and squash.

Thyme

Thyme is one of the most widely used herbs, and garden thyme is the most familiar variety. It has tiny, pale green leaves and a minty, citrusy aroma. Thyme enhances meats, fish, poultry, seafood, and vegetables and is often used in classic French herb combinations such as *bouquet garni* and *herbes de Provence*.

Nutrition Facts

SOURCE: USDA

Herbs

Rosemary
Serving Size: 2 tablespoons (4g)

Calories		5
Total Fat	0g	0%
Saturated Fat	0g	0%
Trans Fat	0g	
Cholesterol	0mg	0%
Sodium	0mg	0%
Potassium	30mg	
Total Carbohydrate	1g	0%
Dietary Fiber	1g	4%
Sugar	0g	
Protein	0g	
Vitamin A		2%
Vitamin C		2%
Calcium		2%
Iron		2%

Sorrel
Serving Size: 1 1/2 teaspoons (4g)

Calories		0
Total Fat	0g	0%
Saturated Fat	0g	0%
Trans Fat	0g	
Cholesterol	0mg	0%
Sodium	0mg	0%
Potassium	15mg	
Total Carbohydrate	0g	0%
Dietary Fiber	0g	0%
Sugar	0g	
Protein	0g	
Vitamin A		4%
Vitamin C		4%
Calcium		0%
Iron		0%

Sage
Serving Size: 2 tablespoons (4g)

Calories		5
Total Fat	0g	0%
Saturated Fat	0g	0%
Trans Fat	0g	
Cholesterol	0mg	0%
Sodium	0mg	0%
Potassium	15mg	
Total Carbohydrate	1g	0%
Dietary Fiber	0g	0%
Sugar	0g	
Protein	0g	
Vitamin A		2%
Vitamin C		0%
Calcium		2%
Iron		0%

Tarragon
Serving Size: 2 teaspoons (4g)

Calories		10
Total Fat	0g	0%
Saturated Fat	0g	0%
Trans Fat	0g	
Cholesterol	0mg	0%
Sodium	0mg	0%
Potassium	120mg	
Total Carbohydrate	2g	1%
Dietary Fiber	0g	0%
Sugar	0g	
Protein	1g	
Vitamin A		4%
Vitamin C		4%
Calcium		4%
Iron		8%

Savory
Serving Size: 2 teaspoons (4g)

Calories		10
Total Fat	0g	0%
Saturated Fat	0g	0%
Trans Fat	0g	
Cholesterol	0mg	0%
Sodium	0mg	0%
Potassium	45mg	
Total Carbohydrate	3g	1%
Dietary Fiber	2g	8%
Sugar	0g	
Protein	0g	
Vitamin A		4%
Vitamin C		4%
Calcium		8%
Iron		8%

Thyme
Serving Size: 5 teaspoons (4g)

Calories		5
Total Fat	0g	0%
Saturated Fat	0g	0%
Trans Fat	0g	
Cholesterol	0mg	0%
Sodium	0mg	0%
Potassium	25mg	
Total Carbohydrate	1g	0%
Dietary Fiber	1g	4%
Sugar	0	
Protein	0g	
Vitamin A		4%
Vitamin C		10%
Calcium		2%
Iron		4%

the recipes

"The discovery of a new dish does more for human happiness than the discovery of a star." — *Jean Anthelme Brillat-Savarin, 1825*

If Brillat-Savarin were writing these words today, he might go a step further and argue that the discovery of a new dish that's both high in flavor and healthy creates more happiness than the discovery of a new universe.

This collection of recipes incorporates the complex flavors, aromas, tastes, and textures of fresh produce in quick and easy-to-make dishes that are a feast for the senses and the palate. These recipes prove that you don't have to sacrifice flavor or skimp on satisfaction to eat healthy. They focus on staple fresh produce ingredients, as well as some you may not have discovered yet. You'll find hearty, mouth-watering dishes that are not only part of Dr. Richter's CommonSense Diet program, but also are sure to become a favorite part of your family's recipe collection. Enjoy!

Dr. Richter's
CommonSensediet

Pork Fried Rice

🕐 **PREP TIME:** 10 MINUTES   **COOK TIME:** 15 MINUTES

1   egg white, lightly beaten
3   oz. diced cooked pork
¼   cup diced red bell pepper
¼   cup diced onion
1   cup cooked brown rice
¼   cup frozen green peas, thawed
2   tbsp. low-salt soy sauce
1   tsp. Thai-style chili sauce
Sliced green onions (optional)

1. Heat a large skillet or wok coated with vegetable cooking spray over medium-high heat 2 minutes. Add egg white; cook 1 minute, stirring occasionally. Remove and set aside.

2. Heat vegetable cooking spray in skillet or wok. Add pork, and stir-fry 1 to 2 minutes or until golden. Add red bell pepper and onion; stir-fry 5 minutes. Add rice, peas, soy sauce, and chili sauce; stir-fry 3 to 4 minutes or until thoroughly heated. Stir in reserved egg. Sprinkle with green onions, if desired.

Serves 2

CALORIES: 240 • SATURATED FAT: 1G • SODIUM: 642MG
DIETARY FIBER: 3G

Raisin Bran Muffins

🕐 **PREP TIME:** 15 MINUTES   **COOK TIME:** 15 MINUTES

½   cup shred of wheat bran cereal (such as All-Bran®)
⅓   cup plus 2 tbsp. skim milk
¼   cup raisins
2   tbsp. honey
1   tbsp. vegetable oil
1   egg, lightly beaten
½   cup all-purpose flour
¾   tsp. baking powder
½   tsp. ground cinnamon
⅛   tsp. salt

1. Combine cereal and milk in a bowl; let stand 5 minutes. Add raisins, honey, oil, and egg; stir well.

2. Combine flour, baking powder, cinnamon, and salt in a bowl. Add flour mixture to cereal mixture, stirring just until moist.

3. Spoon batter into muffin cups coated with vegetable cooking spray, filling two-thirds full. Bake at 400°F for 12 to 15 minutes or until muffins spring back when touched lightly in center.

Serves 6

CALORIES: 166 • SATURATED FAT: 1G • SODIUM: 173MG
DIETARY FIBER: 3G

Cumin-Spiced Sirloin with Tomatillo Salsa

🕐 **PREP TIME:** 10 MINUTES   **COOK TIME:** 20 MINUTES

½   lb. fresh tomatillos, husked, rinsed, and chopped
½   jalapeño pepper, seeded and chopped
2   tbsp. chopped sweet onion
2   tbsp. chopped fresh cilantro
6   tsp. fresh lime juice, divided
2   cloves garlic, minced, divided
¼   tsp. salt, divided
¾   tsp. dried cumin
¾   lb. lean sirloin steak

1. For Tomatillo Salsa, combine tomatillos, jalapeño, onion, cilantro, 2 teaspoons lime juice, 1 clove garlic, and ⅛ teaspoon salt in a food processor; process until smooth.

2. Combine remaining 4 teaspoons lime juice, remaining 1 clove garlic, remaining ⅛ teaspoon salt, and cumin in a small bowl. Pour over steak. Marinate 30 minutes.

3. Grill steaks, covered with grill lid, over medium-high heat about 8 to 10 minutes on each side or to 160°F for medium doneness. Serve with Tomatillo Salsa.

Serves 3

Notes: *Use caution when handling hot peppers. Wear disposable gloves or wash hands thoroughly with hot, soapy water. To broil instead of grill, broil 5½ inches from heat (with door partially open) 6 to 8 minutes on each side or to 160°F for medium doneness.*

CALORIES: 193 • SATURATED FAT: 3G • SODIUM: 175MG
DIETARY FIBER: 1G

Veggie Black Bean Soup

🕐 **PREP TIME:** 15 MINUTES   **COOK TIME:** 15 MINUTES

½   small onion, chopped
½   cup chopped carrots
½   cup chopped celery
1   clove garlic, minced
⅛   tsp. freshly ground pepper
2   cups vegetable broth
2   cups fresh baby spinach
1   (14½-oz.) can crushed tomatoes
⅓   cup chickpeas, rinsed and drained
⅓   cup low-salt black beans, rinsed and drained
1   tbsp. chopped fresh thyme (optional)

1. Heat a large Dutch oven coated with vegetable cooking spray over medium heat. Add onion, carrots, celery, garlic, and pepper. Sauté 5 to 7 minutes or until vegetables are tender. Add broth, spinach, tomatoes, chickpeas, and black beans; bring to a boil. Cover, reduce heat, and simmer 10 minutes. Top with fresh thyme, if desired.

Serves 4

CALORIES: 95 • SATURATED FAT: 0G • SODIUM: 508MG
DIETARY FIBER: 6G

PORK FRIED RICE

CUMIN-SPICED SIRLOIN WITH TOMATILLO SALSA

RAISIN BRAN MUFFINS

VEGGIE BLACK BEAN SOUP

101

VEGETABLE BEAN TOSTADAS

Indonesian Chicken and Vegetable Kabobs

PREP TIME: 20 MINUTES   **COOK TIME:** 10 MINUTES

- ½ cup fresh lemon juice
- 1 tbsp. olive oil
- 2 cloves garlic, minced
- 2 tbsp. chopped fresh mint
- ½ tsp. salt
- ¼ tsp. freshly ground pepper
- ½ (6-oz.) pkg. portobello mushrooms, sliced
- ½ red bell pepper, cut into 1-inch pieces
- ½ red onion, cut into 1-inch pieces
- ½ lb. skinless, boneless chicken breasts, cut into 1-inch pieces

1. Combine lemon juice, olive oil, garlic, mint, salt, and pepper in a small bowl, stirring with a wire whisk.

2. Assemble 2 long or 4 short skewers, alternating mushrooms, red bell pepper, red onion, and chicken on each. Arrange skewers in a glass dish. Pour lemon juice mixture over kabobs. Cover and refrigerate 30 minutes.

3. Spray grill rack with vegetable cooking spray. Place skewers on grill; cover with grill lid and cook 5 to 7 minutes on each side or until a meat thermometer in chicken registers 170°F.

Serves 2

Note: To broil instead of grill, broil 5½ inches from heat (with door partially open) 4 to 6 minutes on each side or until a meat thermometer in chicken registers 170°F.

CALORIES: 270 • SATURATED FAT: 2G • SODIUM: 651MG
DIETARY FIBER: 2G

Vegetable Bean Tostadas

PREP TIME: 15 MINUTES   **COOK TIME:** 10 MINUTES

- 2 (6-inch) corn tortillas
- ½ cup sliced fresh mushrooms
- ½ cup chopped broccoli
- ½ cup shredded carrots
- ½ (14-oz.) can spicy vegetarian refried beans
- 1 plum tomato, diced
- ½ avocado, chopped
- 2 tbsp. reduced-fat shredded Mexican cheese
- 2 tbsp. fat-free sour cream

Sliced green onions (optional)

Chopped cilantro (optional)

1. Heat tortillas over medium heat in a large skillet coated with vegetable cooking spray. Sauté 30 seconds on each side or until golden.

2. Sauté mushrooms, broccoli, and carrots over medium heat 5 minutes or until vegetables are tender.

3. Spread refried beans over tortillas. Top evenly with mushroom mixture, tomato, avocado, cheese, and sour cream. Top with green onions and cilantro, if desired.

Serves 2

CALORIES: 279 • SATURATED FAT: 2G • SODIUM: 259MG
DIETARY FIBER: 11G

INDONESIAN CHICKEN AND VEGETABLE KABOBS

EGGPLANT RATATOUILLE

Cheesy Artichoke Pasta Salad

🕐 **PREP TIME:** 20 MINUTES   **COOK TIME:** 10 MINUTES

1½ cups cooked tricolored corkscrew noodles
⅓ cup chopped artichoke hearts
¼ cup light red kidney beans
¼ cup chickpeas
¼ cup diced red bell pepper
¼ cup diced green bell pepper
¼ cup chopped ready-to-eat sun-dried tomatoes
2 oz. part-skim cubed mozzarella cheese
¼ cup red wine vinegar
2 tsp. olive oil
¼ tsp. salt
¼ tsp. freshly ground pepper
Chopped fresh basil (optional)

1. Cook pasta according to package directions; let cool. Toss pasta with artichoke hearts, kidney beans, chickpeas, bell peppers, sun-dried tomatoes, and cheese. Drizzle with vinegar and olive oil; sprinkle with salt and pepper; stir well. Cover and chill at least 30 minutes. Garnish with fresh basil, if desired.

Serves 2

CALORIES: 405 • SATURATED FAT: 5G • SODIUM: 764MG
DIETARY FIBER: 6G

Eggplant Ratatouille

🕐 **PREP TIME:** 15 MINUTES   **COOK TIME:** 15 MINUTES

½ medium onion, chopped
1 fennel bulb, coarsely chopped
1 small zucchini, chopped
½ red bell pepper, diced
2 cups peeled and cubed eggplant
1 (14½-oz.) can no-salt-added diced tomatoes
1 tsp. dried Italian seasoning
¼ tsp. salt
½ tsp. freshly ground pepper
2 tbsp. chopped fresh basil
Polenta (optional)
Asiago cheese (optional)

1. Sauté onion, fennel, zucchini, and red bell pepper in a large skillet coated with vegetable cooking spray over medium-high heat until tender. Add eggplant, tomatoes, Italian seasoning, salt, and pepper; bring to a boil. Cover and simmer 10 minutes, stirring often. Stir in basil. Serve over polenta and sprinkle with Asiago cheese, if desired.

Serves 2

CALORIES: 153 • SATURATED FAT: 1G • SODIUM: 449MG
DIETARY FIBER: 10G

CHEESY ARTICHOKE PASTA SALAD

Mushroom-Beef Burgers

PREP TIME: 15 MINUTES   **COOK TIME:** 15 MINUTES

- 1   lb. lean ground round
- 2   cloves garlic, minced
- 1/2   cup finely chopped mushrooms
- 2   tsp. Worcestershire sauce
- 1/4   tsp. freshly ground pepper
- 4   whole wheat hamburger buns
- 1   small tomato, thinly sliced

Spinach leaves

1. Combine ground round, garlic, mushrooms, Worcestershire sauce, and pepper. Shape meat mixture into 4 patties. Cover and chill 1 hour.

2. Grill over medium-high heat, covered with grill lid, 4 to 6 minutes or until a meat thermometer registers 160°F. Serve on buns with tomato and spinach.

Serves 4

Note: To broil instead of grill, broil burgers 5½ inches from heat (with door partially open) 3 to 5 minutes on each side or until a meat thermometer registers 160°F.

CALORIES: 258 • **SATURATED FAT:** 2G • **SODIUM:** 309MG
DIETARY FIBER: 4G

Triple Cheese Pizza

PREP TIME: 15 MINUTES   **COOK TIME:** 10 MINUTES

- 1/2   cup part-skim ricotta cheese
- 1/4   cup grated Parmesan cheese
- 1   egg white
- 2   tbsp. freshly chopped parsley
- 1   (7-inch) pizza crust
- 2   Roma tomatoes, thinly sliced
- 1   clove garlic, minced
- 2   tbsp. chopped fresh basil
- 1/4   cup shredded part-skim mozzarella cheese

Crushed red pepper (optional)

1. Combine ricotta cheese, Parmesan cheese, egg white, and parsley in a medium bowl. Spread mixture over pizza crust. Top with tomatoes, garlic, basil, and mozzarella cheese.

2. Bake at 450°F for 8 to 10 minutes or until thoroughly heated and cheese is melted.

Serves 2

CALORIES: 270 • **SATURATED FAT:** 7G • **SODIUM:** 462MG
DIETARY FIBER: 1G

Honey-Ginger Tofu and Veggie Stir-Fry

PREP TIME: 20 MINUTES   **COOK TIME:** 10 MINUTES

- 2   tbsp. low-sodium soy sauce
- 2   tsp. rice vinegar
- 1   tsp. honey
- 1   tbsp. minced fresh ginger
- 1/4   tsp. crushed red pepper
- 1   tsp. dark sesame oil
- 1/2   (12-oz.) pkg. extra-firm tofu, drained and cut into 3/4-inch cubes, patted dry with paper towels
- 1   cup snow peas
- 1   cup sliced shiitake mushrooms
- 1/2   small red bell pepper, sliced julienne
- 2   tbsp. sesame seeds, toasted (optional)

Brown rice (optional)

1. Combine soy sauce, vinegar, honey, ginger, and crushed red pepper in small bowl, stirring with a wire whisk.

2. Heat sesame oil in a large nonstick skillet over medium-high heat. Add tofu and sauté until golden, about 2 minutes. Transfer to a plate. Add snow peas, mushrooms, red bell pepper, and soy sauce mixture to heated skillet and stir-fry 2 to 5 minutes or until vegetables are tender.

3. Top with toasted sesame seeds and serve over brown rice, if desired. Serve immediately.

Serves 2

CALORIES: 241 • **SATURATED FAT:** 2G • **SODIUM:** 546MG
DIETARY FIBER: 6G

Papaya Seafood Salad

PREP TIME: 20 MINUTES

- 1/3   cup white wine vinegar
- 2   tsp. olive oil
- 1/2   cup chopped fresh cilantro
- 2   cloves garlic, minced
- 1   tsp. finely chopped jalapeño pepper
- 1   tsp. dried cumin
- 1   cup cooked and peeled large shrimp
- 1   papaya, seeded and sliced in half

1. Whisk together vinegar, olive oil, cilantro, garlic, jalapeño, and cumin in a small bowl. Pour over shrimp. Cover and refrigerate 30 minutes.

2. Spoon shrimp salad evenly in papaya halves and serve immediately.

Serves 2

Note: Use caution when handling hot peppers. Wear disposable gloves or wash hands thoroughly with hot, soapy water.

CALORIES: 183 • **SATURATED FAT:** 1G • **SODIUM:** 153MG
DIETARY FIBER: 3G

MUSHROOM-BEEF BURGERS

HONEY-GINGER TOFU AND VEGGIE STIR-FRY

TRIPLE CHEESE PIZZA

PAPAYA SEAFOOD SALAD

Garlic Scallops over Pasta

🕐 **PREP TIME:** 15 MINUTES   **COOK TIME:** 15 MINUTES

- ³/₄ lb. scallops (about 10 oz.)
- ¼ tsp. salt
- ¼ tsp. freshly ground pepper
- 3 cloves garlic, minced, divided
- 2 shallots, chopped
- 1 tsp. olive oil
- ¼ cup vegetable broth or dry white wine
- ¼ cup fresh lemon juice
- ¼ cup chopped fresh parsley
- 2½ cups whole wheat pasta, cooked

Freshly grated Parmesan cheese (optional)

Fresh parsley sprigs (optional)

1. Sprinkle scallops with salt and pepper; toss with 1 clove minced garlic. Sear over medium-high heat in a large nonstick skillet coated with vegetable cooking spray 3 to 5 minutes on each side or until scallops are opaque. Remove from pan and keep warm. Cook shallots and remaining garlic in hot oil over medium-high heat 3 minutes or until tender. Stir in vegetable broth and lemon juice; simmer 5 minutes. Stir in parsley.

2. Spoon scallops over pasta; top with sauce. Sprinkle with Parmesan cheese and fresh parsley, if desired.

Serves 2

CALORIES: 464 • SATURATED FAT: 2G • SODIUM: 748MG
DIETARY FIBER: 9G

Garden Frittata

🕐 **PREP TIME:** 15 MINUTES   **COOK TIME:** 10 MINUTES

- 1 tsp. margarine
- 1 cup chopped broccoli florets
- 1 cup chopped asparagus spears
- ¼ cup chopped sweet onion
- 2 egg whites
- 1 egg
- ¼ tsp. salt
- ¼ tsp. freshly ground pepper
- 2 oz. reduced-fat shredded Cheddar cheese
- 2 Roma tomatoes, thinly sliced

Chopped fresh basil (optional)

1. Melt margarine over medium heat in ovenproof skillet coated with vegetable cooking spray. Add broccoli, asparagus, and onion; sauté 5 minutes or until vegetables are tender.

2. Whisk together egg whites, egg, salt, and pepper. Pour eggs over vegetables. Cover and cook until edges are set and bottom is lightly browned, about 2 minutes. Sprinkle cheese and tomatoes over egg mixture. Broil frittata 2 minutes or until lightly browned. Cut into wedges. Sprinkle with fresh basil, if desired.

Serves 2

CALORIES: 202 • SATURATED FAT: 6G • SODIUM: 409MG
DIETARY FIBER: 4G

Carrot-Fennel Soup

🕐 **PREP TIME:** 10 MINUTES   **COOK TIME:** 20 MINUTES

- 1 (16-oz.) pkg. baby carrots
- 1 fennel bulb, chopped
- ⅓ cup chopped onion
- 1 clove garlic, minced
- 1½ cups vegetable broth
- ½ tsp. chopped fresh thyme
- ⅛ tsp. salt
- ¼ tsp. freshly ground pepper
- 1½ cups skim milk

Fresh thyme (optional)

1. Spray a large Dutch oven with vegetable cooking spray. Add carrots, fennel, onion, and garlic; sauté until soft, about 8 minutes. Add broth; cover and bring to a boil. Reduce heat, uncover, and simmer until carrots are tender, about 10 minutes. Stir in thyme, salt, pepper, and milk; cook 5 minutes more.

2. Process mixture with a hand or electric blender, stopping to scrape down sides, until mixture is smooth. Garnish with fresh thyme, if desired.

Serves 4

CALORIES: 109 • SATURATED FAT: 0G • SODIUM: 413MG
DIETARY FIBER: 5G

GARLIC SCALLOPS OVER PASTA

GARDEN FRITTATA

CARROT-FENNEL SOUP

Beef and Couscous Stuffed Peppers

🕐 **PREP TIME:** 10 MINUTES   **COOK TIME:** 20 MINUTES

1	**cup couscous, cooked**
1/2	**cup diced fresh tomatoes**
1/2	**cup soy or garbanzo beans, rinsed and drained**
1	**tsp. dried Italian seasoning**
1/4	**tsp. freshly ground pepper**
4	**large red bell peppers**
1/2	**lb. lean ground round**
1	**tbsp. chopped shallots**
1/4	**cup crumbled feta cheese with garlic and herbs**

1. Combine couscous, tomatoes, beans, Italian seasoning, and pepper in a large bowl; set aside.

2. Cut off tops of bell peppers. Remove seeds and membranes. Cook in boiling water 5 minutes; drain upside down in paper towels.

3. Cook beef and shallots in a large nonstick skillet over medium-high heat 5 minutes or until beef is browned; drain. Toss beef mixture into couscous mixture.

4. Stuff bell peppers evenly with beef mixture and top with feta cheese. Place in a lightly greased 9x9-inch baking dish.

5. Bake at 350°F for 10 to 15 minutes or until bell peppers are tender and cheese is melted.

Serves 2

CALORIES: 478 • **SATURATED FAT:** 5G
SODIUM: 331MG • **DIETARY FIBER:** 10G

BEEF AND COUSCOUS STUFFED PEPPERS

INDEX

Dr. Richter's
CommonSensediet

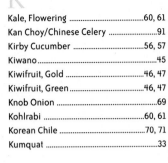